GW00702409

Primary Management and Leadership towards 2000

Edited by C. Eric Spear

Longman

Published by Longman Information and Reference,
Longman Group Limited, 6th Floor, Westgate House, The High,
Harlow, Essex CM20 1YR, England and Associated Companies
throughout the world.

A catalogue record for this book is available from The British
Library

ISBN 0-582-22925-1

Typeset by EMS Phototypesetting, Berwick upon Tweed
Printed in Great Britain by BPC Wheatons Ltd, Exeter

Contents

About the authors

Mike Aylen was closely involved in planning and contributing to management development courses for deputies and headteachers, during his fourteen years of headship in two contrasting Kent primary schools. As an LEA senior primary inspector and an OFSTED registered inspector, he has been responsible for an extensive LEA primary school inspection programme.

Sir Robert Balchin leads the present government's initiative on self-governing schools and is chairman of the Grant-Maintained Schools' Foundation. For six years he was the national Director-General of St John Ambulance. He has been a school governor and county councillor and was knighted in 1993.

Geva Blenkin is a senior lecturer in curriculum studies and early childhood education at Goldsmith's College, University of London. She is currently director of the research project 'Principles into practice: improving the quality of children's early learning'.

Michael Brunt is deputy director of education services in Doncaster, having previously been assistant director of education in Solihull and, before that, assistant education officer in Walsall.

Ciaran Clerkin is head of Selwyn Primary School in Newham, his third headship. He is particularly interested in the integration of deaf and partially hearing pupils into mainstream education. He is an Ofsted inspector.

Rick Collet is school development consultant with the Kent Curriculum Services Agency, having previously been Kent's inspector for multicultural education. He has worked in Cardiff, Bedfordshire, China, South Africa and Eastern Europe.

Elsa Davies is the director of the National Playing Fields Association. She was formerly the education liaison manager of the Institute of Management and, before that, a primary headteacher for many years. She was a member of the National Curriculum Working Group, Chair of the Advisory Centre for Education (ACE) and a BEMAS council member.

Derek Esp is chair of the Society of Education Consultants and a former director of education. He is also an independent inspector of schools, a school governor and vice-chair of a county education committee. He has therefore, experience as employer and employee in many different contexts.

Charles Frisby is head of Riverside Middle School, Suffolk, having been previously headteacher of two Coventry junior schools.

David Hargrave is an educational consultant who was, until 1988, senior inspector for primary and middle schools in Kent. Prior to this he was a teacher, a principal lecturer in a college of education and a science inspector.

Michael Jackson is headteacher of Cinnamon Brow CE Primary School. As the largest primary school in Cheshire, this was one of the county vanguard primary schools which took on its delegated budget in 1990. At present he is part of a county working party which is monitoring the introduction of an enhanced delegation scheme.

Hugh Lawlor is a senior adviser in Kent and an Ofsted registered inspector. He was previously a senior inspector and inspector for INSET and assessment in Kent. He has wide senior management experience in schools and teacher education in this country and overseas.

Sally Manning is one of the county co-ordinators for appraisal in Kent. She has been involved in planning and training for teacher appraisal and the management of headteacher appraisal. She is an assessor for the National Education Assessment Centre (NEAC) which focuses on the professional development for senior managers in primary and secondary schools. Sally was formerly deputy head in the secondary sector.

Chrise Roome is a senior adviser in Kent. He was formerly head of a large, Kent primary school and before that taught in ILEA.

Eric Spear is head of Staplehurst Primary School in Kent. The early part of his teaching career was spent in Zambia and in Swaziland, where he was head of a large, locally managed primary school. As one of the original cohort of 'OTTO' heads, he was a regular contributor to Kent's headteacher management training programme and is a writer on education management. He is a national council member of the National Association of Headteachers (NAHT).

John Thorp is at present a senior lecturer in education at University College, Scarborough. He has had substantial experience of primary schools, first in the Midlands and as a headteacher in North Yorkshire. In his present post he co-ordinates an MEd course in educational management and has recently completed Ofsted inspection training. Dr Thorp has a long-standing interest in the transition between home and school and a child's transfer to secondary school. He has undertaken research into community education in both rural and urban contexts and this has contributed to his particular interest in small schools.

Derek Waters was, for twelve years, director of the ILEA Primary

Management Studies Centre, following his service as headteacher and adviser with ILEA. He has conducted management training courses all over the British Isles and in other parts of the world. He is the author of two books on primary school management. Currently, he is visiting lecturer at the University of London Institute of Education.

Preface

The management and leadership of primary schools will have a crucial bearing on this country's standards of achievement as we approach the end of the century. Primary education is the foundation on which all else is built. There can be no more important issue than to ensure that the management leaders of primary schools are equipped with the right tools for the highly responsible task they are called upon to perform. This book, just like its predecessor *Primary School Management in Action*, will assist considerably those involved in primary schools management to fulfil their roles more effectively.

David M. Hart OBE FRSA, General Secretary,
National Association of Headteachers

Introduction

The forerunner of this book, *Primary School Management in Action*, edited by Ian Craig, was conceived in a time of unprecedented change in education. Not for more than a century has an education act had as much effect on the shape of schooling as did the 1988 Education Reform Act. Though there have been several other significant acts in this century, it is probably the 1870 Elementary Education Act which comes closest to the 1988 Act in its impact on the whole system.

Both were concerned with similar objectives; education for all to certain specified standards, and value for money, achieved through government inspection and financial control. Their differences are contextual. In the climate of the nineteenth century, the 1870 Act was trying to establish a coherent, national system of schooling for the masses. The 1988 Act, on the other hand, was trying to wrest control, from those running it, of an already established system on the grounds that the system was neither cost effective nor offering to its pupils an appropriate education, of sufficient rigour.

Along with a highly prescriptive curriculum and assessment system, now acknowledged to be unworkable and so subject to review, came a vastly increased managerial role for the headteacher, in the wake of the 1988 Act. This weighed particularly heavily on primary school heads whose approach to education had, traditionally, been more hands-on in the classroom and who enjoyed comparatively meagre administrative and managerial support. Suddenly, primary heads who had, hitherto, always given priority to the needs of children, suddenly found themselves cast in the role of chief executive of the board of directors of a company in the marketplace.

The advent of the local management of schools, the increased emphasis on the role and responsibilities of school governors and the progressive diminution of the role of local education authorities has left schools and their heads dramatically and unprecedentedly exposed in this age of accountability and consumer charters.

More than ever before, the primary headteacher needs to develop skills of leadership and management in order to motivate his teaching staff, guide his governors, and satisfy the legitimate aspirations of his parent customers; all in the interests of giving children an appropriate and effective education.

This book aims to be useful to those headteachers, their deputies and senior managers. It should also interest governors, education officers, inspectors and advisers, and the general reader interested in education. One hopes that the occasional politician might learn from it too!

The emphasis is practical and each chapter is written by authoritative and experienced practitioners. Each chapter is brief and to the point, and can be read independently of the others at a sitting. This is not an 'academic work', though many of the writers are distinguished adacemics, but the distillation of successful experience based on soundly grasped theory.

C. Eric Spear

1 Teacher appraisal: a structured approach to staff management

Sally Manning

Introduction

Schools up and down the country have been getting on with the introduction of the national scheme for appraisal without fuss and without the level of national publicity which has accompanied the introduction of other elements of the Education Reform Act. This is perhaps due to the nature of the scheme, and because it draws together strands of staff development processes which were already in operation in many schools.

The introduction of the national scheme has been a protracted affair. The work of the national pilots was started in January 1987 and was published in the *National Steering Group (NSG) Report* in 1989. There was extensive consultation on this document before the statutory orders were laid before parliament, and appraisal for all school teachers became a requirement, starting on 1st September 1991. The majority of teachers will be involved in appraisal by the beginning of the autumn term 1994, and all must be included in the appraisal cycle by 1st September 1995.

I am writing this chapter from the perspective of one who has been involved in the introduction of appraisal into all schools in Kent, one of the largest LEAs. Practically every type and size of school can be found in this part of the country. There are many small village schools, some with fewer than 50 pupils, as well as the large schools which serve diverse urban communities.

Kent LEA launched its own pilot scheme for teacher and

headteacher appraisal in 1990. Approximately 240 headteachers and 600 teachers volunteered to participate in this pilot study which was based entirely on the NSG recommendations. David Hopkins, Mel West and Rob Bollington of the Cambridge Institute of Education (CIE) were involved in evaluating the voluntary pilot scheme in Kent. Their initial report celebrated the many positive aspects of the approach to appraisal, and was invaluable in providing pointers for the introduction of the mandatory scheme. Three years later, in 1993/1994, CIE was invited to carry out a detailed evaluation of the mandatory scheme. Through their evaluation report we have been given an insight into how appraisal is actually operating, the issues which have arisen and the potential benefits for schools.

> It is generally felt that appraisal has helped the school to implement its objectives and to refine its priorities. Appraisal has made an impact on the school. Everybody knows what is happening.
> Extract from a case study on appraisal in an infant school —
> *KCC Evaluation of Teacher and Headteacher Appraisal*

Aims

Appraisal is still seen by many as a sensitive issue. It is clear that many teachers remember the suggestion made in the early 1980s, that appraisal would be a way to 'weed out the incompetents'. Add to that a measure of media misinterpretation; for example: Judgement day — *TES* headline, April 29th, 1994 and perhaps a previous experience of appraisal outside education, and it is easy to understand why some established teachers feel uncertain about the process and its aims.

In 1986, the ACAS independent panel agreed principles with regard to teacher appraisal. The group's aims have provided the foundation for the development of the national framework and their definition still provides an excellent starting point for appraisal:

> The Working Group understands appraisal not as a series of perfunctory events, but as a continuous and systematic process intended to help individual teachers with their professional development and career planning, and to help ensure that the in-service training of teachers matches the complementary needs of individual teachers and schools.
> *Teachers' Dispute: ACAS Independent Panel, Report of the Appraisal and Training Working Group*, 1986

In Kent we have maintained this emphasis on the importance of appraisal as a 'structured approach to staff development' and have encouraged headteachers and managers in our schools to ensure that teacher appraisal is kept quite separate from disciplinary procedures and that it is not linked to pay.

The schools where appraisal is operating successfully have been very clear about their aims. Their appraisal policies include unambiguous public statements such as 'Teacher appraisal in this school is concerned with the professional development of individual members of staff. It will not be linked to pay and conditions of service.'

Appraisal and school improvement

The evidence of HMI inspections shows that planning for improvement has not been a strength in the majority of primary and secondary schools. The OFSTED booklet *Improving Schools* (1994) highlights the key role of effective planning in school improvement. The case study on Little Snoring County Primary School describes the pragmatic approach to development planning adopted by the head after her appointment in 1991. In this 'simple and succinct' plan ten areas for development were identified of which 'the professional development of teachers' was one of the five priority areas. Commenting on the *quality* of improvement, inspectors report that 'The diagnosis of staff development needs and INSET provision are integral to the development plan. They play a significant part in raising the quality of teaching and learning.'

It is not clear from the booklet how these needs were diagnosed at Little Snoring but, in the appraisal regulations, we have at our disposal a process which has been designed to identify staff development needs and to link these needs with the priorities of the school.

Links with school development planning

Appraisal should be set in the context of the objectives of the school, which will generally be expressed in the school development plan. *DES Circular 12/91*

Those schools which have an open, participative approach to development planning have a clear advantage here. If all the staff of the school have been involved in the process of review and identifying priorities, it will be easier for them to talk about their personal contribution to the achievement of common goals.

Job descriptions

> Appraisal should be undertaken on the basis of an established job description. *DES Circular 12/91*

Appraisal can help people to identify priorities and it provides an opportunity to review the job description on a regular basis.

A common priority in a school development plan is the formulation of a policy for an aspect of the curriculum. In this context, the curriculum co-ordinator or leader may use the appraisal process to work out a personal action plan for the development of the policy, while other teachers in the same school may be working on action plans for delivery of that policy.

Placing the appraisal process in the context of the school's and individual's priorities helps to improve target setting, and can help to ensure that outcomes are realistic and can be met.

The role of governors

Governing bodies of LEA maintained schools have a duty to ensure that the school's arrangements for appraisal comply with the LEA scheme whilst the governing body of a grant maintained school, as the appraising body, is responsible for all the arrangements.

In either case, the governors do not have a direct involvement in the appraisal of teachers. However, if they are to be able to play an effective part in supporting school and teacher development, they will need to have an overview of the appraisal process.

Governors should make sure that they are kept up to date with the way in which appraisal is operating so that they can ensure that it is properly integrated into the management of the school. Head-teachers need to include in their regular reports to governors a summary of the targets for action identified by the staff. Thus, governing bodies will be able to see how the appraisal of individual teachers is linked with the tasks and priorities set out in the school development plan. In addition to responding to an existing development plan, appraisal targets, when taken together, will form an important agenda for future action for the school as a whole.

Managing the process

The how and when of appraisal depends on many other factors already operating in the school. In schools where there is a fairly large staff, it is usually phased over the two-year period so that, in one academic year, approximately half the staff are involved in the first stage whilst the other half are in the review stage. This is then reversed in the second year. In some smaller schools it has been possible to carry out the appraisals in a more concentrated period of time which makes the links with the school development planning process somewhat easier to manage.

Whichever approach is adopted, the whole cycle needs to be kept moving forward, as there is a statutory obligation to ensure that appraisal takes place on a two-yearly cycle. There are software programmes available which can help headteachers to plan and keep track of the appraisal process. Schools in Kent have been using the software developed by Educational Key Systems (formerly ESL) which will also collate the training needs identified by staff.

Finding the time for appraisal

A concern raised by some teachers is the time it takes to go through the appraisal process. The introductory phase of the mandatory scheme has been supported by central government through GEST funding. In the long term, schools will need to find ways to support both the process and the outcomes. Time spent on appraisal is invaluable as it provides each teacher with a regular opportunity to review their work and to plan ahead. This needs to be properly integrated into the way the school is managed so that it is not regarded as an extra chore but as a real opportunity to contribute to personal and school development.

The issue of time is of particular concern to those who are appraisers as they will be participating in their own appraisal as well as taking the responsibility for the professional development of up to four colleagues. Some of the practical suggestions which our schools have made are listed below.

- Appoint and train additional appraisers so that the work load is shared amongst a larger group of people.
- Designate a percentage of the school's budget for staff development, and use available funding to 'buy-in' time either by the use of supply cover or through enhancing the hours of part-time teachers.
- Adjust the contact ratio to create additional non-contact time for appraisers. (Where this has not been possible, the headteacher and deputy have often released colleagues on a regular basis.)
- Examine the pattern of meetings with a view to reducing the number and/or length of regular meetings. In some schools there is a meeting each month allocated for 'staff development'. This can include elements of the appraisal process as

well as time for individual activities related to professional development targets.

- Structure staff development days to allow some or all staff to become involved in parts of the process, e.g. preparation meetings, appraisal interviews, writing and agreeing the appraisal statement.
- Use development days for INSET which has been identified by a number of staff as an outcome of individual appraisals. This could take the form of group inset led by a member of the school staff or by an external provider. Alternatively, it could provide time for external training or visits to other schools or for individual planning and preparation.
- Use development days for a number of individual formal review meetings which can be linked to whole-school review and forward planning.

I have found the booklet *Making Time for Staff Development* by Eric Hewton and Michael Jolley useful for reference. In it, they describe different approaches to staff development which have been adopted by a range of schools.

Who will the appraisers be?

The headteacher cannot be the sole appraiser in the school but it is his/her responsibility to appoint the appraisers. It is recommended, in *Circular 12/91*, that no appraiser should be responsible for more than four appraisees. When making decisions about suitable appraisal partnerships heads need to think about:

- who has (or could develop) the necessary skills to be an appraiser?
- in whom do the other staff have confidence?
- who has the experience and understanding to ensure that appraisal serves the needs of the teacher and the school?

Staff in our schools have the opportunity to express 'negative preference', that is, to talk to the head in confidence if there is anyone with whom they do not feel they can work with in an atmosphere of trust and confidence. This helps to establish the kind of professional partnerships where experience and good practice are shared.

The appraisal process for teachers

The regulations provide the framework for the appraisal process and there are certain elements which have to be adhered to in order to

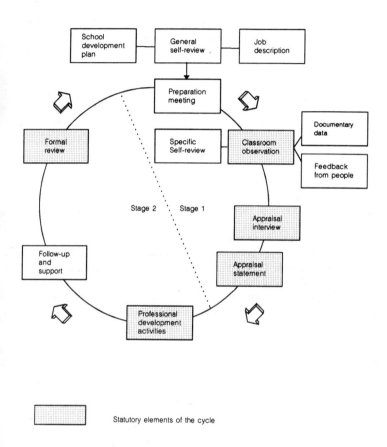

Figure 1.1 The appraisal process for teachers

comply with the legislation (see Figure 1.1) However, schools have built on this framework in a variety of ways which reflect their individual circumstances and approaches to staff development.

The appraisal cycle extends over two years. Experience has shown that, if the first stage of the process is too drawn out, it tends to lose its impact, and managing this with a large number of teachers gets quite difficult. A period of about four to six weeks or half a term seems to be about right for this.

Self-review

Many of those who have already been appraised have stressed the usefulness of self-review before the process gets started. The following are some possible questions for self-review which can also provide preparation for the appraisal interview.

- What are the main priorities of the current school development plan? How do you see yourself contributing to these?
- Are there any aspects of your job description which you think need updating or changing?
- During the past year, which parts of your job have you felt particularly pleased with and have given you the greatest satisfaction? Could these be used to better advantage in the school?
- Which aspects of your job have not gone as well as you would have hoped? Is there something that can be done to support you here?
- What additional things might be done by the headteacher or senior staff to improve your performance in your job? What changes in the school organisation would be beneficial in enhancing your performance?
- What do you think should be your main targets for the period up to your next appraisal?
- What hopes and aspirations do you have for your personal and professional future? What can be done during the next two years, and in the longer term, to develop your professional experience and add to your teaching expertise?

Preparation

If the appraisee has had a chance to engage in some general self-review ideas can be brought to the planning meeting, which can then be discussed, refined and agreed with the appraiser. The areas of focus selected for appraisal tend to reflect the balance of the teacher's job description. For many teachers, appraisal will concentrate entirely on aspects of their 'classroom work' while, for some, it may also include 'managerial responsibilities'. Some of the areas of focus (in addition to aspects of classroom management and practice) which have been selected by teachers in our schools are:

- activities and clubs
- areas of responsibility
- assemblies
- curriculum areas
- display
- liaison with other agencies/middle or secondary phase
- liaison with parents and the community
- managing classroom and welfare assistants
- organisation of resources
- prioritising time
- providing INSET for colleagues
- special educational needs provision.

Once the decision about the focus of appraisal has been taken, more specific plans for the process can be made. Appraisee and appraiser need to prepare for the appraisal interview by collecting information in a variety of ways. They need to decide what information needs to be gathered and how this is to be done.

Documentary data is fairly easy to identify and collect, but it is important to bear in mind that documents must relate directly to the area of focus and that they should not be too detailed or lengthy.

If *feedback from other people* would be helpful, the individuals involved should be identified by the appraisee and they need to be prepared for their meeting with the appraiser. We have found it helpful if this preparation is done by the appraisee who can explain why feedback has been asked for, and outline the sorts of questions that are likely to be asked by the appraiser. This is a particularly sensitive part of the process and, if it is to be used, it is worth referring to the *Guidance and Code of Practice on the Collection of Information for School Teacher Appraisal (Annex A, DES Circular 12/91)* which gives practical and helpful advice.

Classroom observation

The *observation* element is compulsory and is a very valuable source of information in the appraisal process. The regulations specify at least two observations, and it is recommended that these should total a minimum of 1 hour. The experience of being observed is becoming more of an everyday event for teachers but, for some, past experiences of observation have undermined their professional confidence. Unlike headteachers, teacher/appraisers may not have had many opportunities to observe colleagues and they are, almost without exception, very enthusiastic about their role. As one teacher put it '...the opportunity to *observe* is a rare event. As a teacher I have not seen other teachers *teach*. It is the best form of learning for me.' *KCC Evaluation of Teacher and Headteacher Appraisal.*

Successful observation depends on thorough planning and preparation by both appraisee *and* appraiser, a sensitive and supportive approach to observation and feedback on the part of the appraiser, and the establishing of the conditions for an open and constructive dialogue. In appraisal, the role of the observer is not to make an assessment of the appraisee but to create the climate in which teachers can reflect and develop their classroom practice.

The interview

The interview also needs careful preparation, planning and follow-up. This is largely the responsibility of the appraiser but, if appraisal is to be successful, both appraiser and appraisee need to prepare. The purpose of this professional discussion is to review current performance and formulate a personal action plan to meet future needs. In order to create the climate for a relaxed, but business-like, discussion, teachers have sometimes found it helpful to go off-site so that they will not be interrupted by the telephone or distracted by other school activities.

The appraiser's function is not to 'talk at' the appraisee but to stimulate the conversation. Their ability to do this depends on the sensitive use of appropriate listening and questioning skills. The agenda should be known to both appraisee and appraiser in advance and could include:

- a summary of self-review
- an update of the job description
- a review of the areas of focus using the information collected from various sources including classroom observation
- the highlighting of professional achievements
- the setting of targets to meet developmental needs
- hopes for the future.

The appraisal statement

The statement consists of a summary of the main points made by the appraiser and the appraisee at the interview, and should include the conclusions reached and the targets for action. It does not need to be a lengthy document but should highlight achievement as well as setting out the personal action plan for the teacher.

Appraisers have sometimes found it difficult to make notes during the interview. One strategy for keeping a record of the discussion is for the appraiser to compile a brief summary of each section at stages during the interview. The wording of each summary is agreed with the appraisee before the dialogue is taken forward

Confidentiality

When the statement has been finalised, the only people to receive copies should be the appraisee, appraiser and the headteacher. In LEA schools, the CEO, or a representative of the CEO, can ask to see a teacher's statement, although this right does not pass to the chair of governors of a grant maintained school. In any school the *chair of governors* (but no other governor) may ask to see the targets for action identified by an individual teacher — perhaps if there has been a request for specific support and/or funding. In these circumstances, it would be helpful for the headteacher to arrange to meet with the chair of governors and the teacher concerned to discuss the targets and the support which the school is able to provide.

Targets for action

Professional development targets will be identified during the appraisal interview. It is helpful to have a summary of these at the end of the appraisal statement, along with a sensible timescale and some agreed success criteria. There should not be too many targets, as these are more than routine tasks. They should be realistic, achievable and related to the needs of the individual teacher and school in which they work. Targets are recorded on a separate annex to the statement as they form the only non-confidential part of the statement. Targets requiring INSET and/or other support will need to be passed on to the person who is responsible for staff development.

INSET courses often spring to mind when thinking about ways to support professional development. There are some difficulties associated with this. Off-site INSET can be costly, and usually involves the additional expense and possible disruption of supply cover. Available courses do not always match requirements so there has been a shift towards professional development activities which can be planned and delivered at a local level — within a school or consortium group. The following is a list of some strategies (other than courses) which have been used to support professional development in our schools.

- Seek advice from professional association
- Attend meeting of groups outside own sphere
- Seek counselling/support from senior managers
- Delegate
- Exchange ideas with a colleague
- Form a support group
- Gather parents' responses
- Seek an industrial placement
- Invite adviser in
- Job swap
- Job rotate/shadow
- Keep portfolio of progress
- Keep log/diary
- Make detailed lesson plans
- Make use of commercial expertise
- Mentor/mediate
- Mutually observe
- Negotiate time
- Seek new/different areas of responsibility
- Observe a colleague
- Prioritise responsibilities
- Procure additional resources
- Pupil shadow
- Read a book/watch appropriate video
- Research
- Run a course
- Share good practice within a cluster/consortium
- Show parents around the school
- Seek practical help with stress management
- Seek support for middle management
- Team teach
- Find time to talk/reflect
- Use time management strategies
- Use video of self and analyse
- Vary year group responsibility
- Visit other schools
- Work with other staff
- Work with another colleague who has a similar problem
- Write a short paper
- Write a CV.

The impact of appraisal

The appraisee-led approach to appraisal might be perceived as undemanding. However, our experience has been that, if people find that they can *trust* the process and their appraiser, the vast majority would *demand* a rigorous and professionally challenging appraisal in the second and subsequent cycles. The evidence now collected from teachers in our schools bears this out.

> In the first round targets were often suggested by the appraiser and lacked specificity in terms of classroom performance. When targets are led by the appraisee and, where appraisal is systematically linked to development planning and whole school issues, the impact on classroom practice is more acute. (KCC Evaluation of Teacher and Headteacher Appraisal, 1994)

Follow-up, support and review

Regular follow-up and support gives both appraisee and appraiser an opportunity to highlight success, discuss any difficulties and suggest changes to targets. The appraiser can ask the question 'How is it going?' on informal occasions as well as during the *Formal review* meeting which must be held during the second year of the appraisal cycle. The actual timing of the formal review varies from school to school, and even from individual to individual. For those who have long-term targets on the statement, sufficient time to achieve those targets must be allowed before the formal review.

The formal review meeting provides an opportunity for appraisee and appraiser to look through the statement again and reflect on the success of any professional development. The purpose of the meeting should be:

- to review the progress of the appraisee and/or the school in meeting the targets set at the appraisal interview
- to consider whether those targets are still appropriate
- to consider the usefulness of any training undertaken since the appraisal
- to provide an opportunity for the appraisee to raise any issues relating to his/her work
- to consider any career development needs.

When the formal review meeting has taken place, a brief summary of the discussion should be added to the appraisal statement.

Future developments

Appraisal for all personnel

Schools are already tailoring the process to suit their own needs and circumstances. Some have included all their personnel. Where the whole school approach has been adopted, all the staff have been trained together. Observation is usually seen as an optional element of the process for classroom and clerical assistants, although many have found this to be helpful in providing professional feedback about their work.

A shorter cycle

In some schools, the opportunity for professional development is regarded as so important that the two-year cycle is felt to be too extended. In these schools, the process is moving towards an annual cycle by extending the formal review meeting to include an opportunity to set individual targets for the year ahead. This gives teachers a realistic opportunity to respond to the rapid pace of change in our schools today.

In conclusion

Some of the key success factors are:

- commitment of the headteacher and appraisers to the process of appraisal as a vehicle for staff development.
- clarity of whole school plans and priorities.
- open, team approach to school management.
- fair allocation, and use of available resources to support the process of appraisal and the achievement of outcomes.
- thorough preparation and training of all appraisers and appraisees.

The benefits

My experience of appraisal in schools is that, when a school 'gets it right', the potential for change and improvement is enormous.

For schools, it can assist the co-ordination of organisational and individual aims and priorities. Staff are made clear about their individual responsibilities and can work on agreed action plans. Used positively, it can develop the potential of all individuals and enables colleagues to talk in a structured way which can lead to improved communications and a greater exchange of ideas. In the present environment of rapid educational change, it builds a supportive environment in which teachers can develop and respond to the demands placed upon them.

For the individual it provides a better understanding of the job the school expects them to do. Appraisal gives a formal opportunity for professional feedback and recognition of their contribution. It provides an opportunity for everybody to have a regular review of their development and training needs in the knowledge that their individual development will be supported by the organisation. For those teachers looking for promotion, it can help to set out a career path to achieve their ambition. Essentially, however, appraisal is about job satisfaction for all teachers in providing the highest quality of education for all children.

References

HMSO (1989) *School Teacher Appraisal: A National Framework — Report of the National Steering Group on The School Teacher Appraisal Pilot Study.*

The Education (School Teacher Appraisal) Regulations 1991.

DES Circular 12/91.

OFSTED HMSO (1994) *Improving Schools.*

Hopkins, D. and West, M. (1994) *Kent County Council — Evaluation of Teacher and Headteacher Appraisal* Obtainable from the Kent Curriculum Services Agency,
    South Borough Buildings, Loose Road, Southborough, Maidstone, Kent ME15
    6TL.

Hewton, E. and Jolley, M. (1991) *Making Time for Staff Development: A Report for the DES* University of Sussex, Occasional Paper 14.

Further Reading

West, M. and Bollington, R. (1990) *Teacher Appraisal, A Practical Guide for Schools* Fulton.

Jones, J. (1993) *Appraisal and Staff Development in Schools* Fulton.

LEAP (Local Education Authorities Project) (1991) *Appraisal in Schools.*

Hewton, E. (1988) *The Appraisal Interview* Open University.

Poster, C. & D. (1991) *Teacher Appraisal — A Guide to Training* Routledge.

Software

School Appraisal Manager (SAM), Educational Key Solutions, Number One, The Old Yard, Brasted, Kent TN1 1IP

Supporting Self-Review (The Development Needs Analysis — DNA — program which enables primary teachers to reflect on their work in the classroom and other areas of professional practice). MLS (Mast Learning Systems Ltd), 26 Warwick Road, London, SW5 9UD.

Video

Into Appraisal, Focus in Education.

2 Preparing job descriptions: the head's role

Ciaran Clerkin

Job description: the curriculum co-ordinator

In consultation with the headteacher, the curriculum co-ordinator is responsible for:

Overall curriculum management

1. Identifying and determining overall aims and objectives in the subject
2. Determining a curriculum within the subject area relevant to the abilities and needs of pupils
3. Organising the curriculum within school and liaising with feeder schools
4. Evaluating standards of learning
5. Compiling information on assessment and achievement
6. Allocating and supervising resources necessary for implementing the curriculum.

Leadership and human relations

1. Encouraging staff development and support within the curriculum area
2. Motivating pupils and staff by personal influence and concern for individuals

3. Helping to solve problems and resolve conflict by using skills of arbitration and negotiation
4. Helping to establish effective channels of communication within the school community
5. Being an effective member of the school management team.

External accountability

1. Involving parents and governors in school activities connected with the curriculum area, and explaining aims and methods of working
2. Reporting to parents and governors on school policy and general standards of performance
3. Helping to represent the school to the local community through displays and exhibitions of work
4. Liaising with other schools as well as LEA curriculum assessment groups.

Specific aspects of each of these headings are open to negotiation in the light of discussion between the curriculum co-ordinator and the headteacher.

This generic job description for a curriculum co-ordinator represents an attempt to provide an account of the job, its component tasks, and the circumstances in which the job is performed. In this chapter I consider the issues arising from the generic job description in relation to the managerial responsibility of the headteacher. Having briefly discussed the role of the primary head at the present time, I then comment on preparing a job description using the headings cited above as a framework. Finally, a suggested framework is provided to assist the headteacher and the co-ordinator to translate the job description into a more specific action plan.

It is essential that all teachers, including the head, should have straightforward accounts of what is expected from them, drawn up in consultation with interested parties within the school including representatives of the governing body. For reasons of space, however, in this chapter I refer mainly to job descriptions for those with specific responsibility for an area of the curriculum. In doing so, I recognise the danger of overlooking the boundary and possible overlap between jobs and across curriculum areas unless there is regular discussion within the school team about common objectives.

Although job descriptions have now become an established feature in primary schools, headteachers have not always been in sympathy with them. As Geoff Southworth has noted in *Staff Selection in the Primary School* (1990):

Many headteachers perceive them to be too officious and technocratic. Others argue that they usually fail to capture the richness of teaching or damage the degree of spontaneity which an imaginative teacher needs to display. (p.25)

In the past, headteachers often assumed that, because people with responsibility knew what their job entailed, there was no need to write it down. Indeed, some took the view that it might be counter-productive to do so. Others were wary of identifying teachers' duties too precisely for fear of being unable to alter them at a later stage. The increasing prominence of accountability together with a greater emphasis on team management and responsibility in schools throughout the 1990s has changed things greatly. The necessity of clarifying every teacher's obligations has been stressed in a variety of studies and, as Pauline Perry (1991) has noted,

> Real quality cannot be achieved unless each individual who works within an organisation accepts personal responsibility for the delivery of the service.

As part of the move towards greater accountability, conditions of employment for both headteachers and other staff have been laid down in the *School Teachers' Pay and Conditions Document* (DES 1991) which, for the first time, clearly identifies the general professional duties as well as the working time of teachers.

Since the early 1990s, teacher appraisal has also become an established fact in schools, for appraisal to be effective, it is essential that staff have agreed job descriptions which have been put together in consultation with those concerned. To quote Southworth once more, it is clear that a job description

> should not be a straitjacket, nor should it be an imposition from someone 'higher up' the school... A job description should offer some clarity so that we each know what our respective jobs are. (1991 p.25)

The role of the headteacher

Everyone who is in the slightest way associated with education realises that, as a result of changes since the 1988 Education Act, the role of the headteacher has altered significantly. Among the biggest changes have been the introduction of the National Curriculum and Local Management of Schools (LMS). Whatever the changes, the headteacher is not only at the centre of the process but is charged with making sense of change and communicating this to the whole school community. Furthermore, in an environment 'characterised by discontinuity' (Clerkin 1985), an issue of central importance for the head has been maintaining a stable environment and ensuring that careful planning and implementation of policies contributes to school improvement.

Much of the research on school effectiveness over the last 10 years, including *Primary Schools: Some Aspects of Good Practice* (DES 1987), has pointed unambiguously to the quality of leadership provided by the headteacher. Agreed aims relating to academic work and children's personal and social development, coupled with effective delegation and the ability to motivate others, are also key factors in managing schools successfully. Consequently, the head-teacher's role is more concerned with *leading* than with determining the policy formation process. The capacity to encourage continuous improvement, and to manage change as a matter of course, are therefore important considerations. In such circumstances, a col-legial strategy, based on consistent aims and effective communica-tion is likely to be the most effective means of securing the enthusiastic commitment of other staff in the preparation of job descriptions.

The organisation

In a dynamic organisation where individuals are constantly having to modify responses to situations, both internal and external, the head and senior staff have to respond to a range of events occurring in a context of political, social and economic constraints. So, at best, a job description can only offer a single snapshot at a particular time in a school's history. Moreover, as Gray (1981) argues, most job descriptions 'are in reality *notional* structures in that they are a simplified example of what is desired.' Gray claims that, because human behaviour never totally conforms to desired behaviour we must be 'exceedingly cautious' in distinguishing between what is sought and what actually occurs.

It is evident, therefore, that job descriptions are less useful as instruments for *controlling* behaviour than for *offering a framework* for staff to develop their own strengths for the good of the school. Besides, they should be sufficiently flexible to enable teachers to modify or alter their responsibilities in relation to fresh demands.

Preparing the job description

The initiative for preparing a job description for a curriculum co-ordinator may stem from a variety of reasons:

- it could be a vague list of duties hastily assembled in response to an LEA or other OFSTED requirement
- it might be put together during a period of internal re-organisation
- it could be set up as a means of involving staff more fully in school development, or ensuring that individual staff have an opportunity to contribute to school improvement.

How useful a job description is as a practical instrument depends largely on who made it and how it was made. Other important factors are the time and other resources available, the experience of the post-holder, and the actual responsibilities agreed. Although the head and the person in the post may be the main contributors, it is important to involve individuals and groups with whom the teacher must relate to implement the policy. It should be remembered that every job description has its limitations. While it provides a framework for action, a job description does not offer guidance on *how* major tasks should be carried out. From the initial preparation stage, therefore, the head ought to stress the need for review and re-negotiation when interpretations of the role vary with what was originally intended.

For new appointments, the process ought to begin well before the interview. A precise job description provides a means of enabling potential candidates to assess their suitability for the post. Besides, it can be a relevant discussion point at the interview as well as a means of establishing the worth of candidates in relation to the school's needs. A good deal of information already exists in the literature to assist the head at the initial stage, including information from the *Primary Survey* (DES 1978a), the *Cockcroft Report* (DES 1982), *Education Observed 3: Good teachers* (DES 1985c) and *Primary Schools: Some Aspects of Good Practice* (DES 1987).

The generic example cited at the beginning, which has been adapted from Morgan et al. (1983), focuses on the three basic elements in need of analysis in preparing a job description:

- overall curriculum management
- leadership and human relations
- external accountability.

Curriculum management

The key factor in the preparation of a job description is the identification of aims and objectives in the subject area. National Curriculum guidelines can help to provide a clear statement of aims for all pupils. In the preparation of the school development plan, it is likely that a broad statement of overall aims, such as the one contained in the Warnock Report (DES 1978b), will already have been formulated to enable staff and governors to agree together what they seek to achieve for pupils.

When these fundamental agreements have been established, the head and the co-ordinator can work together on drawing up more specific aims related to the school's needs which have to be tackled within an agreed time-scale. Successful management is the art of the possible. So, once the aims related to the job description have been agreed and other staff have been informed of these, considerable skill and judgement will be needed to recognise where the possibilities lie in determining the curriculum and creating situations to enable the aspirations in the job description to become a reality. Complex management skills are involved in the process, for the opening up of curriculum issues can often be an uncomfortable process. Consequently, close attention must be paid to developing effective relationships and sound communication. This will be referred to in the next section.

Curricular continuity

For many years there has been general agreement among those concerned that education should be envisaged as a coherent whole, and that the transition between stages should be as smooth as possible. In reality, however, as Dean (1980) has indicated, this is a concept to which the profession usually pays only 'lip service.' HMI also noted in their *Primary Survey* that the 'importance of continuity in the curriculum of the schools was largely overlooked'. The document *A View of the Curriculum* (DES, 1980) also argues for more thought to be given to curricular continuity. It stresses:

> that between primary schools and the schools which receive their pupils there needs to be not only communication about individuals but also consultation about aspects of the curriculum.

If this aspect of the curriculum co-ordinator's job description is to be more than just rhetoric, certain considerations need to be taken into account by the head and written into the job description. First, adequate cover to underpin teacher release needs to be organised in planning the school staffing budget. This may be achieved in a variety of ways depending on the school's internal policies and financial limitations. Whatever arrangement is made, it should not be at the expense of the effective organisation and management of the school. It is essential too that both teaching and support staff are consulted in advance and their co-operation secured. This helps to keep interruptions to children's learning to a minimum while ensuring that proper communication is maintained with parents and other groups in the absence of a teacher from normal duties.

Secondly, with the help of the school's INSET development plan, the head and the co-ordinator need to reach agreement about training and support for curricular continuity and decide upon an appropriate time-scale for this activity. The competencies demanded include:

- interpersonal skills
- subject knowledge across the curriculum
- an understanding and sensitivity to the internal organisation of other departments or schools.

At the time of preparing the job description, the curriculum co-ordinator and the headteacher may find it useful as well to draw up together a framework establishing the kind of liaison which already exists or ought to be developed between infant, junior and post-primary sectors of the education service locally. This is best done in consultation with cluster groups or other local curriculum support networks.

Evaluation and review

As the general topic of appraisal is being dealt with in another chapter, I propose to look briefly here at evaluation and review of children's work and teacher performance in relation to the preparation of job descriptions. Largely due to the impact of National Curriculum assessment, these processes are now regarded as integral managerial tasks for schools. Consequently, there are important implications for the curriculum postholder and the head.

Much will depend on the degree of trust already existing between staff as well as their willingness to discuss classroom work in an open manner. If evaluation is to be considered as a significant part of the job description, it is vital that opportunities are provided on a regular basis to visit other classes and discuss the content and quality of the work. Clearly, skill and sensitivity as well as training in classroom observation and interviewing techniques are required.

In *Quality in Schools* (DES, 1985b) HMI mention the value of a 'state of readiness' when introducing an individual scheme. For those including evaluation in the job description for the first time, 'pre-evaluation' activities which introduce some of the concepts and attitudes could be examined by the head and the post-holder. The stages agreed as a result could then be presented to others for discussion and subsequently included as an individual target in the job description, perhaps with a date for review recorded. The supportive nature of this part of the job description as well as the evaluative one should be acknowledged. Moreover, attention should focus on the effect of planned activities on learning outcomes for the pupils.

Resources

The allocation of proper resources to deliver the curriculum within the subject area must be considered carefully if the job description is to have any relevance. In preparing the school development plan, the head and others involved must create opportunities for discussion with the post-holder about forward planning and budgeting in relation to the whole curriculum for the school. It is the co-ordinator's responsibility to put together priorities for additional resourcing in relation to the planned programme as well as any new developments which are envisaged. Other staff need to be consulted, and the way in which materials are cared for in individual classrooms should be agreed and carefully monitored. An efficient system of 'booking' for expensive equipment is necessary as well as a timetable which ensures materials in short supply are circulated fairly.

Inevitably, each individual school will regard certain subjects or activities as being in need of additional financial support at a particular time. This may lead to a feeling among staff that some curriculum areas are treated more generously than others. My own experience, however, suggests that a co-ordinator who takes the trouble to submit a well-prepared brief, supported by accurate costings, is unlikely to go empty-handed when funds are being allocated. It is worth remembering too that careful management of resources together with regular feedback on their use increases the chances of favourable consideration when additional finance is being distributed or bids for additional funding are being considered.

Leadership and human relations

The second element in the job description reminds us that the role is concerned not only with tasks and objectives but also with people. As a member of the school management team, the curriculum co-ordinator is responsible for getting others moving, or keeping them moving, in the desired direction. Pupils as well as individual and team members of staff are included in this motivating activity.

How senior teachers lead develops an atmosphere in the school which helps to raise achievement and ensure that learning goals are attained. Much will depend upon the overall ethos, together with the head's leadership style, which sets the tone for standards of achievement, style of management and oversight of work. However, leadership of the kind mentioned earlier in the chapter is not confined to the head alone. On the contrary, there is a variety of aspects of leadership throughout the school to be shared by other staff.

Although leadership duties cannot always be itemised, discussion about the job description should focus on the co-ordinator's role in acting as a stabilising force within the school, clarifying aims and objectives as well as providing encouragement for others. From time to time, it will be necessary also for the post-holder to engage in 'productive conflict' to deal with resistance encountered along the way. There needs to be agreement about resolving problems, and about delegation between the head and the co-ordinator, with decisions conveyed to appropriate staff on the limits of authority in relation to delegated duties.

Managing change

Initiating rather than just reacting to change requires insight, together with the capacity to find solutions to difficulties and win acceptance of these by others. Hence the willingness to persuade colleagues to accept new ideas, including those who may be lukewarm about innovation, is an important consideration for the curriculum co-ordinator.

Waters has noted (1983) that the manner in which responsibility is carried out is of crucial importance. The author argues that:

> while most people will expect the co-ordinator to exercise responsibilities with an air of authority, an autocratic style will be met by resistance and may indeed be counterproductive.

Consequently, the co-ordinator needs to regard the leadership aspect of the job description and the effective management of change as a two-way process, paying careful attention to the attitudes and feelings of colleagues. In his book *Managing Change and Making it Stick*, Roger Plant (1987) emphasises the importance of recognising that resistance to change is a natural phenomenon.

> It does not come from sheer cussedness, it needs to be recognised, understood and managed. This is true of departments as well as individuals. (p.29)

Plant goes on to describe the importance of building trust and expending energy finding out more about the resisting forces within a group to planned change.

A simple but useful model for portraying the critical phases in the implementation of change has been identified by Kurt Lewin (1958 pp.197–213)

- unfreezing
- changing
- refreezing

According to Lewin, the initial unfreezing phase is the most crucial. It is also the stage where the post-holder and others leading the change are most likely to encounter unexpected and unpredictable resistance. The key task therefore is identifying and overcoming initial resistance. At the unfreezing stage, the post-holder could usefully organise a series of training sessions with a focus on a participative approach. At the changing period, staff should be encouraged to set aside old ways and try out the new. An emphasis on careful planning and team development is particularly helpful at this stage. Lastly, according to Lewin, refreezing involves the establishment of a process to firm up the new ways of doing things so that they become permanent and accepted by all staff. In practical terms, the co-ordinator could prepare a set of guidelines for the new procedures or a report to parents and governors describing progress.

External accountability

Accountability in education has been defined

> as a means of maintaining or improving the level of public confidence in the education system (Barton et al. 1980).

As Hewton and West (1992) have indicated in *Appraising Primary Headteachers*, the demand for increased accountability was an expression of concern about standards in schools, teaching methods and spiralling costs set against the background of professional autonomy. Events such as the disruption at William Tyndale school, described by Sallis (1977), focused public attention on doubts about the condition of education. In his famous Ruskin speech, James Callaghan raised questions concerning accountability in the education service, standards in schools and the nature of the school curriculum.

The White Papers *Teaching Quality* (DES 1983) and *Better Schools* (DES 1985d) called for more informed knowledge about the work of staff in schools. In the following year the *1986 Education (No. 2) Act* sought to strengthen ties still further. The annual parents' meeting, at which governors present their report on the school, became a legel requirement and governors were given a greater say in the appointment of staff. The introduction of LMS, increased pressure on resources and freer parental choice all underline the necessity for schools to be more conscious of their corporate image. As a result, marketing the school and managing its reputation among the local community are now regarded as an important area of responsibility for all staff.

The need to define this aspect of the co-ordinator's role in the job description arises, first, because others now have a legal right to know what goes on inside schools. Secondly, effective communication to parents coupled with clear understanding can be a positive influence in raising standards and improving attitudes and relationships among pupils. Finally, experience shows that a school's efforts are more likely to win tangible support from the wider community when staff maintain an emphasis on raising achievement.

The issue of marketing the school is discussed more fully in another chapter. However, for the purposes of preparing a job description, the head and the co-ordinator should consider effective ways of publicising the school's strengths and achievements. This does not mean sweeping weaknesses under the carpet but rather making sure that shortcomings are identified within the school development plan and a strategy towards eliminating them is established within an agreed time-scale.

Most day-to-day contact between parents and teachers about accountability is informal, and cannot easily be separated into tasks and commitments. In preparing the job description, however, the head and the co-ordinator should try to ensure that certain practices are enshrined in school policy. The parents' awareness of what pupils are doing in the subject area is the key element in the process. This is usually best promoted through regular communication on individual progress with class teachers, and by allowing parents access to classrooms at appropriate times. It is also helpful for parents to know how to contact the person with responsibility for a curriculum area when a matter of concern arises. Naturally, the head may wish to be involved in the process too, especially when the post-holder needs to be defended or the parent requires further clarification or support.

As well as encouraging a general atmosphere of openness and enquiry, the co-ordinator can give a powerful lead to staff by making systematic arrangements to explain to parents and governors the school's aims and teaching methods for the curriculum area. An account of curriculum development, together with reports on general standards of performance within each key stage can be provided in various ways, both formal and informal, including a

Selwyn Primary School

Job description

Name of teacher _____

Title of post _____

Responsible to _____

Responsible for _____

Brief description of post

_____

_____

Current responsibilities

1. _____   These tasks *must* be done in
                      relation to the *description
                      of the post.* They do not
2. _____   always have to be done by the
                      teacher but it is the
                      teacher's job to make sure
3. _____   they *are* done.

4. _____

Table 2.1

Key tasks for 1994-95

1. _____

2. _____   These essential tasks, relating
                                     to the *description of the post*
                                     must be done by the teacher.
3. _____

4. _____

Targets agreed with the headteacher/phase co-ordinator

1. _____

2. _____

3. _____

Time scales   1._____   2._____   3._____

Review dates 1._____   2._____   3._____

*The post-holder is also required to undertake duties set out in the School
Teachers' Pay and Conditions Document 1991*

Signed   _____

Headteacher   _____ **Date**_____

Table 2.1 (continued)

seminar for governors, a practical session for parents, news bulletins and displays of work.

A job description as an action plan

Since the introduction of teacher appraisal and the more recent OFSTED arrangements for school inspections, the importance of concise job descriptions which have been agreed by governors and the headteacher has increased significantly. As appraisal becomes a more firmly established part of each school's staff development and review procedures, the function of job descriptions has begun to change. As well as a generic job description of the kind illustrated at the beginning of the chapter, it is now quite common to find a second section relating to mutually agreed targets. For the majority of staff, therefore, job descriptions will in future be reviewed more frequently and renegotiated periodically in relation to the needs of the school as well as each teacher's own career plans.

The outline job description in Table 2.1 was devised by the senior management team as a result of appraisal activities in my own school. We have found it helpful when used alongside a more general job description for each member of staff.

Summary and conclusions

In this chapter I have tried to show that a job description is not merely intended to prescribe minimum requirements or reduce opportunities for initiative. On the contrary, it seeks to promote a firmer realisation of the responsibilities involved in a teacher's work, leading to higher standards of achievement in the school. Throughout the chapter I highlight the fact that leadership is exercised through a variety of formal and informal channels. It involves persuasion and influence to link and reconcile the objectives of the wider school community. Because schools are dynamic, the job description is frequently concerned with change in the system. But, as Paisey (1984) points out, leadership should also be identified with routine maintenance of initiatives:

> The working life of most people in schools, in spite of the uncertainties and complexities which abound, consists essentially of steady application, a good deal of repetition and attempts to make existing relationships work well.

Given the diverse set of duties portrayed in the job description, the management of time is an important consideration. Organising administrative tasks, as well as class teaching, presupposes careful forward planning. Nevertheless, even the most efficient teacher is likely to experience stress occasionally because of discontinuity in the work pattern. The pressure of a host of minor matters which sometimes prevent attention being given to more professional concerns can be a source of frustration. Besides, the teacher may lack the confidence to accept the less pleasant aspects of the role such as resolving conflict or the supervision and correction of others.

The anxiety that arises could be detrimental to overall effectiveness and job satisfaction unless support to cope with it is provided. Both the head and colleagues who appreciate the specific circumstances of the school can exercise an important counselling role here, especially with new appointees. Discussion and training in style and approach as well as assistance with interpersonal skills may be needed. A good way for the co-ordinator to tackle unfamiliar elements of the job description may be through 'bridging delegation', working alongside another person and examining together the methods employed afterwards.

In determining the best use of time, the co-ordinator needs to be clear about priorities and relate activities to these. Discussion on how to create time can, in itself, often enable individuals to define more clearly how they propose to tackle their duties. The crucial decision is between what is urgent and what is important. Within the 'important' category, the co-ordinator and the head need to think about the short term and long term. For both it can be helpful to negotiate intermediate stages in the job description (with 'do by' dates) which others are aware of.

The tasks set out in a job description of the kind referred to in this analysis require those in senior management roles to support the job-holder in undertaking allocated duties. There are plenty of messages in HMI surveys and inspections and elsewhere in the literature suggesting that co-ordinators require time during the school day to enable them to carry out their duties effectively. The consequences for senior management, particularly the arrangement of suitable cover, must therefore be considered carefully.

The delegation of responsibility cited at the beginning clearly implies an increase in decisions which can be made without referral. Consequently, good communication and trust as well as an acceptance by others that mistakes will be made occasionally is important. Inevitably, some aspects of management are inter-related, and the head must recognise this in assigning job descriptions. The precise cut-off point at which one job ends and another begins is often hard to specify. Furthermore, as roles are constantly developing, job descriptions soon become outdated so that review is necessary from time to time. As circumstances change, certain functions within the school may become obsolete with the result that people may need to be informed of redefined duties and, where possible, be involved in the development of new approaches.

Finally, we must not assume that, just because a job description has been constructed and the managerial recommendations above have been acted upon, all will be well. It has to be remembered too that, by nature, we are all functionally imperfect. But, to end on a positive note, people have capacities for development together with the resilience to face new challenges which far exceed any limitations or specifications we may define for them. For the true leader, like Wordsworth's *Happy Warrior*,

> Looks forward, persevering to the last
> From well to better, daily self-surpast!

References

Barton, J., Becher, T., Canning, J., Eraut, M. and Knight, J. (1980) 'Accountability in education', in Bush, T., Glatter, R., Goddey, J. and Riches, C. (eds) *Approaches to School Management* Harper and Row.

Clerkin C. (1985) 'What do heads actually do all day?' in *School Organisation* 5 (4) Taylor and Francis.

Clerkin, C. (1989) 'Leading a team to facilitate change' in Craig, I. (ed.) *Primary Headship in the 1990s* Longman.

Dean, J. (1980) 'Continuity', in Richards, C. (ed.) *Primary Education: issues for the Eighties* Black.

DES (1975) *A Language for Life (The Bullock Report* HMSO.

DES (1978a) *Primary Education in England: A survey by HM Inspectors* HMSO.

DES (1978b) *Special Educational Needs (The Warnock Report)* HMSO.

DES (1980) *A View of the Curriculum* HMSO.

DES (1982) *Mathematics Counts (The Cockcroft Report)* HMSO.

DES (1983) *Teaching Quality* HMSO.

DES (1985a) *Curriculum Matters* HMSO.

DES (1985b) *Quality in Schools: Evaluation and Appraisal* HMSO.

DES (1985c) *Education Observed* HMSO.

DES (1985d) *Better Schools* HMSO.

DES (1987) *Primary Schools: Some Aspects of Good Practice* HMSO.

DES (1991) *School Teachers' Pay and Conditions* HMSO.

Gray, H. (1981) 'The relationship between organisation and management in schools', in *School Organisation*, 1, (2).

Hewton, E. and West, N. (1992) *Appraising Primary Headteachers*, OUP.

Lewin, K. (1958) 'Group decision and social change' in Macoby, E. E., Newcombe, T. M. and Hartley, E. L. (eds) *Readings in Social Psychology*, New York.

Morgan, C., Hall, V. and Mackay, H. (1983) *The Selection of Secondary School Headteachers* Open University Press.

Perry, P. (1991) 'Quality' *Times Education Supplement* June 1991.

Paisey, A. (1984) 'Trends in educational leadership thought', in Harling, P. (ed.) *New Directions in Educational Leadership* Falmer.

Plant, R. (1987) *Managing Change and Making it Stick* Fontana/Collins.

Sallis, J. (1977) *School Managers and Governors, Taylor and After*, Ward Lock.

Southworth, G. (1990) *Staff Selection in the Primary School*, Blackwell.

Waters, D. (1983) *Responsibility and Promotion in the Primary School* Heinemann.

3 The resident inspector: the headteacher's role in monitoring quality

Chris Roome

> Headteachers are uniquely placed to look across the whole school for the purpose of judging its strengths and weaknesses, spotting incipient problems, drawing attention to work of distinction and to aspects of work which call for improvement. Among other things, headship is leadership in quality assessment and assurance and this is a role which will assume even greater importance as the National Curriculum and the Parents' Charter take full effect. DFE 1992

In this chapter, I offer some practical guidance to headteachers on how to implement, in the complex and busy everyday reality of their primary schools, that leadership in quality assurance described in the passage from 'Curriculum organisation and classroom practice in primary schools', a discussion paper by Alexander, Rose and Woodhead quoted above. However, before embarking on the practical advice, it is necessary to outline some important features of modern primary school headship.

Most headteachers in our primary schools have achieved their position because they are perceived as successful classroom practitioners. This is a considerable advantage, and one of the great strengths of the British primary school system. Their experiences in a number of different roles within schools has usually equipped them with a clear understanding of the learning needs of their pupils, an array of strategies for addressing those needs, and a sense of vision about primary schools and the activities which take place within them.

The advent of local management of schools with its accompanying demands for the development of budgeting skills, has meant that most aspiring headteachers have also learnt something of budget management before arriving in the headteacher's office. For some, there is a danger that the appeal of managing a budget successfully, and the opportunities which the process can offer for the flexing of fledgling entrepreneurial skills, can divert headteachers from their prime task: the management of learning within their schools.

Managing a budget is, compared with the task of managing the curriculum and the staff of a school, a relatively simple and mechanistic procedure. Monitoring procedures can be learnt quickly and simply by headteachers, and then properly be consigned to the daily care of an assistant in the school office. The management of the budget will be an integral part of the school development plan, and will serve the main business of the school: the provision of an effective learning and teaching environment. The curriculum and its impact upon pupils, in all its complexity, richness and challenge, is, as always, the proper concern of the headteacher.

> Effective headteachers have a vision of what their schools should become. They will seek to establish this vision through the development of shared educational beliefs which underpin evaluative judgements, school policies and decision making generally. The vision will have at its heart a clearly articulated view of what constitutes the school curriculum (including, very importantly, its relationship to the National Curriculum) and of how planning, teaching and evaluation will be undertaken in order to ensure that the aims and objectives of the curriculum are translated into pupil learning.
> The result is the sense of purpose and direction so characteristic of successful schools. DFE 1992

The stated purpose of the National Curriculum, and the development of the OFSTED cycle of inspections, is to raise standards in our schools. The debate about those standards is not the subject of this chapter, but there can be no doubt that the systematic monitoring of standards of achievement, and the quality of learning and teaching taking place within the school, is the prime responsibility of the headteacher. The programme suggested below could be accomplished in two/three hours per week, and if implemented, would safeguard the headteacher's leadership role in quality assessment and assurance.

I argue that heads should establish a monitoring structure within

their schools, based on a typology which examines three key
elements of the school's activities:

> Planning: the regular monitoring of curriculum planning
> Process: the regular monitoring of classroom practice
> Product: the regular monitoring of pupils' work — the learning
> outcome.

These three elements should be monitored in a systematic fashion.

Planning

> With the introduction of the National Curriculum and the
> School Development Plan initiative, there has been a recogni-
> tion that teachers must plan together to ensure consistency and
> progression across classes and year groups and that formally
> structured short and long term planning are essential to effective
> classroom teaching. DFE 1992

It is important to establish a coherent set of planning systems.
Curriculum planning is an essential part of a well-ordered school.
There should be a clear understanding of the different types of
planning to be undertaken, and it should involve all the teaching
staff. Long-term planning, i.e. that which encompasses a key stage,
should provide a framework within which individual teachers can
plan their termly and weekly work. This should also incorporate the
school's decisions about time allocations for the various National
Curriculum subjects. Long-term plans need to form an important
part of the school's curriculum documentation, and all staff should
have their own copies to hand. (Useful advice can be found on this
matter in *Planning the Curriculum at Key Stage 2* NCC 1993)

In order to facilitate the headteacher's monitoring role, consideration should be given to producing a common format for medium-
and short-term planning which is used by every teacher. Such
planning should be seen by the headteacher on a regular basis.
Medium-term plans, i.e. those which cover a class for a term, should
be submitted to the head at the beginning of each term. Copies of
these can be made to form a useful file in the head's office, or they
can be read and commented upon and returned to the teachers. Such
planning should contain a clear statement of what the pupils are
expected to learn, and should be closely linked to the school's long-
term plans.

Short-term plans, i.e. those covering a week's work should be
written in a common format, and a copy supplied to the headteacher.
Such planning can be confined to a sheet of paper, and should
include headings such as:

- National Curriculum subject
- learning to be achieved (including relevant NC attainment targets)
- learning activities to be undertaken
- resources to be used
- evaluation of session/day, assessment of learning outcomes.

By adopting such a procedure, the head can oversee the staff's planning, and build up a duplicate set which does not have to be returned to teachers by a specific time. It will also be useful in an emergency involving staff absence when the head may have to fulfil the role of on-site supply teacher.

Over time, the headteacher will be able to see if the planned learning relates to National Curriculum requirements, and how particular lessons fit into sequences in order to achieve progression. The headteacher will be in a position to evaluate how well the school's planning procedures are working. In addition, there will be opportunities to judge whether each teacher's planning is taking sufficient account of individual pupil need. However, while examining plans is a necessary component of in-school quality assurance, it must be complemented by a programme of regular classroom observation in order to evaluate how closely teachers' planning is reflected in classroom practice. There is a need, therefore, to move into the fleshy reality of the classroom to observe the process of learning closely.

Process

Headteachers should establish a regular routine for the monitoring of classroom teaching. The programme for these visits should be discussed with staff, and the criteria to be used in evaluating classroom practice agreed. In this matter, headteachers can make use of *The Handbook for the Inspection of Schools*, which not only gives a wide range of criteria but also provides an example of the classroom observation form to be used in OFSTED inspections of schools. Such a form can be adapted for use in the school, and at the same time provide teachers with the useful experience of being observed in their work for the purpose of evaluation. Headteachers may wish to use a number of strategies for this activity. They may wish to work alongside the classteacher, help with a group, or sit and observe in a more formal manner. I would argue that headteachers should observe their teachers formally on a regular basis, make notes in the classroom, and work with a clear commitment to discussing their observations with the teacher promptly, in order to provide opportunities for in-school professional development.

Among the key issues headteachers will need to consider during classroom observation will be:

- How closely is the teacher's planning related to the classroom practice?
- How clear are the learning objectives?
- Are the pupils engaged upon their tasks?
- Does the lesson have sufficient challenge, pace, rigour and interest?
- Is the teacher in command of the subject matter?
- Are the differing abilities of the pupils sufficiently well catered for?
- What is the quality of the relationship which exists between the teacher and the class?
- Are pupils being encouraged to develop as autonomous learners, who co-operate readily with each other?
- How well does the teacher use questions?
- Are pupils given sufficient opportunities to talk purpose-fully?
- How are issues of classroom control resolved?
- How well are resources deployed?

By posing and answering such questions within a programme of planned visits to all the classrooms, the headteacher will gain valuable insights into the quality of the teaching and learning processes, and be able to make evaluative judgements based on evidence. Further confirmation of the standards being achieved, and the quality of learning and teaching taking place within the school, can be obtained by a systematic examination of pupils' work — the product

Product

All headteachers see examples of pupils' work in the course of their everyday duties. Often, it will be sent specifically to them for commendation or censure. However, such a system needs to be supplemented by a manageable method of looking at a sample of pupils' work in a systematic manner. This can be accomplished by instigating a programme which involves regular inspection of books and other items produced by pupils. There are several ways in which this can be achieved, but the chosen method should be manageable, and allow sufficient time for realistic sampling.

A useful strategy is one whereby each class teacher in turn is required to provide six, i.e. about 20 per cent, full sets of work for inspection at the end of one day. (A regular day each week helps to systematise this practice.) The six are chosen by the classteacher to represent the spread of ability in the class, and are examined by the headteacher in the classroom after school.

Examining the work in the context of the classroom is an important part of the process, for the work seen can be related to the displays in the classroom, and also to the planning, copies of which are already available. (See above section on Planning.) By setting aside an hour a week for this purpose, the head can look systematically at a sample of work throughout the school. It is especially useful if the head works through the classes in their age order, thereby gaining further insight into the progression of pupils across the key stages. In the majority of primary schools, all classes can be sampled in this way at least once a term, and in the largest schools headteachers should ensure that all classes are sampled in some way on a termly basis. This will require a greater investment of time.

Judgements can be made about marking, the application of school policies, standards of presentation, the balance of tasks, and the opportunities provided for pupils to produce self-generated writing. Further opportunities to review work can also be taken when the headteacher is in the classroom observing learning. A different perspective is obtained if the headteacher can discuss with a pupil their work and progress. Again, pupils can be chosen by the teacher to reflect the spread of ability in the classroom. During this time too, opportunities can be taken to hear pupils read, observe them using apparatus, including computers, and observe how well pupils co-operate with each other.

This basic programme of systematic sampling of work produced by pupils can be varied in its details. Single subjects could be examined, or complete sets of books related to a subject component of the National Curriculum.

Whichever procedure the headteacher decides to adopt is not as important as the decision to instigate such an examination of work on a regular basis. It is important therefore to ensure that the task is manageable within the schedule of each busy week.

No man is an island, entire unto himself

wrote John Donne, and no school exists as an island either. All headteachers need therefore to monitor the standards being achieved by their pupils in the ways described above, and in addition, to use some form of standardised tests to provide further evidence of pupil achievement. While SATs will partly fulfil this function, there is still a need for headteachers to test specific groups within their pupil population at regular intervals throughout the primary phase. Reading and mathematics are monitored most commonly in this way in many schools. Frequency of testing and target age groups are matters to be decided in the light of the school's circumstances, as is the use made of the information obtained.

In his 1992/3 report on *Standards and Quality in Education*, HMCI wrote:

> Heads and other senior staff should develop and implement strategies for the systematic monitoring of the work of their schools in order to evaluate standards of achievement, curricular strengths and weaknesses (including time allocations) and the quality of teaching and learning. OFSTED 1993

The type of programme outlined in this chapter, whereby headteachers monitor planning, process, and product, and produce standardised test data for some key areas of the curriculum, would meet the requirements outlined above, and enable headteachers to exercise their leadership role with regard to quality assessment and assurance. In addition, headteachers could also report confidently to their governors on the quality of education being provided by the school.

The business of schools is learning, and it is the central responsibility, and accountability, of the headteacher to ensure that all pupils have access to a vibrant curriculum, and the opportunity to be taught and to learn effectively.

References

DFE (1992) 'Curriculum organisation and classroom practice in primary schools — a discussion paper' Alexander, Rose & Woodhead.

NCC (1993) *Planning the Curriculum at Key Stage 2.*

OFSTED (1993) 'Standards and quality in education 1992–3' *The Annual Report of Her Majesty's Chief Inspector of Schools* (HMCI).

OFSTED (1993) *The Handbook for the Inspection of Schools.*

4 Leadership and management: a style for the 1990s

C. Eric Spear

I once rang a colleague, the head of a large secondary school. 'Is Mr X available?' I asked the secretary who took the call. 'No, I'm afraid not', she replied, 'he's busy dictating.' For one fleeting moment my imagination toyed with the ambiguity. It conjured a vision of Mr X, enthroned on the stage of the assembly hall, issuing edicts like bolts of lightning which were received by suppliant minions scurrying forth to deliver them to subservient staff in every corner of the school.

It is the image of the headteacher assiduously cultivated by fiction and one which persists in the minds of many outside schools. Indeed, there are, no doubt, weary headteachers everywhere to whom the role, so described, would come as a welcome relief from the reality which is so different from this fictional image.

One of the problems of headship, especially a new one, is that everyone will have his different expectation of the way you should play the role and will try to impose that view upon you by the way he treats you. It takes time and practice to develop the style which best suits your personality and beliefs. To begin with you inherit the role of your predecessor but, like a second-hand suit, it only fits where it touches. Nevertheless, there will be those who insist that you wear it whilst there may be others who will want you in teeshirt and jeans!

Whatever style you adopt you must bear in mind that many of the models of yesteryear are unlikely to serve the needs of tomorrow. In the days of the elementary board schools, forerunners of today's country primary schools, and well beyond, the headteacher personified the school and was perceived to be personally controlling all that went on within it. It is probably still true that headteachers are seen as having a close identity with their schools but there is a well developed and growing awareness, both within schools and in society generally, not only that the head does not control all the forces acting upon the school or within it, but a feeling that the headteacher should not have this monopoly over the school's destiny. The authoritarian model of the headteacher worked in the past because it was a reflection of a more authoritarian society than exists today.

The 1988 Education Reform Act gave greater emphasis to the role and responsibilities of school governors. They are now expected to play a much more active part in the management of schools and the formulation of school policies.

The Citizen's Charter initiative has emphasised the accountability of schools to their customers and the wider public.

The commercialisation of schools has caused many to look beyond traditional fund-raising ventures towards business and industry sponsorship.

All of this means that the number of people and organisations to whom the school, and particularly the headteacher, must maintain 'diplomatic relations', has increased considerably. The headteacher should not have to do this alone, of course, and is entitled to expect that the school governors will shoulder some of this burden.

The head stands, in many ways, in relation to his governors as his elementary school predecessors did to their school boards and will do so even more if his school opts out of LEA control. It thus becomes necessary for heads to exercise their managerial role 'upwards' in advising and guiding the governors, as well as 'downwards' in leading the staff.

All heads, through participation in the work of their governing bodies, already have some knowledge of what corporate decision-making involves. You only have to imagine how you would feel if you were now treated by governing bodies as heads were once treated in some instances in the past. 'Old timers' remember being summoned to the 'office' to sit outside the meeting until summoned to present their report and then being dismissed so that the meeting could continue to make judgements about and decisions on 'their' schools. Such a procedure strikes as inconceivable today, yet sometimes headteachers are guilty of treating their staff in the same way. The complexity of the demands on today's primary school places great strains on the structure of its organisation. It bears particularly heavily on the autocratic headteacher, not only because he becomes burdened with more and more complicated and important decisions at a faster and faster rate, but because he has to find ways of ensuring that the staff implement his decisions.

He cannot command these changes in the sense of issuing edicts to be obeyed. His staff, educated as autonomous professionals, operating in a society whose climate has shifted away from authoritarianism towards participation, will resent such a management style and will tend to subvert proposals for change by, at best, simply going through the motions of conformity while ignoring the spirit of the proposals. Now that the imposition of a national curriculum and assessment procedures by central government has occurred, some of that professional autonomy has been eroded. This makes it even more important that headteachers should give the fullest recognition to the value of what professional autonomy is left if active participation in implementing innovation is to be promoted.

Authority, responsibility and leadership

By virtue of his office the headteacher is set in authority over the rest of the staff but it is obvious that this fact alone will not empower the head to gain acceptance of and compliance with new ideas. The exercise of authority has been described and analysed in various ways but a simple model suffices to explain the derivation of different types of authority.

1. Bureaucratic authority derives from a person's position. You have the authority of your title, 'headteacher', and everyone will expect you to exercise this authority though, as we have already seen, everyone will not agree on how it should be used. Your position will be underpinned by the often separately described, but closely related, legal authority which is supported by the law, rules and regulations. You start out with this authority as a 'given' when you are appointed head.

2. Professional authority derives from your command of the professional skills, knowledge and understanding of the job that your subordinates are doing. Your length and variety of experience enhances this type of authority, though it can count against you if you are seen to be relying upon distantly past experience and have not obviously kept in touch with recent developments. All heads should possess this type of authority. It is the type of authority which you can acquire by study and training.

3. Charismatic authority derives from personal charm and magnetism which most are tempted to think they have but which few actually possess. It is, therefore, risky to rely on this type of authority alone, though as an additional element

to support the other types of authority it is a bonus. Alas, it is difficult to teach and difficult to learn so not much use as an element of inservice training or in staff development programmes. It is no substitute for professional authority as easily charmed appointing bodies have sometimes discovered, too late! You have to recognise that there may be informal staff leaders who possess greater charismatic authority than you as head anyway, so that reliance on this type of authority may lead to your being out-manoeuvred by a member of staff.

The present-day head has to recognise that he is not just a more highly qualified and experienced teacher than the rest of the staff (not always true nowadays anyway) but that he is a leader who must inspire professional respect and loyalty. He is also a manager — a manager of people. It is a well rehearsed aphorism that 'management is getting things done through other people', and the success of a school depends, to a very large extent, on the head doing just that.

Motivating people to give of their best is the major task confronting all managers. It is not simply a question of offering 'bribes', even in situations where the manager has command of resources financially to reward effort. This news will come as a relief to headteachers because they do not have that type of power anyway.

Students of management are always made aware of the work of two writers in this field, McGregor and Herzberg, whose theories crystallise much thinking on the subject of the motivation and management of people.

McGregor's Theory X and Theory Y sum up two extreme views about the nature of people in organisations.

Theory X states that the average person is lazy and does as little work as possible, prefers to be led and lacks ambition, puts personal needs before organisational needs, dislikes change and is gullible and easily manipulated.

Theory Y states that people are not by nature passive or resistant to organisational needs but only become so in response to the way they are treated by the organisation. People have the capacity for hard work on behalf of the organisation, for ambition and personal and professional development, and it is management's job to create the circumstances where these potentialities can be realised. Individuals can gain personal satisfaction through the fulfilling of institutional goals.

It is obvious that these propositions are extremes and that many people's make-up contains elements of both. Your own philosophy will need to take account of the fact that these characterisations are 'ideal types'. You will have to make up your own mind towards which you most incline because that will powerfully influence the way you choose to manage people.

If you largely subscribe to Theory X you are likely to believe in an autocratic view of headship where you make all the important decisions for people and persuade them, either by reward or threat of punishment to do what you see as being in the best interests of the school irrespective of the views or personal needs of individual teachers.

Theory Y protagonists are more likely to see their headship role in terms of satisfying the individual, professional needs of the staff thus motivating the staff to serve the needs of the school.

What are these needs which will motivate staff? More importantly, what is it which demotivates them? The second theorist known to all students of management is Herzberg who proposed that there are two distinct facets of organisation which reflect those factors in the institution which act as 'motivators', or satisfiers and those dis-satisfiers which Herzberg refers to as 'hygiene factors'.

Herzberg says that those things which give rise to most dissatisfaction among workers are policies and administration, supervision, working conditions, interpersonal relations, money, status and security. The motivators are achievement, recognition, challenging work, increased responsibility, growth and development.

Herzberg points out that it is not enough simply to remove causes of dissatisfaction, such as improving working conditions and paying people more money. People need to be more positively motivated by the job itself, by the nature of the work and the sense of responsibility and achievement it offers. Most teachers will, at least, agree that the nature of their job is a major source of satisfaction and motivation, but they may be surprised that money itself is not a motivator. The lack of money may be a demotivator but paying people more money doesn't necessarily increase their motivation. Studies have shown that, when asked what is important to them about their jobs, what they find most satisfying, people generally do not give a high priority to financial reward. They are more concerned with achieving success, experiencing a sense of professional fulfilment and having their achievements recognised by others.

All of this has obvious lessons for the headteacher in his management of staff in schools. In brief, it means sharing the management of the school with the rest of the staff and offering them genuine opportunities to participate in decision-making.

The head has a duty, not only to the long-term image and success of his school, nor only to the short-term goals for the education of the transient child population. He has, also, a responsibility towards promoting the professional growth of his staff, both as regards their present affectiveness as classroom teachers and their potential within and beyond the school.

The style of management the headteacher adopts, therefore, needs to take account of these factors and he must have regard to such issues as how decisions are to be taken and by whom, for making decisions is only half the job, the other half is getting them effectively implemented. The method by which decisions are arrived at has a direct bearing on how, and even whether, they are given practical effect at the 'chalk face'.

Autocrat or democrat?

It is too simplistic to suggest that all we need is a good dose of democracy to replace the autocracy of the head and all will be well. It depends on how democracy is interpreted for one thing. Does it mean everyone being equally involved in every decision? Such an approach to problem-solving would be extremely time-consuming, inefficient and not guaranteed to come up with the best solution anyway. Everyone knows the old saying that a camel is the result of a horse having been designed by a committee! If you consulted everyone before taking any decisions, staff could well become annoyed by your apparent inability to make up your mind about anything.

On the other hand, even a benevolent dictator can't always get things right, and people who feel that they can never really influence the courses of events tend to become passive and resigned, hardly what a school needs in these demanding times. Outright autocracy leads to resentment and an unwillingness to exercise initiative on the part of subordinates. They, in turn, will always 'play safe' rather than take risks by behaving imaginatively or exploring new ideas. The autocratic head who manages to impose uniformity and conformity on his staff is not only minimising the potential of his most expensive and adaptable resource, his staff, he is also fooling himself. For who really believes that people can be moulded into identikit look-alikes. A head may, by exercising his bureaucratic authority, achieve uniformity and conformity in the superficial and most trivial aspects of school life, but those which are fundamental to a school's purpose are not susceptible to change by directive. To achieve a consensus view on the philosophy of the curriculum, for example, requires much patient debate and mutual exploration. It also requires great leadership skills.

The fact is that the head is not just a manager, a term which smacks of coping with the routine of everyday organisation, he is the leader of the school, a term which perhaps conjures up more of a vision of someone positively shaping the organisation, showing others the way, and encouraging them to follow where he is going. The difference between the autocratic head and one who engages his staff in corporate decision-making is the difference between driving and leading. By corporate decision-making I mean involving others on the staff in making decisions either as a group or individually both with the head, and, sometimes, in his absence. The difference between autocracy and corporate decision-making reflects the difference between the role of a master and the role of a manager.

One point has to be clearly established at the outset. Legally, the headteacher is responsible for the internal management, organisation and conduct of the school. No staff group can assume that responsibility. Nor can they indemnify the head against the consequences of their decisions. To that extent the decision-taking capacity of other members of staff is circumscribed. That does not mean, however, that the head should always take all the decisions alone. There is a difference, not merely a semantic one, between decision-making and decision-taking. Making a decision involves all those factors which contribute to arriving at a proposal for action. The agreement to give effect to the proposal is decision-taking. The former allows much scope for all staff members to subscribe their views. The latter is ultimately the province of the head or those to whom he chooses to delegate that authority. There will be some decisions on which he will always have to have the final say. There will be others where this is unnecessary, even undesirable. It all depends on the type of decision being made.

The decisions that are made in a school may be broadly characterised as those of principle and those of practice.

Decisions of principle lay down the ground rules. They establish, if an organisation is to be coherent, standards and beliefs which inform all other decisions. Decisions of principle embody the philosophy of the school. An example of this type of decision would be either to stream or teach mixed ability. Vertical grouping might be another, though it must be recognised that practical consider-ations may sometimes make such decisions as the latter unavoidable, regardless of principles.

Decisions of practice, on the other hand, are lower level, though none the less important for they may more immediately and practically affect what goes on in the school on a day-to-day basis.

There are different levels of decisions of practice including those which have such a long-term effect that they set precedents which can become principles. The decision to use this rather than that textbook or the decision to use one or other published reading or maths schemes may begin by being a practical decision, but its long-term influence may be more akin to a policy decision because the philosophy of the authors will permeate the thinking of the users.

Other practical decisions will be less far reaching in their consequences, and may set no precedents for the future. The decision to line up children in the playground at the end of break rather than let them walk in informally may reflect the philosophy and ethos of the school, but it is a decision that can be changed easily and quickly if there are practical reasons for doing so.

In the foregoing examples, such decisions affect everyone in the school. It would be unwise, therefore, for one person to take these decisions without reference to the views of those who have to implement them. Plainly, if people can understand the reasoning behind a decision and can be persuaded of the benefits it will bring they are more likely to make a sincere attempt to implement it. But what if they understand the reasoning but disagree with it?

This is a real dilemma for the head who believes sincerely that he has a good idea which will benefit all in the organisation if only they will give it a try. Should he impose the decision in the belief that once people have been forced to do something the self-evidence of its virtue will become apparent? While there is some virtue in this view, it is a dangerous philosophy to rely upon wholesale. Nevertheless a strong positive leader should not shrink from giving a lead at times, even when all about him doubt the course he has set. You need to be an experienced and confident head to do this though and be very sure you are right.

Perhaps it is better to reserve this approach for the less important and reversible decisions. For example, you want an established member of staff to try teaching an age group different from that she is normally used to taking. You may be able, by exercise of authority, to make the change in the hope that, by the end of the year, she will have been converted by the experience. On the other hand, there is always the danger that she will have her worst fears confirmed. At least you can then return her to her previous age group. You need to know your individual staff members really well as personalities before employing this tactic.

If you cannot persuade your staff of the value and benefits of a change you propose, and you don't know them individually well enough to forecast that they will be converted by the practice, even if the theory doesn't appeal, then maybe it is the wrong moment to insist upon or to impose the change. A half-hearted or hostile implementation of an idea will condemn it to failure. I recall an exercise in staff profiling on a course where someone wrote of a teacher, 'Miss X is always ready to try out new ideas and determined to make them fail'. Presumably Miss X had been on the receiving end of a large number of imposed decisions in the formulation of which she had played no part.

Sometimes there simply isn't time to do anything other than take the decision yourself. Where it seems to make no real difference to anyone else except you, it is quite legitimate to take the decision yourself anyway. Sometimes, though, there may have to be a decision which affects everyone but which has to be made on the spot without reference to anyone else. A decision to evacuate the school-building after a bomb-threat phone call, or to close the school because the water supply has been frozen up, are two dramatic, but not unusual, examples. Both have happened to me. These are leadership decisions and are taken in the full knowledge that you are entirely responsible for the consequences, and that you may have to justify the decisions after the event, when hindsight will be available to those who judge you. Sometimes these decisions turn out to be wrong, but, as long as they were responsibly taken on the best evidence available at the time, no reasonable person can justify criticising you.

On the other hand, there will be times when other views can be solicited before you make a decision which will, nevertheless once made, still be your responsibility. The decision to regard the bomb threat phone call as a hoax and to re-enter the building could be one of these. It would be taken after consultation with the rest of the staff, and after advice from the police, but it would still be your decision.

Fortunately, most instant decisions are not as momentous as these. It may just be a matter of, with both of you with diaries in your hands at that moment, making a date for the school photographer to call. Such arrangements will be made with due regard to known calendar and timetable commitments and subject to revision if it turns out to be really inconvenient for the rest of the staff. For this reason, such arrangements should be made sufficiently far ahead of the date to allow changes to be made, and for the staff to be given plenty of notice of the event. A date set for next term would be a reasonable on-the-spot agreement in these terms, a date set for next week would not.

Generally speaking, if people can know what options are being considered before a decision is made, they are more likely to accept a decision than if they only hear about the decision after it has been taken. Hearing about the options beforehand implies, of course, that people will have an opportunity to make their views known, and will expect to have them taken into account, so that there is a real opportunity to modify or change the final decision.

The main difference between the teaching staff and the head is that they do not have the authority to 'tell' the head to adopt an idea, they have to 'sell' it to him. The wise head will also sell, rather then tell, when it comes to implementing his own ideas.

It is not always wise to enter into a debate with a very firm commitment to one particular solution to a problem. Sometimes this amounts to prejudging a situation before all the evidence has been heard. A wise head will prepare himself by thinking through all the alternatives he can think of in advance of a staff meeting called to make a decision on some matter, but he may not have thought of some of the alternatives which others have. Keeping an open mind, and not closing one's options too early, are the signs of a wise negotiator.

Delegation

Another general principle in decision-making is that, ideally, decisions should be taken by those closest to the level of implementation. Decisions about classroom practices, for example, should be made with the fullest contribution possible from classroom teachers because it is at their level that the immediate and practical consequences will be felt daily, not in the head's office. Delegation may be to an individual or a group but it must be clear to all concerned at the outset what is being delegated, to whom and within what confines decisions are to be made.

Decisions on curriculum matters are probably those which require the most complete staff involvement if they are to be implemented successfully. Such decisions cannot usually be taken quickly and require lengthy and skilled negotiation and periodic review. This type of decision-making process can be frustrating for the impatient, but the alternative of an imposed scheme of work is, as experience has often shown in the past, largely an exercise in self-deception, for if people are not committed to a procedure they may present the outward signs of conformity but will remodel the spirit of it to suit their own beliefs and practice.

True delegation is not just giving a job to someone or to a group, all the decisions and procedures having been minutely worked out beforehand. There would be little point in that. It would be offering very little responsibility to the delegate and wouldn't have off-loaded much of the work from the delegator. Of course, it is often easier to do things oneself than to get someone else to do it. It is often necessary to do things oneself if one wants things done in a particular way, but the question then has to be asked, 'Even if this is an excellent way of doing something is it the only excellent way?' A harder question to face is, 'Even though my way may produce the best result in terms of the specified task, will there be additional, incidental benefits to be gained by allowing someone else to apply their own, second-best solution, which will more than compensate for the effects of a less than perfect conclusion to the task?' Teachers make these decisions every day in the interests of their pupils' education. In art and craft work, for example, is the production of a prespecified artefact a more important consideration than the pupil's exploration of his own ideas and his experience of handling tools and materials, even if, in the latter case, nothing concrete is produced at the end? It is a matter for judgement when the one course is more appropriate than the other.

The manager has to balance the value of the immediate task being done in a specific way against the long-term growth and development of the staff, and the organisation as a whole. People only learn to do things well by doing them, sometimes doing them not so well to begin with. They cannot learn everything by simply watching someone else do it well, though they can learn much from others' experience and mistakes. All heads know that, however many courses and lectures about headship they attended before they became heads, there was nothing like the real thing for promoting rapid and effective learning. The same principle applies lower down the management chain.

If you really want something done your way, don't delegate the job. It is very demotivating to be delegated to perform a task, and then to feel that the delegator wants to operate the delegatee by remote control. It insinuates a lack of trust and confidence by the manager in that staff member.

Staff participation — the pros and cons weighed up

It is perhaps, appropriate at this point to summarise the arguments for and against autocracy and 'corporacy' in school management.

Autocratic management depends upon the will of one person, the headteacher. The effective exercise of autocracy will lead to swift decisions and consistent decisions being taken by the person who is, after all, supposed to be the senior person paid for taking responsibility for everything to do with the school.

The problems with autocracy are that the person exercising it has to be infallible, will need to spend an inordinate amount of time and effort persuading people to implement decisions in exactly the way they were intended to work and will almost always provoke resistance every time a decision is made. The autocratic head has also to contend with a general move, in society at large, away from authoritarian to participative practices and a teacher force which is more professionally aware of the forces which interact to promote healthy management structures in schools.

The headteacher who promotes corporate decision-making in schools is delegating some of his authority to others lower down the management chain. This ensures that teachers understand the reasons for decisions and, by being involved in making them, become more committed to them and their implementation. It increases their interest in, and satisfaction with, their job and motivates them more surely than old-fashioned 'carrot and stick' methods.

The problems with the corporate approach to decision-making are all soluble, but need to be recognised in advance so that the advantages are not lost through failure to avoid the potential pitfalls.

First, not every staff member is immediately ready to assume full-blooded participation in the decision-making processes in the school. Those who previously have been used to an autocratic regime will not necessarily welcome the increased involvement and greater responsibility that is implied by a corporate approach to decision-making. Corporate decision-making is not a more permissive form of management. It actually requires people to work harder than they were expected to do under an autocracy. This will quickly become obvious to those who become involved in corporate decision-making and it may not, at first sight, seem much of an incentive to some members of staff. Handled with patience and sensitivity, however, people will begin to appreciate that the personal benefits which accrue will more than compensate for the extra work and responsibility.

Teachers unused to participating in decision-making and with little experience of shouldering real managerial responsibility will need training for their new role. To begin with, it may be difficult to get decisions made at all, and meetings will tend to be long, argumentative, and inconclusive. This can be frustrating for all concerned, but it can be a valuable self-learning process for the staff and one which it is often necessary to go through before progress can be made. Skilled chairmanship by the head will be particularly necessary at this stage. It is probably better to concentrate on simple, relatively unimportant problems at this learning stage. Strangely, it is the apparently simple decisions which often generate the longest debate and the strongest opinions. Perhaps that is because, in these matters, everyone feels sufficiently confident to express an opinion.

Be aware that there will be many areas where staff may not have an opinion, and will feel insecure being placed in a position where they have to help to make decisions without feeling that they understand the issues involved. This is the time when they will look to the head for leadership, and it will be his task to demonstrate his command of the pros and cons to assist and guide the uncertain towards making an informed choice.

Group problem-solving is slower than individuals making decisions but it should lead to a richer solution which has been formed by the collective thinking of several minds. Because all those minds have contributed to the solution, they will have a better understanding of the problem and a more ready acceptance of the actions decided upon.

Finally, be aware that often opinion is not unanimous about a particular course of action or a particular decision. You must decide at the outset how conflict is to be avoided even though agreement may not be total. You may decide that a majority vote is the best way of resolving a deadlock, but this can be divisive and leave a sometimes substantial minority disgruntled. Consensus decisions, on the other hand, may end up as compromises which do not entirely satisfy anyone. With practice, groups get better at making decisions and learn that every member may find himself in a minority at times but that he must sometimes be prepared to 'go along' with decisions for the good of the group, and for the achievement of a decision. Good advanced groundwork by the head amongst individual members is an important way of avoiding open public conflict in a large meeting. People may often be prepared to speak more frankly in very small groups of two or three and also are often more tolerant of opposing views. If some of the difficulties can be faced and argued through before a large meeting, this will speed the decision-making of the meeting itself. The ideal number for good decision-making is probably four or five, the maximum number ten or a dozen. Primary school teachers will recognise that the majority of primary school staff will fall within these limits, and so have something going for them to begin with. Larger primary school staff must decide how they are going to be divided up for the concentrated 'committee work' which goes into decision-making before its conclusions are presented for public affirmation by the whole staff.

The most important decision, however, is made by one person, the headteacher. The decision is to eschew autocracy and embrace corporate decision-making. You can't ask a committee to decide that for you!

References

Everard, K. B. and Morris, G. (1985) *Effective School Management* Harper and Row.
Glatter, R. et al. (eds) (1988) *Understanding School Management* OU Press.
Handy, C. (1994) *Understanding Organisations* (4th edn.) Penguin.
Handy, C. (1984) *Taken for Granted: Understanding Schools as Organisations* Longman/Schools Council.

5   School-centred financial management

Michael Jackson

Local management of schools (LMS) has been the most significant development for primary school management this century. The government believes that:

> Effective schemes of local management will enable governing bodies and headteachers to plan their use of resources — including their most valuable resource, their staff — to maximum effect in accordance with their own needs and priorities, and to make schools more responsive to their clients — parents, pupils, the local community and employers. *Circular 7/88*, para 9

From April 1994, almost all 26 000 schools in England and Wales have managed their own finances. Many schools have welcomed this increased freedom and flexibility, and would argue that their schools have become more effective with the introduction of LMS. At the same time, there are many people who still see LMS as a burden which is preventing them from doing their job properly. They see financial management as something which takes them away from the teaching of, and caring for, children.

LMS is working most effectively in those schools that have recognised that a coherent approach is needed to the whole management of the school. Budgeting should be an integral part of the whole school planning and decision-making process. A school's budget is simply a way of costing and then implementing those plans. LMS will be judged on how adequately it enables schools to respond to the needs of its children.

The Audit Commission in a recent report said:

The objective of delegating financial management from local authorities to schools was to enpower schools to use their closer knowledge of pupils and their communities in determining how resources could be applied to greatest effect. A further aim was to improve efficiency by enabling schools, through their day-to-day management, to use resources efficiently. Local management was also intended to strengthen accountability by more sharply focusing responsibility for the management of resources on schools themselves. Audit Commission (1993)

Whether we like it or not, the delegation of budgets to schools has meant that words like accountability, clients, efficiency, effectiveness and managers, are with us and are not going to go away. As we move towards the year 2000, headteachers are going to have to accept the extension of their chief executive role, and the subsequent displacement from the core act of teaching. They will need to be the people with the vision of where the school is going and with the managerial expertise to plan and budget for the journey.

The school development plan

Since the introduction of local management, it has been the intention of the government and of many LEAs to extend the areas of delegation:

The Government intends to extend the benefits of LMS. His aim is to build on the progress that has already been made towards pupil-led funding and delegated management, so as to increase schools' control over resources and thereby improve the standards of education which they provide. *Circular 7/91*, para.3

If these delegated finances are to be used effectively by the school, it is essential that there is a well thought out and comprehensive plan in place. This enables the school to set attainable and observable targets, and to assess where it is now with respect to those targets. With such a framework in place, the school is then able to design an implementation strategy. It is essential that the school development plan drives the budget and not the other way round.

Once the school development plan has identified the school's short-, medium- and long-term priorities, then it is important to attempt to cost out these priorities. The ideas set out by Caldwell and Spinks in *The Self-Managing School* would give schools a framework to aim for. They demonstrate the relationship between policy-making, planning and resourcing. If we were to take an example from their work, *Special Needs*, the main headings of this programme of work would be:

1. *Purpose:* this would identify the specific aims of the programme of work.
2. *Broad guidelines:* this would indicate in a general way what is required, what the learning difficulties of the children were and how they might be overcome.
3. *Plan for implementation:* this would identify, in more detail, how the programme is to be implemented. This would include the resources needed including teaching and non-teaching resources.
4. *Resources required:* in this section the teaching, non-teaching, materials and equipment are set out in greater detail and the respective costs calculated.
5. *Evaluation:* this section would indicate how and when the programme would be evaluated.

The above educational programme would be aimed at a specific group of children within the school. At the same time, there would be a direct link with the schools overall policy on special needs. This illustrates how policies are translated into educational programmes for children through planning and budgeting.

In secondary schools, it would be possible to have subject specific programmes directly linked to subject policies. This reflects how teachers work, and how the children learn. In primary schools, we would want to take a different approach. Here, it would be necessary to have programmes of a more general nature for a specific age range of children, e.g. Key Stage 1 or Key Stage 2. Such programmes would reflect how the school was organised, and would relate to a number of curriculum policies.

As schools become more adept at handling the schools finances, so they will be able to cost more accurately how they are going to put into action the school's policies, through the school's development plan.

The role of the headteacher and the governing body

It must always be remembered that LMS delegates the school's financial budget to the governors. This is a major financial responsibility, and one that many school governors have yet to grasp. It is the governors alone who can legally set and approve a school's final budget. Those governors who go through such a process without any access to a school's development plan may be accused of, at best, merely 'rubber stamping' the process, or, at the worst, abdicating their responsibilities.

It is essential that the whole budget cycle be well thought out and accessible to all the staff of the school. A suggested cycle may look like this:

1. *Review or audit:* where staff look at where the school is. This would involve reviewing the previous year's plans.
2. *Re-definition of the school's aims:* ensure that everyone involved in the school is aware of these aims.
3. *Establishment of school development plan:* determining where the school is aiming for, what are its short-, medium- and long-term targets, in some sort of priority order.
4. *Budgetary process:* at this stage, budgetary information is available and the process of costing the school's development plan will begin.
5. *Implementation of the plan:* it may be that different parts of the plan will have to be implemented in stages, according to financial restraints.
6. *Monitoring and evaluation:* this will be done by various groups within the school. It is important that the senior staff are in a position to bring all the different ideas together.
   The cycle would then begin again.

At all stages of the cycle, it is important that governors have some input, or are at least kept informed. It would make sense for some governors to be involved with teaching and non-teaching staff at all stages of the planning cycle. This can be done either by involving individual governors, as and when they are available, or, as is becoming more the case, to have a well-structured system of governor sub-committees, each one taking responsibility to be involved with the staff at one or more of these planning stages.

Monitoring of the school's budget is an essential procedure. In many schools, budget managers, whether they be headteachers, secretaries or LEA staff are involved in regular reviews of the budget to ensure that expenditure follows predicted patterns. Headteachers should then ensure that the governors receive regular reports on the progress of the budget. It is a good idea that the finance sub-committee have a thorough review on the progress of the budget against the school development plan at a half-yearly stage. This allows any unexpected, and therefore unplanned, changes to be implemented.

The recent Audit Commission report noted some areas of concern with regard to the amount of authority headteachers had to spend the schools budget. It stated that only 10 per cent of headteachers reported that they had any limit on their authority to spend money. It went on to say:

In a small but noticeable number of schools there have been questionable practices... Some of these practices are questionable in themselves. Others raise questions because governors had either not been asked for their consent or had not been informed of all the relevant consequences... Audit Commission (1993)

The report then goes on to recommend that governors should reconsider their decision to allow headteachers to spend money without limit. It is important to get the balance right. On the one hand, governors need to remember that financial responsibility is delegated to them not to headteachers, but that, if headteachers are to manage the schools effectively on a day-to-day basis, they must be given the power to do so. Headteachers need to remember that the management of the school is a partnership, and that the governors are very powerful and important partners who need to be kept informed.

Accountability

Part of the thinking behind the Government's 1988 Education Reform Act and the introduction of LMS was to make schools more accountable. With the introduction of LMS, it became necessary for LEAs to allocate a budget to all schools and, more importantly, to make this information accessible to many people. At the same time, governors became obliged to make a financial report to parents on an annual basis, as part of their annual report.

It must be remembered that governors have been given stewardship of public funds. It is, therefore, essential that schools and their governors develop clearly defined mechanisms for accountability.

At the same time, schools and their governing bodies need to remember that they are accountable to the children in their care and to the parents. Schools need to become much more accurate with the process of matching budgets to development plans and priorities. It is understandable that many schools are very cautious when they first are delegated responsibility for the school's budget. It is this caution that is partly the reason for the substantial balance of income over expenditure that many schools at present have.

In a number of schools, this carry forward figure is known by all and properly accounted for in the school's long-term planning. In other schools, this sum of money seems to come about almost by accident, and there are no clear plans as to what it will be used for.

Many schools end the financial year with balances of unspent money in their budgets. Almost all schools allow for some contingency in case of unexpected events, and this is quite reasonable. Before LMS, local authorities used to do the same. Some schools may have large carry forwards because they have long-term objectives identified within their school development plans. It is important that this information is shared with parents, especially if they have children who may leave the school before they can benefit from the savings in current expenditure.

In some authorities, the size of some individual schools' carry forward figure is causing concern at all levels. There is some evidence that some schools are holding excessive balances, and that with some there is a progressive unjustified growth in balances. The Audit Commission report talks about the significant amounts of money held by some secondary schools, and quotes some schools as holding balances up to £200 000. It then goes on to say that it is difficult to understand what unforeseen circumstances could merit holding balances of £200 000 as a general contingency. It needs to be remembered that, even though the figures in primary schools, of excessive balances, may be much lower, in terms of percentage of the schools' budget they are in fact much higher.

If the schools and their governing body are to be held accountable to parents about how the school's budget is being spent, then more attention needs to be given to this question of unspent money. As the Audit Commission reported:

> Whilst the establishment of an appropriate level of balances at the start of local management of schools was sensible, such balances should not be allowed to increase without rational justification... One effect of balances is that a sum approaching 5% of the annual grant for school education is not being used. Another effect is that schools are seeking to achieve 100% of the required output with 95% of the resources. It is appropriate that schools should hold balances as a contingency and for specific projects outlined in the school development plan. It is the element of balances held for no reason which causes concern. Audit Commission (1993)

Conclusion

The introduction of local management of schools was intended to allow schools to determine for themselves the particular needs of their schools and their children, and then to have the financial flexibility to meet those needs. Those schools now into their fourth year of LMS speak enthusiastically about the increased opportunities they now have for greater self-management. At the heart of many of these schools, will be a clear and agreed school development plan which has the needs of the children at its centre. Such a plan will be the driving force behind all financial planning.

If schools are to benefit from this new-found freedom and increased opportunities, there is a need for strong leadership. This does not mean a return to the traditional, autocratic style leadership, but rather to a style of leadership which encompasses partnership. The leaders of our schools will need to have a commitment to and a capacity to articulate a vision for where their schools are going. They will need to work with staff and governors to plan for the future and to use the resources within their control to implement that plan.

References

Audit Commission (1993) *Adding up the Sums: Schools' Management of their Finances* HMSO.

Caldwell, B. J. and Spinks, J. M. (1988) *The Self-Managing School* The Falmer Press.

DES (1988) Circular No. 7/88 *Education Reform Act: Local Management of Schools.*

DES (1991) Circular No. 7/91 *Local Management of Schools: Further Guidance.*

Davies, B. and Ellison, L. (1992) *School Development Planning* Longman.

Preedy, M. (1993) *Managing the Effective School* Open University.

6 The deputy as trainee head

Derek Waters

The advertisements for primary deputy headteachers placed in the professional press by school governors provide clear indications both of the calibre and experience required for the post and the range of tasks and responsibilities the successful candidates will have to carry out. They are expected to be 'excellent classroom practitioners' have 'a sound educational philosophy', 'experience of curriculum leadership' and 'possession of excellent interpersonal skills in working with staff, parents, governors and the wider community' (No doubt in this case it is assumed that the same would apply to pupils.) The new deputy headteachers would have to 'contribute to the overall management and development of the school with vitality and imagination and in the management development of LMS'; in another example they would have 'a leading role in curriculum and staff development and share with the head in the management of the school'. It is quite evident that what is being offered is a position of shared leadership, shared power and shared responsibility. What a far cry this is from not so many years ago when in a report (DES 1985) the Welsh Office HMI stated that deputy heads in primary schools were carrying out lower level tasks than the curriculum leaders. Perhaps older readers can recall some of the mundane tasks that such people carried out, e.g. totalling the registers on a Friday afternoon, collecting the staff tea money, and looking after the cycling proficiency campaign. Those deputies more fortunate in their headteachers than others saw their bosses as mentors and, when in due season they were promoted, they were ready to take over the onerous duties that this seniority brought.

Many headteachers realise that, apart from this altruistic and professional responsibility they have for the development of the deputy, they must share their workload with their senior colleague if they are to survive and the school is to flourish. Many headteachers, particularly those of experience had the good fortune of having had management training provided by the LEA or the then DES; or took it upon themselves to attend weekend and vacation courses, often subsidised by a local authority. Relatively speaking, the cost of such courses was not high. Today, there has been a severe cutback on such courses and, where they exist, funding is severely limited to enable staff to attend. Such courses that do exist need to be studied carefully to assess, to see if they meet precisely the deputy head's training needs, full course details with content, objectives, methodology and information about the staffing. Further information can usually be obtained. Most helpful is a recommendation of the course by a local adviser or someone who attended the same programme on a previous occasion. One does not become a manager by reading books; nevertheless, carefully selected titles, of recent publication date, especially by practitioners are well worth studying. Sadly, little has appeared in print about the work of the deputy head. I argue that the role of head and deputy should, in the best of all worlds, be interchangeable. Therefore, what the head and deputy should do in advance of a new school year is to decide upon the range of activities in which each should engage. What is more probable than this scenario is that the head could suggest a new task which would provide valuable experience. Similarly, the deputy could take the initiative and ask whether a particular facet of the job could be transferred in this way. What is important in such arrangements is that the rest of the staff, the governors and parents should know of this re-allocation of duties, so that everyone will know whom to approach on a particular subject. Only one major obstacle stands in the way of this remarkable example of hands-on experience. Everyone, and in particular the headteacher, is extremely busy to the point of not being able to do many things as well as they should be done. So this essential element of deputy head training is going to depend upon the good will of the head. In a report to ILEA in 1985 Norman Thomas (formerly Chief Primary HMI) recommended:

> We believe that nearly all the deputy heads should be on the way towards becoming heads, and the heads should give them as much pre-training and experience as possible.

But circumstances are very different now. What must be evident is the practical contribution that the deputy is making towards meeting the demands on the school. It would be expected that the deputy would be fully involved in the school programme, sometimes as a leader and at other times as a participant. But, in addition, there should be a planned programme to meet the specific needs of the deputy head. This assumes a willingness and a competence on the part of the headteacher to engage in this activity and, similarly, a co-operative attitude and an ability to benefit on the part of the deputy. Mutual respect and a sound working professional relationship between the two senior members of staff are prerequisites for the success of such a programme. The term 'programme' has been deliberately chosen, since the activities and experiences would be planned to cover a period of two years. While much that will be proposed will need to be carried out while the school is in session, some items will have to be done outside those normal hours, and both parties will need to commit themselves to this arrangement.

Where the head, because of pressure of work, is unable to give the same commitment to the task as the deputy is willing to offer, it will be important for the deputy to seek the opportunities which are suggested later in the chapter. It will be necessary for the deputy to indicate that the activities are suggested to enable the head's responsibilities to be carried out in the case of absence and to assist with personal career development. To enable some things to take place, the co-operation of other teaching and support staff may be required, and the deputy must be clear about what (s)he is requesting by way of assistance and why this is necessary. Some arrangements can be suggested which will be to the mutual benefit of all parties concerned.

Advisers and local inspectors who will be involved in preparation for headship courses and in appointments will wish to see evidence of training initiatives adopted in school, and will want to encourage the active interest of the headteacher in this process. In recent times, some LEAs have designed courses which require the attendance of both heads and deputies, thus acknowledging the key leadership roles which each holds.

Gaining experience

In order to deputise properly, even for a very short time, the deputy head ought to know everything the head knows in relation to the school, and what has to go on to make it function effectively and efficiently. So, there is a need systematically to list all the tasks which the head engages in during a typical year. It could be useful to keep a professional diary to record experiences undergone with comments upon them. Alternatively, a large notebook can be obtained, with different headings given to each page, an index to indicate cross references, and the facility to annotate the reports with personal comments. Ideally, if time can be found, the deputy and head should have regular discussions about the entries made in this training logbook to check accuracy, seek further clarification, indicate links and where further development or reinforcement is required. In the absence of such regular advice from the head, a critical friend, e.g. another deputy or another head, can be asked to provide the counselling service. It is suggested that such discussions be confined to positive comments about the deputy's training progress.

Administration

Because of the demands of recent Education Acts 1993 and other legislation, there has been a great increase in the administrative work of the school. While a good secretary can relieve the headteacher of much of this, its sheer volume and complexity is turning the head into an administrator with less opportunity to be a professional leader in the school. The deputy could, to the school's advantage, take over more responsibility for the day-to-day running of the institution. Since the proposal is that the deputy should share the head's workload, administration must be included. Attendance at courses and conferences on such items as local management of schools will mean that the demands of tasks will be shared, but also that, on promotion to headship, the deputy is already familiar with the theory and practice of financial management.

Headteachers will want the school to run efficiently in their absence and it makes good sense to show deputies both the standard forms and accompanying instructions for their use. The opportunity for training in a practical way will be to show with real examples how the details are filled in and procedures followed. On the next occasion when a return is required, the deputy can carry out the prescribed procedure. In larger primary schools, much of the administrative work is carried out by the secretary, and in some areas it is she who would be the obvious tutor to seek help from. Deputies should, in the normal course of events, assist the headteacher with administration, but they should seek experience of all such work at different times. While they may not have to do all of it when they become headteachers, they need to know all about it, since they have to append signatures thus accepting responsibility.

The deputy should know about the filing system in operation and have access to it. Communications from the DES and LEA, including those marked confidential, should be available to the deputy. Letters will also arrive from other sources, including parents, and the head can be helpful to the deputy by discussing the appropriate form of reply to each since there will be no LEA guidance in this area. The deputy could be invited to suggest a suitable response, with the head commenting on this afterwards. It could well be that a mutual consideration of some correspondence could improve the quality of the reply. In most cases, and certainly in those which are sensitive, a copy of the reply should be kept. The examination of a series of letters and replies could be useful to a deputy.

In the absence of the head or involvement somewhere else in the school, callers and those who telephone should be invited to speak to the deputy.

Experience of this kind should be seen as valuable training, as well as serving the needs of the school. Such interviews and even telephone calls can be stressful, and the deputy needs to be in possession of the facts, if the matter is going to be dealt with adequately. In cases of doubt, it is wise to listen carefully and sympathetically, promise to investigate promptly, and to call back or arrange another meeting. A careful discussion with the head after investigation should be followed by a sincere request to be invited to continue to deal with the case or alternatively attend the promised interview.

At other meetings, for instance, when children are transferring to their secondary schools, as well as being made familiar with procedures, the deputy should ask to sit in on the parental choice sessions.

Ritual practices

The deputy should be taking regular assemblies of the whole school. The head may be observed conducting such events, but it is imperative that practice is gained. Some deputies feel a degree of reluctance to have other staff attend assemblies; it is better if they do, since it will be more normal for the children, and some early feedback can be requested from senior colleagues. Wise deputies always have an instant assembly ready in case the head is unavoidably detained and sends a note with the cryptic message 'carry on'. Certain special assemblies, harvest festival, Christmas and Easter celebrations, often require a different form of leadership. Once again, responsibility for this can be shared with the head. Some schools hold prize days or leaver's days, and the form of these should be noted carefully. The deputy usually has a role to fulfil on these occasions, and some enlargement of this can be suggested to gain further experience.

Visitors are a regular feature of some schools: HMI, LEA advisers, governors, students, other teachers and prospective parents. The deputy can volunteer to carry out this escorting duty following some careful planning and liaison with colleagues. A checklist can be prepared following such experiences and used subsequently as a guide.

Most schools make good practical arrangements to welcome the new intake of children and their parents in advance of the new term. As well as knowing the whole procedure, the deputy should ask to attend the welcoming session to see what goes on; how information is gathered from the adults; what the future pupils do at this time; how the new teachers are introduced, and so on.

The deputy, especially if new to the school, should be observant of all the other ritual and practice which goes on, to assess its value to the social organisation of the institution. In one school, the head might meet the staff informally before the children come in and, to all intents and purposes, conduct a staff meeting; in another, the staff may have a social gathering once a term; in a third place the head may take all the children in the hall to allow staff to carry out classroom organisational tasks for the following week. The examples are legion, many of them idiosyncratic, yet most serve a useful purpose. Those that are might be noted for later use by a promoted deputy, suitably modified to suit the new context.

The governing body

By examining the Rules and Articles of Government issued by the LEA, as well as the plentiful literature on the subject (e.g. Wragg and Partington, 1990 and Leonard, 1989), the roles, rights and responsibilities of governors can be discovered. New legislation in parliament has increased the powers of the body, as well as clarifying their position *vis-à-vis* the LEA and the headteacher (1986 and 1988 Education Acts).

If the deputy is the elected staff member, then regular attendance and active involvement at the termly meetings will provide valuable experience. Where this is not the case, then the head should ask the chairperson if the deputy can observe on a regular basis. The latter would not be allowed to speak unless invited, and would have to leave during the discussion of any confidential matter (unlike the elected staff governor). It may be possible to attend staff interviews with the chairperson's aggreement and to be allowed to ask questions, but (s)he would not be allowed to vote in the selection process.

It should be helpful to the head for the deputy to get to know the individuals on the governing body as well as possible, so that the responsibility of welcoming them to the school to special events or for routine visits can be shared.

The professional role

The deputy must always be seeking to improve personal classroom practice and provide a good example of professionalism to colleagues. Varied teaching experience should be sought. On a yearly basis, this should not be difficult to arrange but, in addition, opportunities should be sought with colleagues to exchange classes for one period a week. This experience over an extended time should enable the newly appointed head to discuss primary practice, throughout the age range, with knowledge and confidence. Visits to other schools to observe good practice can be a regular feature of the training process. Often, the chance to look around one's own school and discuss in open, frank and positive terms with colleagues what is going on in the teaching and learning process is overlooked. The newest recruit to the profession has much to offer the experienced teacher and the deputy should be ready to receive new insights from those ready and able to offer them. Such professional discussions should boost the confidence of colleagues, especially those new to the profession. The deputy may be designated staff member responsible for the professional and pastoral care of probationer teachers and students on teacher training. Many LEAs have formulated programmes of induction which incorporate a school-based element. There needs to be a degree of flexibility within the whole programme, and this applies particularly within the school setting. This responsibility demands considerable skills in terms of providing assistance in various forms with such matters as classroom organisation, resource provision, motivation of children, and work planning. In addition, the need to build up and maintain a good relationship with a new colleague is paramount. This role of the deputy could include staff development. The success of this enterprise will depend largely upon attitudes and feelings of goodwill, co-operation, trust and mutual support fostered in the professional setting of the staffroom.

Where another member of staff has been appointed to take responsibility for staff training, the deputy head should offer the fullest co-operation as well as taking an active interest in the programme.

Curriculum responsibility

It is important for every teacher to have the opportunity to exercise leadership in some aspect of the curriculum (Waters, 1983). The role in this respect for the deputy should offer opportunities both to help the school and the individual. In some schools, either because there are too few members of staff, or because there is a special expertise available, the deputy will assume a curriculum responsibility. With the advent of a national curriculum, a wider role can be anticipated. To provide a broad and balanced curriculum, a co-ordinator will be required, and the deputy could be the most appropriate person for this task. In any case, it will be important to be familiar with all the documentation which is being sent to the schools by the DFE and LEAs. An active part will be expected from the Deputy in regular school based INSET, particularly on the organisation side but also in terms of providing active learning situations. Allocation of funding to curriculum areas will involve the deputy in decision-making activities with senior colleagues.

Managing meetings

It will be unfortunate if the headteacher insists upon chairing every meeting in the school, thus preventing other members of staff taking on this responsibility. The deputy should ask for opportunities to take on this role, and then have the chance to discuss the process afterwards. As well as general business meetings, there will be gatherings of all or part of the staff to discuss curriculum matters, the organisation of special events, and emergency matters, e.g. a discipline problem, a new directive from the education committee and so on. The size of the staff and the nature of the business will dictate the level of formality which is required. However, many meetings are regarded as disappointing because no decisions are reached or action agreed upon. To aid in this process of managing meetings in a business-like manner, the chairperson must prepare adequately. This must include agreeing date, time, duration, place of meeting and its purpose. The form and amount of preparation that all, as well as particular members must undertake. The meeting itself should start on time and work steadily through the agenda, with the chairperson ensuring that different viewpoints are expressed and listened to attentively, summarising, seeking suggestions for action, and so on. The keeping of records of the meeting is vital so that, where agreements and action have been agreed, this is firmly stated with the people responsible for carrying out the decision by a definite date. It is a useful idea to adopt a flipchart for some, if not all, meetings so that everyone can see what is being recorded by way of suggestions and decisions. The formalities and courtesies must be observed by the chair who sets the tone of the meeting. Follow-up includes writing up the minutes, as well as prompting individuals to deal with issues they have taken on.

Parent organisations

Where there is a formal parent organisation, whether a PTA or not, the deputy should be actively involved both to support the head and to gain experience in dealing with parents as a body. Once again, opportunities for committee work and other forms of leadership can arise, as well as for formally addressing the parents. The most successful groups are those which have developed a pattern of fundraising, social and educational activities, and see themselves as being an active support of what the school is trying to achieve. The deputy is in a unique position to set a powerful example to the staff, be a source of practical and creative ideas and an energetic worker on behalf of the organisation

Deputising

There will be occasional opportunities for the incumbent to carry out a deputising role. Sometimes this will be for a short period, e.g. part of a day or the whole of one. There is unlikely to be supply cover for such occasions, and so class responsibility will continue. Only emergencies are likely to arise, to be dealt with, if a competent secretary is on hand to deal with routine matters. However, problems can happen, and the deputy should be ready and able to deal with a crisis. The head should alert the deputy when a difficulty can be anticipated and in any case should, in a training setting, have prepared the person concerned for most eventualities. The local office or a neighbouring head can be contacted in a case of real difficulties. Where there has been an incident, the deputy should make a written record of it, and discuss it and the action taken as soon as the head returns. In the case of a longer absence by the head: from illness, course attendance, or during an interregnum period, supply cover should be available and so the acting head can adopt the new role.

Familiarity with the day-to-day running of the school will be of great value. While the LEA can anticipate that no major changes will be made, it will expect more than a caretaking role to be carried out. Regular but not over-frequent discussions with the head would be a wise plan to adopt. In the case of a head-designate, arrangements should be made to communicate from time to time, so that the transfer of position can be made smoothly. Such behaviour should ensure a good working partnership later. While the new position for the deputy is different, good relationships even if slightly more formal, must be maintained if the school is to run satisfactorily, and a comfortable transfer back to former duties is possible. Occasionally, the deputy can be invited to take on the acting headship in another school. This too provides some good opportunities for learning and a real knowledge of whether the position of headteacher is exactly what is desired. While there are some advantages in being an acting head in a different school, the development of new and possibly brief relationships with staff, pupils and parents makes particular demands upon the individual. To refuse such an opportunity may be unwise, however challenging or even uninviting the situation appears. Reflection on events and decisions will be useful to the deputy in deciding on further training needs.

Appraisal

A regular process of appraisal will involve all staff, including the deputy and the head in the two-year cycle. Appraisal should be regarded as a two-way exchange of views about the past and present with a view to creating an even more satisfactory and satisfying future. The deputy, after self-evaluation, should work with the head to build up a suitable agenda for discussion.

The final outcome should include the setting of realistic targets for development. These might include some change in the job definition as items like financial aspects, curriculum developments, working party membership are included. The removal of some responsibilities could mean further opportunities for other members of staff to enhance their roles. The latter proposals can provide an opportunity for the deputy to be actively involved in the development of other colleagues. In large schools, or where the deputy becomes an acting headteacher, there will be appraisal interviews to conduct. To be able to carry out such activity, training opportunities should be sought. The deputy will be responsible for the appraisal of some staff.

Conclusion

These proposals are a far cry from the days when the deputy's responsibilities did not extend further than the preparation of the playground rota and collection of tea money, and that person being 'dumped' in a head's chair totally unprepared to face the challenges of that post.

It is a demanding training programme which has been suggested in this chapter, and should be seen as the practical element to complement the more theoretical input from one of the planned training courses mentioned at the beginning of the section.

Much will depend upon the head, the relationship with the deputy, and the time available. Even without the headteacher's full particpation there is much that can be done to prepare for headship. This book in its various ways will suggest further important areas for consideration to enable the deputy to engage in the process of self-skilling. As educational budgets are reduced, more responsibility will be thrown back on staff to equip themselves for more senior positions. The art of management is concerned with successfully operating within the resource framework. Those who succeed best are those who are positive about the constraints and learn to manage themselves and their own development in a systematic way.

References

DES (1985) *Primary Education in Wales* HMSO.
ILEA (1985) *Improving Primary Schools* (The Thomas Report).
Leonard, M. (1989) *School Governors Handbook* Blackwell.
Waters, D. (1983) *Responsibility and Promotion in the Primary School* Heinemann.
Wragg, E. C. and Partington, J. A. (1990) *A Handbook for School Governors* Methuen.

Further reading

Craig, I. (1988) *Managing the Primary Classroom* Longman.
Craig, I. (1988) *Primary Headship in the 1990s* Longman.
Donnelly, J. (1990) *A Handbook for Deputy Heads* Kogan Page (written with Secondary Deputies in mind).
Everard, K. B. and Morris, G. (1990) *Effective School Management* Harper.
Fullan, M. (1992) *What's Worth Fighting for in Headship* OU Press.
Glatter, R. (1987) *Understanding School Management* OU Press.
Southworth, G. (ed.) (1987) *Readings in Primary School Management* Falmer Press.

7 Managing the subject-based curriculum

Charles Frisby

I want to suggest that:

1. the revival of the subject as the basis for the primary school curriculum is a positive step.
2. the subject co-ordinator has, first of all to establish the subject firmly within the thinking about the development of the school
3. the main task of the co-ordinator in designing and implementing a scheme of work in the subject is to give attention to the ways in which the content can be most effectively delivered
4. this suggestion should challenge the orthodox view that primary schools should be organised on a basis of non-specialist, autonomous class teaching. Rather, the subject-centred curriculum can be delivered most effectively by adopting a team-based, specialist approach which requires that methods of teaching become a matter for the whole school, rather than for individual teachers.

The 'subject' is now to be re-established in primary schools.

Although the content of the NC is being changed, modified and slimmed down, it seems unlikely that the current basis will be overturned in favour of the 'unified curriculum', whatever that means, and so it looks a safe bet that the NC subjects will provide the framework for the primary school curriculum into the next century.

For a generation, two powerfully attractive but erroneous ideas have dominated the rhetoric of primary practice. 'We teach children not subjects' was, I suppose an attempt to assert that primary teaching possessed a kind of esoteric professional mystique, in the hope that the status of primary teachers relative to their colleagues in secondary schools would consequently be enhanced. The other shibboleth, 'knowledge is a seamless robe' became the theoretical basis for the practice of much 'topic work', which was often great fun but which seemed to promise only that children would perhaps be infected with a smattering of subject related knowledge as they went about doing traffic surveys and making collages with screwed up, stuck on tissue paper.

Such flummery did considerable harm to children themselves, since children have to be taught something, and they will learn it only if it is well thought out, structured and delivered competently by the teacher within some recognisable intellectual framework, and it did no good to hardworking primary teachers, whose relative status declined, contrary to expectation, as they sought a distinctive curriculum and pedagogy at odds with the traditional subject base of the secondary school curriculum, into which their pupils would eventually transfer.

It *may* be true (though I doubt it), that to young children knowledge is indeed a seamless robe. But then, the primary purpose of schooling is to lead children from this state of innocence into the culture of the universalistic meanings of the public forms of thought.

And yet the reality of practice in many schools seemed to be in conflict with the received ideology. In my experience, most teachers taught some subjects, mathematics, reading, even some history and geography, certainly music and PE. And, many of them felt rather guilty about it, as if they knew that they were being politically incorrect. The tension arose because, instead of acknowledging the subject as being of the first importance, they became rather half-hearted in applying it.

Now, of course, the 'subject' is fashionable again, as is the timetable, the balanced curriculum calculated in the relative number of minutes spent on each subject, and the evaluation of results as attainment targets, SATs and league tables. And so, the primary school faces a new future as a place where teachers perform in order to enable children to attain a recognisable body of skills, concepts and information. There is nothing necessarily mechanistic about this. Nor need the performance of teachers be strait jacketed or dulled. Most parents and probably most teachers would agree that it is wholly fair that all children in schools from Darlington to Devon should have access to a common core of school knowledge, and so what I would want to propose is that the subject should not be hidden from children, nor should it become clouded by too much blurring at the edges. Children actually enjoy doing subjects because it gives them the security of knowing what they have learned. We should celebrate the restoration of the subject in our primary schools, and perhaps the first and most important job of the subject co-ordinator might well be to make a convincing case for the subject as a separate sudy within the school, and to overcome any ideological and psychological hang ups on the part of colleagues.

This might be difficult, of course. One objection currently paraded is that children do not learn in linear, logically ordered ways, according to a syllabus, that learning is 'messy'. Indeed, it may be, but children will certainly not learn a coherent body of knowledge if it is not presented coherently. There can be no harm in presenting the subject for a change as logical, in the expectation that children will see it that way for themselves. Another, is that a subject presented as a syllabus of attainment targets is arid, irrelevant and, most to be avoided, 'boring'. Not so. It has been a major failure of the past twenty to thirty years that, in the teaching of mathematics in primary schools, for example, we have simply perpetuated the notion among today's young parents that mathematics is difficult and 'boring' though acknowledged as useful. Yet these are the very parents who, as children were to be liberated from the oppression of mathematics as mystery by integration into the real world through topic-land. Teaching mathematics as a subject from the earliest years at least gives the teachers some chance that children will discover something of its elegance and excitement, both of which attributes will motivate their learning far more than mere utility.

But, the most convincing argument for single subject teaching is that it is both more efficient, as measured by the effect on the teacher's nerves, and more effective, as measured by children's attainments. I once saw a serious article in a prestige mass circulation American magazine which was illustrated by a double-page spread photograph of what purported to be a scene from the classroom of a 'progressive' English primary school. In it, small groups of 8 or 9 year-old children were at work in an 'integrated day'. Some were doing measuring, others writing, some playing the recorder, some climbing on frames in a corner, some painting and modelling, and so on. I doubted that this was an actual classroom, no teacher could have remained sane in such a situation, but the point was being made that good primary practice required teachers to plan for, deliver and evaluate all aspects of the curriculum for all abilities of children all at one go! The fact is that the integrated day never did work because it never could, and after years of trying to make it work, frustrated teachers will now abandon the attempts with hefty sighs of relief.

There is also a marketing advantage in displaying, or even presenting to parents, a timetable for their child's class which specifies subject lessons quite clearly. Most parents still cling to the idea of school knowledge as Maths, science, history, geography, etc, because these are the forms of curriculum organisation they experienced most recently themselves. They readily understand such an arrangement for their primary school.

Having firmly established the subject as a framework for the curriculum, what needs to be considered next?

The NC orders specify the general content, and even some operational indicators of what might be expected in demonstrating understanding on the part of the pupil. Beyond this the school needs a scheme of work, setting out in some detail the weekly, monthly or termly objectives and some guidance on how they are to be attained. My own preference is for a scheme which is compiled as a result of teaching the subject over a period of time. But, the most effective scheme will be the one which teachers collaborate with by bringing together their collective recorded experience. This means that teachers will need to pool their lesson plans and evaluations.

This, in itself, might prove to be a radical departure from existing practice. Until very recently, most primary schools in my experience, did not make much of lesson notes, forecast or record books. Many teachers regarded forecasting and detailed planning as a restriction to the process of creative teaching, and I have often heard teachers of young children say 'I don't know what I will be teaching next week' or 'If you teach the same topic more than twice it gets boring'! Invariably, the massive extra work-load involved, consequent upon changing the curriculum content, or the un-certainty in waiting for some exciting event to occur before planning a scheme, meant that most teachers had their curriculum planned by the schools' TV service. Since the object of a scheme of work is to provide continuity and coherence, it is nonsensical and counter-productive to keep changing it. A school which operates a system expecting teachers to change their curriculum content year by year is wasting a valuable resource, namely the teachers' understanding and expertise with the delivery of the subject. If we are to improve the quality of learning by raising the standard of teaching, then teachers need to have opportunities to practise their teaching of particular aspects of a topic more than once. In teaching the same content for say, a four or five-year period, a valuable stock of resource materials can also be built up, and added to the guidance in the scheme of work.

A major advantage of having explicit statements of attainment is that teachers can work together over a prolonged period on the most effective ways to present ideas to children and evaluate the outcomes. Most of the KS1 and KS2 music NC, for example, can be carried out effectively by a group of non-specialist teachers working together with guidance from the specialist co-ordinator. But the non-specialists will first need to work with the co-ordinator on introducing certain ideas, and follow up using detailed plans for weekly or even daily practice, provided by the specialist. When these procedures have been followed for some months, then the school will be in a position to put together a first draft of the scheme of work, and all the teachers will have an influence and they will have learned from experience what works best.

And so an essential requirement is for the subject co-ordinator to work with teachers and their classes regularly in order to introduce new aspects of the curriculum. This, of course, means some non-contact time has to be planned into the school timetable, together with some resourcing for cover from the INSET budget, and the school development plan will contain references to curriculum development which are more than pious hopes. The plans will have to be costed and the benefits made explicit.

The SDP might specify two or three subjects each year over a four-year period for particular attention. And, since it is not manageable to free two or three co-ordinators all at once to work with colleagues, the school could decide to use a form of specialist teaching.

The idea of specialist teaching is, again, one of those primary school no-go areas which should be radically challenged. There are after all some precedents. Most primary schools have always regarded some subjects as being in the province of the specialist. All that needs to be done is to extend the notion in the pursuit of higher standards.

Suppose a school were to decide to produce detailed schemes of work for mathematics, art and English, and to target their implementation within the school year. A co-ordinator would be appointed for each subject to work along with colleagues in preparing work and particular lessons. The simplest way of doing this would be for the maths co-ordinator to teach a regular session or sessions to all classes, while the art and English co-ordinators did the same. A timetable could be worked out depending on the number of classes. The co-ordinator would prepare and introduce the work, and leave detailed notes for the class teacher to follow up. Copies of the lesson notes would also be available to all teachers, since it does no harm for teachers of R classes to know what Year 6 are doing, and vice versa. Problems and successes would be recorded by the class teacher and reviewed regularly by the whole team with the co-ordinator leading.

Apart from the heightened efficiency which such specialist involvement promotes, there is an effect upon the general morale of both teachers and children. Children as young as 6 can very easily become fed up with their teacher, as indeed he/she can of them, and it does everybody the world of good to have a change. Children benefit from regular contact with a reasonable number of teachers throughout the week, especially if the teachers have a clear direction in delivering the subject. Teachers very soon begin to feel that children are making progress because the lessons become much more sharply focused, and all teachers feel good when children make progress. There is also the greater possibility of tackling successfully the difficult problem of differentiation in applying the curriculum. All teachers expect differentiation of outcome, depending upon the abilities of pupils, but few schools to my knowledge have successfully addressed the difficulties of differentiation of application because, under the traditional system whereby the class teacher is expected to deliver all subjects at all ability levels, there is just too much work involved. When teachers meet together as part of an 'evaluation team' to assess the results of their work as specialists, then point is given to the meetings, and there is a feeling that things are being achieved, and the fact that co-ordinators are appointed for a limited period to carry out specific tasks means that all the school's staff can be offered management opportunities.

But a sensible experiment with specialist teaching leads to a much more fundamental questioning of existing practices in primary schools. In particular, we should, I think be prepared to challenge the traditional role of teacher autonomy in favour of a team approach.

The effective school is one where the whole is greater than the sum of its parts. Given that the most powerful resource, and the most expensive, is the expertise of its teachers, the most effective school is the one which can combine these individual talents and keep them working towards commonly agreed goals.

Consider the following fictional but by no means fanciful scenario.

Mrs B. is a teacher of the traditional kind. Kindly but firm she is known to children and parents alike as a 'strict' teacher. She has been in the school for twenty-five years, and some of the parents of her present class were taught by her. Indeed, many of these parents have made representations to the headteacher, asking that their own children be placed in Mrs B's class. Mrs B. relies a great deal on chalk and talk. It works for her. Her children do as they are told; they must put up their hands to ask a question or to ask permission to leave their seats. The classroom is very quiet, and there is an atmosphere of calm and hard work. The children seem to be 'on task' for quite sustained periods, and their work is neatly presented and meticulously marked.

Mr C. down the corridor doesn't believe much in chalk and talk, not because it is unfashionable but because after years of experience he has come to believe that it does not work very well for the kinds of learning outcomes he has in mind. His children spend most of their time doing group work, problem-solving and 'projects', and Mr C. acts mainly as a guide and counsellor. The children come and go as they need to, about the classroom to use resources, to the library, to the toilet. Mr C. is too busy working with children to attend to trivial requests. The children present their work mostly in folders which are carefully compiled and inventively embellished. There is about the classroom an atmosphere of purposeful endeavour, and relationships are excellent.

Both these classrooms are effective mainly because the teachers know what they are doing and believe in what they are doing. Both styles of classroom management are effective, both have a place in any school. They can and often do co-exist.

Such teachers may give value for money, in terms of quality of learning and standards of achievement, but now the school should go for continuity and consistency.

And since the meat of the subject matter to be conveyed is already prescribed, then the subject co-ordinator will need to look not just at what is being taught, but how it is being taught to achieve the best results.

If the 1960s began the process of encouraging and promoting a wide variety of practice such that many different approaches were to be tolerated within the same building, each teacher working in an idiosyncratic way, then perhaps the next few years will require a much more formal, planned and rigorous approach to ensuring that there is continuity and consistency of pedagogy, so that all classrooms are using all styles as appropriate to the learning outcomes.

To continue with the examples. Clearly, there are advantages to both styles of teaching and classroom management. Outcomes for children are beneficial in both classrooms but we need to be more specific about what the outcomes are. Apart from the skills, understanding and knowledge, what else is being learned? Can we make the 'hidden curriculum' more explicit? Mrs B. might say that it is important for children to learn to follow instructions carefully, to recognise legitimate authority, to present work neatly and so on, while Mr C. would perhaps suggest that the children in his class are learning self-reliance and initiative. Maybe at intervals of a year or more, both these clusters of admirable behaviours are being learned. But, under a system of almost total autonomy, there seems little doubt that children will need to unlearn many of the things they learn with Mr C. in order to be successful with Mrs B. Mrs B. will spend a fair proportion of the first term grumbling at Mr C. while training her new class, and Mr C. fumes with resentment and frustration because the skills he has fostered are now disregarded.

What is needed, logically, is a whole school policy which relates teaching and classroom management styles to the intended learning outcomes.

The school may wish to promote, for example, pupil choice of resources as an operational objective of a wider aim to encourage pupils to become more responsible for their own learning. It seems reasonable to expect that Mr C's methods would be more likely to deliver such an outcome. On the other hand, such a desire is not incompatible with the wish to have children learn to present their work neatly, to have mastery of a number of mechanical skills or to understand the position of legitimate authority. Mrs B's methods would promote these things very well.

Given that children will learn whatever it is we would want them to learn by practising in a consistent environment over a sustained period, it makes sense to suggest that both teachers can learn something from each other, and that maybe they can both adopt some of each other's ways.

There is of course an immense difficulty in bringing this about. Teaching is not just labour intensive, it is personality intensive. Many teachers will say that they cannot be convinced that they are able to adopt what to them are alien 'philosophies' of teaching; that they perform best when they can do as they think best, or do what they have always done. Well, yes. And it does seem apposite therefore that the popular debate over many years about teaching styles has been mainly concerned with teachers being categorised as 'traditional' or 'progressive'. Perhaps these categories would not have gained such currency if we had been seen to be more flexible. Whatever, the situation must change, since the demands of the modern curriculum and the rising expectations we must have of our children are too great to be met by individual, idiosyncratic teachers working away at autonomy. An attack on the problem will come partly through INSET of the kind I have suggested, and of other kinds, but if in the end teachers find it impossible to adapt, then the issue is one for the management of the school. The forms of specialism then might refer not just to the subject content but to the methods of its delivery, and the school might want to arrange things so that aspects of the curriculum even within a subject should be delivered by specialists with the appropriate techniques. It may be that Mr C. should teach mathematics problem-solving skills using group discussion throughout the school or a section of it, while Mrs B. teaches long multiplication skills using chalk, talk and plenty of practice to children seated in rows facing the blackboard. This is not as fanciful as it might seem. We have been half-way there already. Many years ago I remember children doing 'English' and 'creative writing' as separate aspects, they even had different exercise books. The same thing happened with 'sums' and a particular brand of problem solving mathematics ('Fletcher Maths' at the time). I see nothing wrong in principle with this. In practice, we simply need to ensure that whatever is taught is taught well, and that means by teachers who have the skill and the time to develop a subject to the highest level possible.

In thinking about the development of a whole school approach, what might be undertaken then is a comprehensive curriculum audit, which would take account not simply of the time spent each week on each subject, but of how the time is spent. At the simplest level, teachers could be asked to report on how much time they spend on working with groups, whole class interaction and individual attention, and on 'housekeeping' and general supervision. It is always interesting to do this, since the results invariably show a very wide range of practices even within the same stage of a subject. The individual reports could be monitored by classroom observation, perhaps as a part of an overall appraisal process.

At a deeper level, we might ask more searching questions of any or all of these methods. What is going on in the groups? Is the group structure being used primarily as a more convenient means for didactic contact, or are discussion and leadership skills being fostered in a deliberate attempt to enable children to understand strategies for learning? And, what of the outcomes? How do children evaluate their experiences of learning about, say, aspects of the Roman invasion by working in groups? Are there systems through which children can communicate their feelings of progress or difficulty, such as a group log or diary? And, is there a management system within the classroom for ensuring that all children receive an appropriate share of the teacher's quality time? We are all aware of the dangers in letting quiet little Lucy in the corner get on with things while fussy Frankie demands all the attention. But, if there is no system for the rational application of teacher time to the class, and which children understand and accept, then of course the most attention-seeking children will continue to seek attention because they are rewarded for doing so. Some years ago, I heard a very good story about a teacher of 6 year-olds who became frantic because of the constant demands on her time by children requiring attention to relatively trivial matters. It was suggested that she employ two capable children to book appointments for her. This they did by having a wall diary into which was written the appointment time and the reason. When the system had been in operation for a few days, the teacher was amazed to discover that the demands on her time almost disappeared. It seems that most of the problems were being solved by the two children who were making the appointments. This is a nicely illustrative little tale, and whether it is wholly true does not matter. The point is that, in order to give teachers time to teach, there must be clear strategies for classroom management. If these strategies are successful for one teacher, then there is no reason why they cannot be successful for any other, and the effective school will find ways to make them universal.

The major advantage then of having a clearly defined curriculum based on subjects is that the stability of subject content leaves much more scope for teachers to concentrate on the more important issues of quality of teaching and learning, and to share their experiences for, in spite of the millions of teaching hours spent in the primary schools of the country, we are still not at all sure why it is that some things work while others never will.

8 The quest for a general teaching council

Robert Balchin

Not long after I had begun my first teaching post, an elderly colleague was helping me to fill in a form for the inland revenue. 'What should I put for "job description"?' I remember asking. 'You don't have a job, you have a profession, put "schoolmaster — not in holy orders" ' was his firm reply!

Teachers have been referring to themselves as members of a 'profession' for hundreds of years but what exactly do we mean by 'a profession' and the epithet 'professional'? Have they something to do with a willingness on the part of a practitioner not to withdraw his labour? Do they denote some particular qualifications or skills? Do they imply values which mean that the teacher has more than a mere 'job'?

At first sight, it seems easy to draw some clues from the *Oxford English Dictionary*'s definitions of 'profession': 'originally, the public declaration, promise or vow made by one entering a religious order.' There is the implication here maybe that there are some special rules to be kept in a 'profession'. Also we read: 'a calling in which the knowledge of some department of learning is used in its application to the affairs of others', so 'knowledge and learning' appear to be involved and are to be applied perhaps to other people rather than to things.

If the criteria for the use of the word 'profession', however, were very tight in Chaucer's time, by 1600 a news sheet could contain the words: 'Their profession is to robbe and steale from their neighbours', and it was clear to the reader just what the author meant: that

80

larceny was how they gained their livelihood: indeed there is the hint in the use of 'profession' that they were rather good at it! Police today often refer to a particularly successful crime as a 'very professional job'; barristers and doctors are allowed to enter their 'professions' after a very rigorous training, and recruiting posters urge prospective soldiers to 'join the professionals'. Although the Victorians might have hesitated to use the word 'professional' of someone engaged in a manual craft, preferring to reserve the word for clergy, soldiers and the like, it makes perfectly good sense today to speak of someone as a 'professional builder' or 'builder by profession'. In fact, I suspect, if the word 'profession' does mean more than 'job' nowadays, it merely implies that there are some special skills to be acquired, perhaps over a period of time, but what those skills should be, or to what ends they should be used cannot be teased from the normal usage of the word, at least since the seventeenth century.

If the results of this admittedly skimpy analysis seem unsatisfactory, however, it is because there do seem to be occasions when the meanings of 'professional' or 'profession' seem very precise indeed. The doctor knows, for instance, the exact implications of the words 'professional misconduct'; 'unprofessional behaviour' covers a limited number of actions for a teacher, and a 'professional cricketer' goes on to the pitch pledged to obey certain rules.

Certain groups of people, therefore, use the words 'profession' or 'professional' of themselves only when certain extra criteria, additional to those which specify the acquisition of some special skills, are in use. Briefly, these are that the 'professional' should be elected or admitted to his 'profession' only by his fellow 'professionals'; that one of the conditions of admission is his agreement to a code of conduct (thus 'forcing back' into the meaning the original notion of religious vows); that only his fellow 'professionals' can expel him from his 'profession' and that only the 'professionals' are allowed to perform the tasks of the 'profession'. Thus, solicitors and actuaries, for example, have to pass certain examinations and to reach certain training standards established by a group of their older and more experienced colleagues before they are allowed to practise. They subscribe to a strict code of behaviour which has been devised by their colleagues; they can be expelled by them under certain circumstances and are not allowed by law to practise their skills, at least in this country, unless they are on a list kept by their colleagues. Finally, the most important of these additional criteria is that the foregoing shall not just provide extra status for practitioners but shall also afford special protection for the client. To be more precise, solicitors manage their 'profession' by electing certain of their number to the Law Society, which regulates the training of law students by insisting that the institutions which offer law courses meet certain curricular criteria (on pain of having their students excluded, or course), which establishes rules for professional conduct and which strikes those who are guilty of breaking them from the society's register of solicitors. Only those on the register are allowed to practise in the United Kingdom, thus ensuring that clients using a solicitor's services can be sure that he/she is well trained and honest, and have a remedy if he/she should prove not to be.

It was probably this restrictive use of the word 'profession' that was intended in the founding Charter of a body called the College of Preceptors when it was issued in 1849, for this new institution was charged 'with the purpose of promoting sound learning and of advancing the interests of education...' by affording facilities for the teacher for the acquiring of a 'sound knowledge of his profession'. The college had no firm home but was a group of schoolmasters convinced that it was necessary for them and their colleagues to become organised in a way that teachers had never seen before.

Teachers hitherto, and indeed for a long time to come, were mostly untrained in any formal sense and usually had a lowly status in the community. Their calling had been damaged by the activities of a minority of appalling incompetents who only a few years before were castigated by Dickens in his resounding preface to *Nicholas Nickleby*:

> Any man who has proved his unfitness for any other occupation in life was free, without examination or qualification, to open a school anywhere.

Only too aware of the Wackford Squeerses in their midst, many teachers were determined to make their calling exclusive: they would find a means of excluding the iniquitous and the inept from their ranks.

At about that time, medical men also wanted to dissociate themselves from the untrained quacks who harmed their standing, and were feeling their way towards the General Medical Council which was established in 1858. So successful were these early pioneers in setting standards for their new 'profession' that in a few decades, their calling had become a prestigious one.

The reasons were not hard to see: underpinning 'professionalism' is the clear presumption that, if the members of a club or group themselves are the sole arbiters of who shall be allowed to join them as colleagues, then they will insist on high standards on entry in order to preserve their own status and they will exclude all those whose activities are likely to bring their fellows, by association, into disrepute. This presumption has important consequences for the client of the 'professional', of course, for he can expect a better quality service. A correspondent to *The Educational Times* wrote in 1877:

> A clergyman can be suspended ... a barrister may be debarred, a solicitor may be struck off the rolls, a doctor may be deprived of his degree and — paradox as it may appear — professional pride is fostered by these very penalties and dangers.

Satisfied that the experiences of doctors after the creation of the General Medical Council proved this presumption correct beyond doubt, teachers pressed Government throughout Victoria's reign for a 'professional' council of their own. Examinations of high quality could be set, and a register kept of those who had qualified but unless no person could practise as a teacher if his name was not on the register, then 'professional' status would never emerge. This needed changes in the law analogous to those of the 1858 Medical Act to make registration compulsory.

Bills for the compulsory registration of teachers appeared two or three times during the last years of the nineteenth century; Sir Richard Temple's Bill (1891) would have confined registration to secondary teachers in England and Wales as a first step towards general registration. The examining bodies which provided secondary level teacher qualification were to be allowed eight representatives on the registering council, the crown was to have four, and four were to be elected from amongst the listed teachers.

By this time, however, a new phenomenon was on the scene. The growth of the trades union movement had encouraged teachers to gather themselves into associations and unions and these new bodies also wanted to be represented if a registering council came into being.

Teachers, of course, had ceased during the two decades since the Foster Act to be mostly employed privately or to be self-employed or in the service of the churches and other education supplying institutions, and became the payees of the state through the Board Schools. Where there is one paymaster, collective bargaining is made easier and gradually the National Union of Teachers, the Teacher's Guild, the Irish National Teachers' Association and the Educational Institute of Scotland grew to be influential bodies. They sponsored, together with the Headmasters' Conference, Arthur Ackland's Bill for the registration of teachers. It was more comprehensive than the Temple Bill, and extended the necessity for registration to elementary school teachers as well as those in Scotland and Ireland. It was considered by a Select Committee at the same time as the Temple Bill, and evidence was heard for months. Everyone agreed that the principle of a 'professional' register for teachers was an excellent one, and that there should be an independent council to administer it. The questions which could not be answered were: which teachers should be listed and who should sit on the council? At length, the arguments could not be resolved, neither Bill received a second reading, and there the matter rested for a further ten years.

The Board of Education Act of 1901, however, gave the new board the duty of establishing a Teachers' Registration Council, and shortly after, a twelve-person Council came into being: six teachers from the various unions and associations and six government appointees. The new council decided on a form of registration which was immediately boycotted by the National Union of Teachers, representing the elementary school masters and mistresses. These were all, of course, government employees and certificated (and therefore listed) by the education department. The plan was that these teachers should be transferred en bloc compulsorily to the new register whereas the secondary and independent school teachers were to register individually and voluntarily. The NUT repudiated the whole concept as being unduly divisive and, by the end of 1904, only 144 people had tendered their names and the whole scheme died of inanition.

The movement for teacher registration gained in strength again just before the First World War and a new Teachers' Registration Council was constituted by Order of the Privy Council in 1912. The council this time was much larger, to take account of all the interests involved and eventually comprised 50 members: 11 drawn from the universities, eleven each from the elementary teachers and the secondary teachers, together with certain appointees of the crown and other bodies.

The register had no divisions, and all teachers registered voluntarily. The hope, of course, was that so many would do so that compulsion could be later introduced with few political difficulties.

At last things seemed to be going well and, in 1929, when some 78 000 people were listed on the register, George V dignified them and the council by allowing them to be called, collectively 'the Royal Society of Teachers'. Members could place the letters MRST after their names and wear a distinctive academic dress if they so wished.

Alas, a further Act making it a matter of compulsion for all teachers to register never came and the Royal Society of Teachers, with only £100 in its funds, quietly folded during the war years and was wound up in 1949 by an Order in Council. Its proponents had signally failed to get Government to supply it with the necessary authority to make teaching a 'profession': all the time that teachers could practise without the necessity to register, it was powerless to improve standards.

The Royal Society of Teachers failed because it came too late: the state in the years before World War II was becoming looked upon as the 'natural' provider of schooling. Independent schools were thought by many observers to be on the decline, divisive leftovers from Victorian times. The principle of the state as the purveyor of education became enshrined in the 1944 (Butler) Education Act and, by that time, 95 per cent of teachers were on the state payroll. A hundred years before, when the quest for an autonomous teaching 'profession' had begun, the employers of teachers were many and diverse, and the teachers themselves without a voice to speak for them. Now, nearly all teachers were local authority employees, and had organised themselves in a growing number of unions and associations.

In the post-war era, those teachers who still hoped to create a real 'profession' have had to face two problem areas: could the powers concerned with the admission, induction and possible exclusion of teachers, by now firmly vested in the Minister (later the Secretary of State) for Education, be prised away from the Government's grasp and passed to an independent body?

Would the teachers' unions see it as being in their best interests to promote such an independent body?

Both areas are fraught with difficulties. If a general teaching council were to come into being, using the general councils of the other 'professions' as models, it would have to be conceived along the following lines:

1. All teachers presently practising would have to elect some of their number to the new council.
2. Teachers would have the majority of seats on such a council, although there would also be representatives of say, the Department of Education and Science, the local authorities, the universities and other teacher training bodies, perhaps the churches and also some kind of 'client' interest (representing parents' associations). This predicates a large council (fifty/sixty seats)
3. All currently practising teachers would have to register with the new council and pay a fee (perhaps once and for all, perhaps annually). No teacher would be allowed to teach, by law, unless registered.
4. The new council would devise a code of practice to which registering teachers would be obliged to subscribe.
5. The Government would hand over its lists of those currently barred from teaching (List 99) to the new council and with it the right to exclude or suspend teachers who were found guilty of 'professional' misconduct from the register (and thus from teaching).

6. Government would pass the sole right to accredit courses of initial and inservice teacher training to the new council.
7. Government would give the new council control of the probationary period for novice teachers and the power, of course, to decide whether admission to the register would follow at the end of it.
8. The new council would advise Government on the question of teacher supply.

It is clear that immense political embarrassment could result if, during a period when a large number of teachers were required in schools, Government handed to a new autonomous body the power to constrict the supply of entrants to the 'profession'. If it is conceded that a General Teaching Council would set higher standards for would-be teachers (and this, of course, is the presumption which underpins the whole concept of 'professionalism') then either there would be fewer teachers, or higher salaries would have to be offered to attract better candidates. Neither choice has proved palatable to post-war Governments as the attempts to establish a General Teaching Council during the 1960s and 1970s demonstrate.

In 1966, a working party representing all the teachers' unions and associations then extant asked the Secretary of State to consider proposals to create a general teaching council for England and Wales. His reply was in no way encouraging.

The changes the associations are seeking would involve a transfer of control over the fundamental matter of teachers' recruitment from the Government to the proposed Council.

This he was not prepared to countenance at a time of teacher shortage.

In 1968 they tried again. This time, the Secretary of State, Edward Short (now Lord Glenamara) was more sympathetic for he had been a teacher himself. This initiative resulted in the Weaver Report (DES 1970) which was the product of a committee comprising representatives from the Department of Education and Science, the teachers' unions, the universities and teacher training interests and the local education authorities. In the two years in which it struggled to find a solution acceptable to Government, the committee considered many patterns on which to construct the new council. Its final proposals, however, kept the reins of teacher supply firmly in the hands of the department. The authority to register teachers, to oversee probation and to discipline them (and if necessary strike them off) was to be available to a new teachers' council, but the management of teacher supply was to go to a different body and one which would have only five teacher members (out of twenty-nine seats) to represent their colleagues in the country's primary and secondary schools. The reason for two bodies was clear: the school population had expanded so much in the 1960s that local authorities had difficulty in filling teaching posts and even had to advertise abroad. A general teaching council created on the lines discussed above would have made recruitment more difficult. The National Union of Teachers refused to back this hybrid solution saying, quite rightly, that a real 'profession' required that all aspects of admission and supply should be devolved to one body with a majority of teachers. The NUT was probably wrong to have refused a Council with even the limited powers on offer because a time would come in the 1980s when the birthrate would fall and thousands of teachers would be looking for jobs, which would not be available. Government nervousness about teacher supply would probably have diminished enough for the remaining powers to be handed over, and today perhaps teachers would be members of a 'profession'.

The dramatic increase in the number of teachers required to service the schools of the 1960s and early 1970s meant that the unions and associations recruited members as never before. These unions, especially the National Union of Teachers, the National Association of Schoolmasters (later to add the Union of Women Teachers) and the 'Joint Four' (see below) soon became accustomed to pronouncing on, and being consulted about, what were known as 'professional' matters and to 'speaking for teachers' in the news-papers and on radio and television. Clearly, a new and independent general teaching council, especially if it became as prestigious in time as, say, the Law Society could be perceived as a threat to the status of the unions unless their own involvement in it could be guaranteed.

They conceived therefore a concept of a 'professional' council in which, although all teachers would be obliged to register in order to practise, only those who were in membership of one or other of the unions would be able to take part in the government of the 'profession'. The teachers' seats on a general teaching council would be allocated only to those who were sent there by their unions; those teachers who did not choose to join a union were to have no mechanism by which they might be represented.

The formal reasons for this model were that it would be difficult for other constituencies to be arranged for teachers and, anyway, an election of some thirty or forty people by half a million practitioners would lead to practical difficulties of representation. Thus the *Weaver Report* recommended that the teachers (a majority) on its proposed semi-autonomous Council were to be appointed from the ranks of the unions as follows.

- National Union of Teachers: 10
- National Association of Schoolmasters (now NAS/UWT): 3
- Joint Four (now AMMA and SHA): 6
- National Association of Headteachers: 2
- Association of Teachers in Technical Institutions: 2
- Association of Teachers in Colleges and Departments of Education (now NATFHE): 2

The seats were to be allocated roughly according to the numerical strength of the organisations concerned, except in the case of the heads' unions. The NUT later repudiated this division as not reflecting accurately enough its number of members; this, and its rejection of the other proposals concerning the powers of the proposed council, caused the whole question of a general teaching council to be put back into that limbo in which it presently resides.

The concept of a general teaching council has always caused a frisson of difficulty for those teacher unionists who have conceived of teachers as an organised labour force marching solidly in step with their brothers and sisters in the other 'white collar' and 'blue collar' unions. They find it hard to accept the values of a 'profession' with its special overtones of exclusivity. I suspect that the NUT's opposition to the Weaver proposals was founded in part on a belief that, if unity on 'professional' matters were to come, it ought to be through the aegis of the NUT. Some at least of its ruling members believed in those days (I am not sure whether they do now) that all the unions and associations ought to unite into one mega-union which would itself one day command the powers of a 'profession'. That this is muddled thinking, I shall show later.

The impetus for Weaver came partly from the success of Scottish teachers in achieving the establishment of a General Teaching Council for Scotland in 1865. The conditions for its creation were far more benign than in the south: teachers were not in such short supply and there was really only one union to speak of, the Educational Institute of Scotland. The council has the powers delineated earlier in this chapter. Teachers in Scotland elect members to represent them as follows:

- 11 are elected by primary teachers
- 11 by secondary teachers
- 3 by the further education sector plus 4 principals and 1 lecturer from colleges of education.

In addition, there are a further nineteen members representing the churches, the universities, the local authorities and the Secretary of State for Scotland, making forty-nine in all. Elections are held every four years and teachers are obliged to pay a small annual subscription to remain on the register. This provides the finance for the council which has a number of subcommittees to deal with aspects of its work. One is responsible for pre-service training (the Visitation Committee), one for probation, one for discipline, one for public relations, one for registration, etc. (It is an interesting aside to note that the register, of course, is held on a computer. One of the reasons advanced against the notion of an English council used to be that it would be impossible to record nearly half a million teachers' names accurately. Now the National Trust holds details of its million members on a computer tape which would fit into a large briefcase!)

There are currently some 80,000 registered members of the General Teaching Council for Scotland, but alas only a minority of them seem to take an interest in its work, for at election time there is a disappointingly low poll — something of the order of 33 per cent. In its twenty-eight years of existence the Council has worked hard to raise standards. Opinions are divided as to whether or not it has succeeded. To be fair, it is hard to find a standard with which to compare it. Conditions before its foundation by statute in 1965 were very different from those which obtain now; only recently have those whom it admitted in its first decade held positions of senior responsibility in schools. There is one other problem too, which may help to explain teachers' lack of interest in electing representatives to it: it is widely perceived as being union dominated. (It may be difficult, of course, for a teacher who is not backed by the Educational Institute of Scotland to obtain the kind of publicity which may win general teaching council votes.) This perception may be misplaced but still the biographies of many of the teacher members of the Scottish Council show active participation over the years in the organisation of the Educational Institute of Scotland.

In the early 1980s, a group of teachers, of whom I was one, requested the College of Preceptors which still existed to espouse once again the cause of teacher professionalism and the GTC. Alas, its council was dominated by union interest groups, and it refused. Therefore, I founded a pressure group of teachers who called themselves CATEC (campaign for a general teaching council) to try to bring the idea of a 'professional' council for teachers back once more into the arena of public debate. We were successful in persuading the then Secretary of State, Mark Carlisle, (now Lord Carlisle of Bucklow) to issue a statement. A lawyer himself, he was in favour of the principle of a teachers' council and said as follows:

> I will give all the help and encouragement I can to the establishment of such a Council, but I must emphasise that it would defeat the whole object of the exercise if Government

itself were to set up such a Council. Such a Council, as with the Law Society, would be independent of Government — a separate self-regulating body for the teaching profession.

CATEC carried out both informal and official talks with unions and associations to see if there was any room for agreement amongst them.

It was clear from the start that the concept of a general council was unwelcome to the National Association of Teachers in Further and Higher Education (NATFHE). Some of their members (especially those teaching certain technical or trade subjects) were not qualified in the sense of having undergone formal teacher training, and saw perhaps a future in which they would be excluded from registration. The other unions, especially the NAS/UWT, the Professional Association of Teachers (PAT) and the heads' associations, were broadly supportive of a new initiative, though it proved impossible to take up the challenge issued by Mark Carlisle before he was replaced as Secretary of State by Sir Keith (now Lord) Joseph, who publicly stated that he saw 'a great deal in the idea of a general teaching council for teachers, but little for their pupils.' He was said also to equate the notion of a general council with that of a 'closed shop', and it is worthwhile spending some time in the examination of such a criticism.

The term 'a closed shop' is usually applied to an area of work in which an employer agrees that he will employ no one who does not belong to a certain union. Hence, expulsion from the union, or failure to be admitted to it, means no work and no livelihood. Admission to the union depends on a promise to keep to its rules, and continued membership on actual obedience to them. So far there is no discernable difference between the notion of a 'profession' and that of a 'closed shop'. Both a 'closed shop' and a 'profession' demand the following of certain rules and, in both cases, the rules could be said to be promulgated to better the lot of the follower.

For instance, both a medical doctor and a newspaper printer have to possess certain skills before they can work; both are assessed by tests and examinations. Without these skills, the doctor would not be able to save lives, or the printer to keep his machine rolling. Both have to make certain promises before being allowed to work: however clever the surgeon, unless registered to practise; however dextrous the printer, if a 'closed shop' operates, unless he joins the appropriate union, there will be no employment for him.

We have to look more carefully at the relevant requirements for registration with a 'professional' body and for joining a union before the difference is apparent. The necessary and sufficient qualifications for, say, registration with the General Medical Council are all directly related to the skills required by a good physician or surgeon. The standards required on entry are clearly set down and both they and the code of conduct are a matter of public record. Anyone who reaches the required published standard and assents to the Code of Conduct will be admitted to the register and may practise. In a 'closed shop', however, admission is to a degree arbitrary and entry criteria bear no relationship to the skills needed for the job (as some employers have found to their cost) and are concerned only with a willingness to obey the rules of the union concerned. The arbitrariness arises because I could possess the necessary skills, I could offer to promise to obey union rules, there could be work available, but even though I have reached the required standard the union could still refuse to have me in membership because I was, for instance, unknown to the local committee. The nature of the rules reveal further differences. The rules of a union 'closed shop' are concerned only with the furtherance of the interests of its members especially with regard to pay and conditions of service. Those of a 'professional' body are concerned with standards of service and ultimately benefit the clients, although they may indirectly enhance the status — and possibly therefore the pay — of the practitioner.

Finally, the aims implicit in each term reveal clear differences also. A 'closed shop' restricts a client to the use of one group of employees, by threat of the withdrawal of labour, solely with the aim of gaining improved pay and conditions for its members. A 'profession' restricts a client, usually by statute, in order to protect the client from inferior service, and this has only an indirect bearing on pay and conditions.

If it is difficult to separate those criteria needed before a 'closed shop' operates and those which are the requisites of a 'profession', then it is no wonder that confusion exists when we look at the concept of a general teaching council as envisaged, for instance, by the *Weaver Report*. In the absence of a 'professional' council, the teachers' unions and associations have adduced to themselves some of the roles of such a council. They claim, with some justification, to represent the views of teachers on qualifications for entry, on inservice training, on disciplinary matters and indeed some of them have their own 'codes of conduct'. Some unions take their roles as quasi- 'professional' bodies very seriously, and genuinely try to look after client interests as well as those of their members. The Professional Association of Teachers members' code of conduct eschews strike action under any circumstances (although, as we have seen, there is nothing built into the concept of 'professionalism' which requires this, laudable though it may be. Indeed, there could conceivably be times when a 'professional' ought to withdraw his labour for the better protection of his clients). Here is a teacher writing in the journal of another union:

> If the union were unguarded enough to take these recommend-
> ations further we might well be suspected of subordinating the
> real interests of children to the creating of employment for
> teachers.

Immediately the dichotomy is evident: is the union there to
protect the teacher or the children?

If we assume that a teachers' union's duties are primarily
concerned with improving the pay and conditions of service of its
members (whatever else it may be free in a democratic society to do)
then there are clearly disadvantages for the clients if a general
teaching council becomes dominated by union interests. If a
majority of teachers appointed to such a council are there because of
their commitment to the values of their unions, then there is the
danger that they could constrict the flow of practitioners into the
'profession' (by imposing arbitrary entry requirements), in order to
coerce employers into better pay deals.

The quasi-judicial nature of a 'professional' council also makes it
difficult to see how a union dominated body could deal reasonably
and fairly with discipline cases. A teacher accused of gross
misconduct could find himself being judged and struck off by
members of the very union that is defending him. If they belong to
other unions, the position could be worse given the internecine
instincts of the teachers' unions and associations nowadays!

1986 saw the creation of yet another initiative to keep the idea of
a GTC alive. The Universities Council for the Education of Teachers
(UCET) was upset by the creation by the Secretary of State of a new
body of government appointees (CATE) to oversee the quality of
education courses for prospective teachers. The establishment of a
general teaching council would, of course, provide the opportunity
for the powers given to CATE to be wrested from government
hands. Accordingly, representatives of the various teachers' unions
and associations were invited by UCER to a series of discussions,
and a sub-committee produced criteria for a GTC. Almost inevitably, acrimony arose amongst the unionists about representation and
even about the whole concept of a general council. The UCET effort
died down, was prodded into life again in 1988 by a separate move,
by the headteacher of an independent school to form an elected
'national teaching council', and died down again.

More recently, the Select Committee on Education recom-
mended, in 1991, that the Government should reconsider its stance.
No moves have been forthcoming, although both Kenneth Clarke
(Secretary of State for Education and Science 1990–2) and John
Patten (1992 to 1994) have speculated from time to time in public

about the possibility of a body similar to the Royal College of Nursing.

It is quite clear, however, that only a general teaching council which is quite separate from unions and associations could concentrate on client interests, and, indeed, all the while that governments remain the employers of teachers, it is the only model to which 'professional' powers are likely to be entrusted. If a future council is to gain for teachers the respect which is the hallmark of a 'profession', it must not be concerned in any way with salaries or conditions of service and those who run it must be elected (whatever the practical difficulties) by the teaching body as a whole.

The intentions of those who, like myself, wish to see the establishment of a general teaching council must always be tested on one touchstone, and that is the question: 'Will your proposals, as well as enhancing the status of teachers protect and benefit children and their parents?' Only if the answer is 'Yes' will a real teaching 'profession' come about.

References

DES (1970) *A Teaching Council for England and Wales (The Weaver Report)*, HMSO.

9 School development planning

Hugh Lawlor

Planning is not new — headteachers have always had to decide what needs to be done, by whom and by when. What is different today is the speed and number of demands and challenges confronting schools.

It is now essential to manage the considerable number of challenges facing schools and, more critically, to ensure that externally imposed change takes place within the agreed aims and culture of each school. By managing and controlling such change schools can ensure that learning remains the most important activity.

What is a school development plan?

It is an overall plan that allows the school to control and manage changes within its own aims and value system. Priorities for development, for example, the preparation of a school assessment policy or ways of improving communications to parents, are planned in detail for one year, with accompanying action plans and working documents for staff. An outline plan for the next two years is also prepared.

Preparing the school development plan

At the preparatory stage, the headteacher, staff and governors may have an initial discussion on the advantages of development planning, either for one school or within a consortium of neighbouring schools. At this meeting it may be helpful to have the assistance

94

of an external adviser or consultant. In the discussions that take place, it is worth remembering that development planning is about improving the quality of education as well as implementing externally imposed changes. Development planning is a partnership between the headteacher, teachers, governors, support staff, parents, the community and the LEA. All partners share a commitment to develop and improve the school in order that learning and teaching can be as efficient and effective as possible. This shared commitment and responsibility requires mutual support, and a recognition that each partner has a contribution to make to the process of planning. In this partnership, the headteacher will act as a chief executive and, as such, will need to involve and inform the governors throughout the process.

Stage One: mission, aims and objectives

Before embarking on the preparation of a school development plan or a review of a school's needs, it is crucial to establish a shared understanding of the aims and values of the institution. There needs to be a clear statement of the school's mission and aims. These statements of intent are unlikely to change unless the external pressures are altered radically. Such a mission statement will encompass the values and aspirations of the school. Drafting this concise statement with governors, staff and parents is an essential part of the planning process. The aims of the school will relate to the mission statement and describe the main purposes of the school. Until a school has established a clear mission and set of aims, it is not possible to determine its needs, or to begin looking at those areas which require immediate development. This part of the planning process can be lengthy and time-consuming, but is always worthwhile. A clearly stated mission and aims for the school will help to place changes in a specific context, give direction, and provide the framework within which developments can be organised and managed.

Just as the mission and aims for the school are broad statements, the related objectives are specific, identify clear outcomes, and are measurable, for example, to develop the basic skills of listening, talking, reading, writing and mathematics to the maximum for each pupil; to help pupils understand the cultures, religions and values of others.

> At the end of stage one you will have a concise mission statement, a set of aims, and a series of objectives for the school.

Stage Two: review of strengths and weaknesses

An audit is a systematic way of looking at the strengths and weaknesses of the school. Some weaknesses can be remedied immediately and others may need to be included as priorities in the school development plan. Schools can use a variety of schemes for the audit: GRIDS (guidelines for review and internal development in schools) or, the National Curriculum Council's *Curriculum Guidance Number 3, The Whole Curriculum*, are popular published schemes. Many schools prefer to undertake their own reviews, or modify a published scheme, and increasingly use external support from the LEA or independent consultants. In many schools a simple questionnaire and a staff development day are used to involve all staff in the process. The involvement of governors and non-teaching staff at this stage varies considerably. The participation of non-teaching staff and governors in the audit has several specific benefits as well as consolidating the shared understanding of the values of the school.

The resulting long-list of priorities might include: subject policies; assessment, recording and reporting; a review of planning; teaching and learning styles; management and organisation; resources; roles and responsibilities of staff; matching tasks to pupil needs; behaviour and discipline; home–school contacts. It is not necessary at this early stage to categorise priorities into headings, but rather to focus on the identification of needs.

It is becoming increasingly important to link staff appraisal schemes with whole-school reviews. In some schools, the review process takes place before teacher appraisal so that the priorities identified in the review can form part of the appraisal interview.

> At the end of stage two you will have a long-list of priorities identified by the audit.

Stage Three: constructing the school development plan: determining priorities

Detailed plans are now constructed for the year ahead, with the priorities for the next two years prepared in outline. Using financial years has the advantage of relating the costs of priorities to the overall school budget. In drawing up the plan, it is helpful to have a strong sense of realism and a recognition that the plan should be a flexible management tool. A number of factors will need to be considered in constructing the plan:

- the mission and aims of the school
- specific objectives of the school
- national initiatives, including any recent legislation
- LEA policies
- school commitments and policies
- the outcomes of the audit (i.e. any weaknesses that require attention)
- finance available
- a realistic assessment of the number of priorities that can be tackled (particularly significant for small schools).

The priorities for the year ahead and those for the next two years can now be categorised under a number of headings. For example:

- Pupil care
  e.g. discipline policy; equal opportunities policy; special educational needs policy.
- Curriculum and curriculum development
  e.g. developing and implementing subject policies; assessment, recording and reporting; teaching and learning styles.
- Staffing
  e.g. staff development; appraisal; roles and responsibilities; induction programme; pay policy.
- Management and organisation
  e.g. management structure; internal and external communications, organisational changes.
- The community
  e.g. links with LEA and central government; partnership with governors; liaison with local schools; marketing.
- Site and accommodation
  e.g. internal decoration and refurbishment; external maintenance.
- Financial resources
  e.g. review use of computerised system; investigate income-generating schemes.
- Monitoring and evaluation systems
  e.g. for reviewing progress of priorities; for monitoring pupil and teacher performance; for relating costs of priorities to the overall school budget.

Once the outline plan has been agreed by the governing body, it should be widely publicised and contain:

- agreed priorities for the next year grouped under headings
- an estimate of costs, and how these relate to the overall budget
- time targets

- success criteria for Year 1
- outline of priorities for the following two years using the
  same headings.

> At the end of stage three there will be an outline plan for the
> year ahead with priorities categorised, estimated costs, time
> target, and success criteria, and some priorities identified for
> the next two years (see Figure 9.1)

Stage Four: drawing-up action plans

Action plans are working documents, and should be prepared for
each priority, and can include a 'link governor' who will be available
for consultation and support. The action plan will be *concise* and
consist of:

- a description of the priority
- specific objectives for the priority (i.e. targets)
- set of tasks in order to achieve objectives
- who is responsible for the tasks
- time targets
- any resource implications (including staff development,
  materials, etc.)
- success criteria against which objectives can be judged
- review, including any meetings to assess progress.

> At the end of stage four you will have concise action plans for
> each priority for the year ahead (see Figure 9.2)

Stage Five: evaluation of school development plan and process

Implementation of the plan and its evaluation are essential components of the process. Action plans use success criteria and progress
checks to ensure that evaluation is a strand that runs throughout the
process of change. Priorities will have different timescales for
implementation and it is therefore whorthwhile building in two short
sessions during the year when the management team (including if
possible the 'link governor') and those responsible for action plans
meet to assess progress. An annual report on progress to governors,
parents and pupils can be brief but is an important part of the
process.

Figure 9.1 Outline school development plan

	Year 1 (1993–94)	Estimated cost	Time targets	Success criteria	Year 2 (1994–95)	Year 3 (1995–96)
Pupil care	1. Complete school discipline policy 2. 3.	1. £100 2. 3.	1. Autumn 2. 3.	1. Document produced	1. Review discipline policy	1. Review equal opportunity policy
Curriculum and curriculum development	1. Establish science policy and schemes 2. 3.	1. £100 2. 3.	1. Summer 2. 3.	1. Policy and scheme produced	1. Review design and technology	1. Review history and geography policies
Management and organisation	1. Review internal and external communications 2. 3.	1. £350 2. 3.	1. All year 2. 3.	1. Results of staff and parents survey	1. Training for SMT	1. Review D/H role
Staffing	1. Develop pay policy 2. 3.	1. Nil 2. 3.	1. Autumn 2. 3.	1. Policy produced and agreed by governing body	1. Continue appraisal process	1. Review roles and responsibilities
The community	1. improve links with secondary schools 2. 3.	1. Nil 2. 3.	1. Summer 2. 3.	1. Improved communication between schools	1. Review school brochure	1. Enhance links with community
Site and accommodation	1. Continue programme of redecoration — Rooms 9 and 10 2. 3.	1. £500 2. 3.	1. Spring 2. 3.	1. Classrooms redecorated	1. Continue programme of furniture replacement	1. Provide staff resources area
Financial resources	1. Review use of SIMS financial system 2. 3.	1. Nil 2. 3.	1. Spring 2. 3.	1. Report produced for governing body	1. Transfer cleaning contract to direct labour	1. Review cleaning contract and specification
Monitoring and evaluation	1. Maths co-ordinator to evaluate overall achievements in subject 2. 3.	1. £500 2. 3.	1. Autumn and Spring 2. 3.	1. Brief report to HT and oral presentation to governing body	1. HT to monitor classes	1. Review monitoring role of HT

Notes: 1. Some priorities will continue into the next year(s) — just as in some years there will be no priorities under some headings.
2. Details will be contained in the action plans (including who will be responsible for each priority) — which can be attached to the outline plan.
3. Examples are from Featherby Junior School, Rainham, Kent.

Action plan 1993–94

Priority
A review of internal and external communications
Category: management and organisation

Objectives:
1. That teaching and non-teaching staff understand daily routines and feel informed about any changes
2. That teaching and non-teaching staff know the roles and responsibilities of all staff
3. That the staff handbook is considered useful, clear, up to date and effective, and
4. That all external communications are well presented, clear and easily understood.

Tasks
1. Devise a brief questionnaire for all teaching and non-teaching staff on internal communications, roles, and responsibilities.
2. Ask the school adviser/consultant to assess effectiveness of staff handbook.
3. Undertake survey of parents, governors, sample of LEA staff, and local secondary schools on the quality of communications

Staff responsible
Deputy headteacher
Link governor: Mrs A. N. Other

Time targets
1. Questionnaire and surveys in Autumn term, 1993
2. Short report from school adviser/consultant by early in Spring term 1994
3. Report from deputy headteacher to head and governing body by end of Spring term, 1994
4. Presentation to governing body early in Summer term 1994, with any recommendations agreed with the headteacher.

Success criteria
1. High percentage of questionnaires and surveys returned by teaching and non-teaching staff, parents, governors, LEA staff, and local secondary school staff
2. Report from school adviser/consultant identifies strengths and weaknesses of staff handbook
3. Satisfaction of headteacher and governing body with final report and any recommendations.

Resources
1. Cost of questionnaire and surveys   50
2. Supply cover for deputy headteacher for 3 days   300
                                                            Total: £350

Review
1. Feedback to teaching and non-teaching staff on questionnaires and surveys in Spring term, 1994
2. Progress meeting with headteacher and chairman of governors at end of Autumn and Spring terms
3. Recommendations to be implemented in following Autumn term, with review by deputy and head in following Summer term.

Figure 9.2   School development plan

At this stage, the priorities for the second year of the plan can be adjusted and confirmed and work can begin on action plans for the next year. It is important that lessons from Year One are incorporated and that changes in national and local policies are included.

Throughout stage five you will be reviewing the action plans and at the end of the stage will have:

- a brief progress report for governors, staff, parents and pupils on progress in Year One
- after consultation adjusted and/or confirmed the priorities for Year Two and begun to prepare the action plans for the year ahead.

School development planning and OFSTED inspections

The school development plan is a major source of information for OFSTED inspectors, and will be scrutinised by them in advance of an inspection. It will provide evidence of the school context, in particular, its aims and values, priorities for change, how these changes will take place, and how the changes will be evaluated. The plan will also be a reflection of the quality of management in the school, at all levels throughout the organisation. Inspectors will look to see the extent to which the plan has been prepared in consultation with staff, governors, parents, and that it has been agreed by the governing body. They will assess how the priorities reflect the mission, aims and objectives of the school, and how they are costed, and how costs relate to the overall budget and planning cycle. The revised *Handbook for the Inspection of schools* makes several references to school development planning and how it will be evaluated. Inspectors will use the school development plan as one of the sources of evidence when evaluating factors such as the efficiency of the school, management and administration, and resources and their management. The *Handbook for the Inspection of Schools* contains the evaluation criteria that will be used as well as the judgements on development planning that will be included in the inspection report. Finally, on receiving notification of an OFSTED inspection it might be advisable to include specific preparation in the school development plan. Similarly, it will be necessary to adjust the priorities in the plan after an inspection in order to address the key issues identified by the inspection team.

Recommended reading and guidance

School Development Plans Project:

(i) Planning for School Development (1989)
(ii) Development Planning — A Practical Guide (1991).

The publications above are part of the DES project on school development planning.

References

Davies, B. and Ellison, L. (1992) *School Development Planning* Longman.
Hargreaves, D. H. and Hopkins, D. (1991) *The Empowered School* Cassell.
National Curriculum Council (1993) *Planning the National Curriculum at Key Stage 2.*
OFSTED (1993) *Handbook for the Inspection of Schools* HMSO.
Skelton, M., Reeves, G. and Playfood, D. (1991) *Development Planning for Primary Schools* NFER-Nelson.

10 A multicultural policy for all primary schools

Rick Collet

The publication in 1985 of the Swann Committee Report (DES 1985) turned out for many authorities and schools to be a significant milestone on the route to multicultural education. There are flaws and inconsistencies in its 800 pages, but, because of these imperfections (not in spite of them), it provides a useful state of the art description for many of us of a concept which is still emerging, surrounded, like most new educational concepts, by its share of controversy, apathy, and misunderstanding.

Perhaps the most striking feature of the progress made is embodied in the Report's title *Education for All*: here was a Committee, established in 1979, to enquire into the education of children from ethnic minority groups, which after six years' deliberation and gestation, came out with an unambiguous statement of the central validity of preparing all children for life in a multicultural society. The key steps in Swann's argument are as follows:

1. The fundamental change that is necessary is the recognition that the problem facing the education system is not how to educate children of ethnic minorities, but how to educate *all* children.
2. Britain is a multiracial and multicultural society, and all pupils must be enabled to understand what this means.
3. This challenge cannot be left to the separate and independent initiatives of LEAs and schools: only those with experience of

substantial numbers of ethnic minority pupils have attempted
to tackle it, though the issue affects all schools and all pupils.

4. Education has to be something more than the reinforcement
   of the beliefs, values and identity which each child brings to
   school.

5. It is necessary to combat racism, to attack inherited myths
   and stereotypes, and the ways in which they are embodied in
   institutional practices.

6. Multicultural understanding has also to permeate all aspects
   of a school's work. It is not a separate topic that can be
   welded on to existing practices.

7. Only in this way can schools begin to offer anything
   approaching the equality of opportunity for all pupils which
   it must be the aspiration of the education system to provide.

Here was a ready-made agenda for an initial staffroom discussion.
First, do we agree? If not, can we spell out the alternative philosophy
it is proposed to follow, e.g. 'it is *not* necessary to combat racism...',
etc. Secondly, to what extent are we already implementing this
agenda, and how can we go further? What might our school look like
and feel like if we finally arrived?

We could turn for reference to see how some schools that have
become multiracial in recent years have responded to a visible ethnic
minority presence: how this has often forced the staff to re-think
basic principles, about the nature of the school, its responsibilities as
transmitter of culture(s), appropriate professional development,
relationships with homes and parents, and so on. Good practice has
been documented (e.g. Twitchin and Demuth 1985) from which all
schools can draw some constructive lessons, and learning resources
which have been devised for multiracial areas are of a quality to
stand on their own merit in mainstream libraries (Klein 1986). A
computerised database is now available, which provides access to
information on multicultural education materials produced by small-
scale community publishers and local authority centres around the
country (AIMER 1993).

Still, the majority of schools are basically 'all white', and there is,
as Swann documented, a disturbing tendency for those schools to cry
'we have no problems here' when asked about their attitudes to
multicultural education. The first essential point to recognise about
'multicultural education' is that, in its fullest realisation, it is totally
synonymous with good educational practice in general. So a
multiracial school doing its best by its black pupils would, equally,
be giving its white children the best possible education. Conversely,
an all-white school, providing a sound education for all, will
inevitably be 'doing' multicultural education, whether explicitly or

not. For a sound education is one that is up to date, and gives the pupils the knowledge and skills to function in contemporary society. Since that society is pluralist, a good education must, by definition, reflect and utilise cultural diversity. Failure to include a broad pluralist perspective constitutes, in Swann's terms, a 'fundamental miseducation'.

This is recognised and affirmed within the *Education Reform Act 1988*: paragraph 17 of DES Circular 5/89 on the School Curriculum and Assessment is unequivocal:

> It is intended that the curriculum should reflect the culturally diverse society to which pupils belong and of which they will become adult members. The requirements apply to *all* pupils — regardless of age — registered at *all* schools, including grant-maintained schools.

Section 1 of the 1988 Act, in fact, extends the central purposes of the curriculum to emphasise the promotion of pupils' 'cultural development and the development of society.' Such a perspective involves the sharing of cultures within a national identity, rather than 'teaching culture' or 'cultural preservation'. Details of content are less important than the re-orientation of attitudes and objectives which determine curriculum selection and inform teaching processes and learning experiences.

'Sound educational principles' will include staff development policies, without which it is impossible to assimilate Swann's notion that 'multicultural understanding has to permeate all aspects of a school's work.' As Jon Nixon (1985) explains:

> Permeation becomes a cyclical process. Small-scale innovations create the need for a coordinated policy, the development of which requires consultation with a wide range of agencies and interested parties. This round of consultation and informal evaluation in turn creates the impetus for renewed innovations at the classroom level, thereby triggering the process once more. Conceived in these terms permeation as a whole school strategy takes a great deal of time and patience to develop. For it relies upon the willingness of teachers to modify, not only their practice, but also their attitudes and assumptions. The task of changing perceptions is central to the permeation process.

Where conditions for this process exist in a school, what might we observe as elements of good multicultural practice?

Let me take, as an example, what I shall call Cygnet Junior School. It is a decent 1950s building in a neat urban setting, sharing a site with the feeder Infants' School. About half of the school's 300 children come from council housing, the remainder from private housing. Ethnically, the school is predominantly southern British–English, with some pupils of New Commonwealth origin, and a few of other European origin.

However, within this virtually monoracial school, there is a successful ethos of multicultural education, to the extent that, if through a trick of demography, the catchment area were to turn multiracial overnight, the systems and philosophy of the school would not need radical restructuring: it is already providing an appropriate education for all. And the school's experience in attending to the individual needs of all the children would ensure that any special provision, such as English language tuition, was conducted on a sound educational base. As Swann points out, the best place for pupils to learn the language of study and academic opportunity is in the classroom, not withdrawn in the corridor, but this needs understanding by all teachers of the role of language in education.

The starting point here for the teacher–pupil interaction is always an acknowledgement of what the child *can* do, rather than a checklist of failures and deficits. The educational ethos for all children ensures that a pupil for whom English is a second language will be received into the school initially with efforts made by the staff to ensure that the first language, the mother tongue, is recognised and celebrated and appreciated by peers, and only then to move to an analysis of underachievement in a particular area and assistance.

This positive ethos was endorsed by the Kingman Report on English teaching (HMSO 1988):

> It should be the duty of all teachers to instil in their pupils a civilised respect for other languages and an understanding of the relations between other languages and English. It should be made clear to English-speaking pupils that classmates whose first language is Bengali or Cantonese or any other of the scores of languages spoken by the school population... have languages quite as systematic and rule-governed as their own.

Such a school is an enabling rather than disabling environment. There is no way that pupils can be expected to acquire the necessary understanding and respect for each other's personalities and cultures without first having a base of individual self-awareness and self-respect, and having this reflected in the pupil–teacher relationship. Equally, unless we have an appreciation of our own and our peers' skills and talents, we lack the conditions for collaborative learning, for problem-solving activities and negotiation, for experiencing successful participation in a shared activity: another essential aspect of preparation for life in the wider society.

At Cygnet Junior, there is a coherence in the curriculum,

evolving through collaboration with the Infants' School, to ensure continuity of approach. The head has taken care to appoint on to the staff a teacher with Infant experience and training as well as a teacher with a secondary background, to ensure this continuity, and to maintain credible liaison systems. It is sad how much of the average pupil's school life is spent by teachers disparaging what has been done in the previous phase or even the previous class. It is encouraging, therefore, that the National Curriculum

> provides the basis for genuine continuity both within and between schools through a clearly defined common framework of attainment targets, levels of attainment and programmes of study (NCC 1989).

This should help to eliminate the demotivating effects of this part of the so-called 'hidden' curriculum which is, of course, not hidden from pupils at all. The integrity of the child's school career will suffer if there is no evident integration between the various components, and disillusionment and cynicism about the system soon result. Faced with incoherence, disjointedness and unfairness, black pupils and some working class children often more readily express disaffection and resentment than some middle class children, acculturated not to make a fuss, but the latter feel the hurt no less. If we genuinely believe that education is a three-way partnership between pupils, teachers and parents, then we must work hard to ensure that the partnership systems within our part of the triad are setting a good example. At Cygnet, there are joint staff discussions with both the Infants and the Secondary schools. The school's aims and objectives are explicit, realistic, and dynamic, not immutable. Policies are evaluated with parents and governors, so that each partner knows what to expect and what is expected of them.

At Cygnet, the pupils are led to be responsible participants in their own education. With regard to 'basic skills', each child has a regularly updated graph of personal strengths and weaknesses, based on diagnostic assessments. A pupil can see that her reading skills are developing well, for example, but this term needs to concentrate on some element of mathematics, say, or graphic work. Peers, parents and the teachers can then be drawn upon for assistance in self-motivated, independent learning programmes, which, by encouraging experimentation in a range of techniques, let the pupils learn about their own learning. The knowledge and skills base thus acquired is important in itself, but more significant is the awareness of one's capabilities, a gift that develops the potential to continue learning in adult life.

Recently, Cygnet pupils worked on a language project, an integrated whole-school activity, with appropriate tasks and goals for each year group. Examples of languages were collected and analyzed, ordinary homes, as usual, providing quite extraordinary resources. As usual, too, a cluster of parents and grandparents became fascinated as well and brought in, with the same degree of involvement as the children, stamps and coins and other regalia. An English boy proudly found a Punjabi newspaper in the local shop, but needed his Asian classmate to get some value from it. Swahili and Chinese appeared, and stimulated exploratory groups, while another group patiently transliterated the names in the register into the Cyrillic alphabet. Folk tale and song blossomed beside computer languages, and the Domesday Project incorporated a survey of all the language competence locally, including those learned at school and for casual interest. An assembly on the Wordhouse (Fisher and Hicks 1985) vividly illustrated the give and take of English and other world languages, and this underlying concept of inter-relationship and inter-dependence was not lost on the pupils. They had had another opportunity to see the world from someone else's point of view, surely a key component of a sound education. They had experienced again the concept that difference is not to be equated with deficit: that other systems have validity besides our own, and that our familiar language, culture and lifestyle should not be perceived as norms from which all others are inferior deviations.

There had been extended opportunity for practice in basic skills, for information and study skills, for disciplines such as geography, history and (with all the imported foodstuff packaging) home economics. Underpinning this — or perhaps 'permeating' it — is the school's philosophy on multicultural education being put into practice. It is modest, but clear and uncluttered.

To develop in every child a critical understanding and respect, both of their own cultural background and the cultural background of their neighbours, so that:
- children may be helped to make sense of themselves with particular reference to the culture of which they are part
- children may be helped to decide what kind of person they wish to grow into
- children are better equipped to become responsible members of their community, respectful of the views and cultural backgrounds of their neighbours.

This statement, which needs to be read alongside allied statements on moral education, religious education, and other areas of experience, has been formulated and negotiated by the staff together. It is accessible to parents, governors, to the pupils themselves, and the schools connected with Cygnet. The process of permeation, described by Nixon, is constantly in train.

The activities described above in the thumb-nail sketch of the languages project are, of course, replicated each term in countless primary schools up and down the country. What perhaps makes schools like Cygnet rather special is the 'accountability' element, the fact that each staff member can articulate what they are doing, and why. The philosophical and policy base set the context for the practical activities and their conduct and evaluation feed insights back into the policy, cyclically.

No one plods on until the holidays with an exhausted topic, nobody begins the task of finding a theme for next term by dusting down the resources cupboard, no one advances that frequently heard, but least educational, argument: 'we've always done it this way'. Some school activities, methods, assemblies, systems were designed for other times and other people, possibly with a desire to turn out white, male, middle-class, Christian replicas of ourselves and our cultural totems. Perpetuating this immediately disadvantages a large proportion of all our pupils, and obsolete systems, no longer appropriate or necessary, can be racist in outcome if they disadvantage and humiliate ethnic minority pupils, for example, in matters such as dress and diet, totally monocultural learning materials, arrangements for parents' evenings, and so on.

Our world, our society and our culture are changing fast, and teachers, if they are adequately providing for their pupils, must at least reflect this change, if not promote it. A fresh look at our practices and procedures may result in abandoning some irrelevant rituals, but not with the result that our pupils will be victims of turmoil and insecurity, because proper policies will be there to maintain stability, coherence and a steady goal.

The pupils at Cygnet Junior are being equipped to cope with change and its implications, through a key component of their curriculum: 'Education for a Developing World'. The starting point of the policy statement is the overall aim:

> To encourage and develop social awareness and responsibility so that children are led to an understanding that we live in a complex and interdependent world.

There follows a list of objectives in terms of attitudes:

1. the development of an interest in events and situations which will lead to questions about causes — not only how? and why? but what?, where? and when?
2. the development of a sense of empathy, that is, a capacity to imagine what it is like to be in someone else's position
3. a growing respect for the ideas, opinions and rights of other people

4. a concern and respect for the evidence of others and for the experience which others have had
5. an understanding of roles and responsibilities.

Then comes a set of objectives in terms of skills, including information gathering, testing evidence, organising material with appropriate oral and written activities, exploring attitudes, values and opinions, working in groups, and so on.

The realisation of these objectives should lead the pupils to:

- a better understanding of themselves
- a better understanding of and response to other people
- a clearer understanding of their immediate community and the wider society of which they form part
- an understanding of their ability to influence the direction of their personal development.

Five key questions are then posed for consideration:

Issues: What are the issues which affect people's lives?
Values: What sort of world do people want to live in?
Problems: What are the problems in the world today which prevent people living as they would like?
Background: What is the background to these issues and problems?
Action: What can be done and what is being done about them?

Through this consideration, three key concepts should emerge, those of interdependence, responsibility and change. Only when we have reminded ourselves of some of the pitfalls and prejudices (of both teacher and pupil) that may initially cloud discussion, do we start to examine some possible topics that will incorporate these concepts, skills and attitudes:

- my family: a starting point for consideration of how a society works
- local community: including 'my school as a society'
- waste, celebrations, work and responsibilities: 'who does what for whom?', etc.

After working through the project, the staff became concerned that this theme of 'Education for a Developing World' might be becoming isolated from the curriculum and be too distant and issue-based, 'bringing the world into the classroom', rather than starting from the needs of the child. They are now working, through a 'whole-school' inservice activity, to re-cast the guideline document to ensure a projection outward from the individual and the immediate environment of child, home, school and community. A valuable contribution to the discussion is the teachers' handbook (Button 1989) which includes a section on how the National Curriculum can be given a global dimension.

Placing the pupils as the central focus assists both their independence and interdependence which is exemplified in all sorts of ways within the school. Pupils know how to respect each other as human resources and that it is worth working together. Other adults, besides the classteacher, are regularly in the classroom and are drawn into the learning process. Assemblies, always open to parents, make little attempt to ape adult worship, but seek to celebrate the worth of some shared experience, some particular achievement within the school or community. A school council, of staff and pupils, and a school meeting, organised by the pupils themselves, debate and negotiate aspects of administration or facilities and maintain the school ethos. An understanding of the unacceptability of racial abuse, name-calling or graffiti starts here, not with an edict from above. The head 'makes' the school policy, not by promulgation, but by providing the conditions in which the policy will emerge from among the participants themselves.

This corporate, participative, model of school policy is endorsed by the Elton Committee (DES 1989) when it recommends, for example, that:

> Headteachers and teachers should encourage the active partici-
> pation of pupils in shaping and reviewing the school's behaviour
> policy in order to foster a sense of collective commitment to it
> (R76). Additionally: Headteachers and staff should work to
> create a school climate which values all cultures, in particular
> those represented in it, through its academic and affective
> curricula. R90

A useful analysis of the features affecting the failure and success of innovation within the school is provided by Robin Richardson (1985). Though written with reference to the implementation of the Swann Report in schools, his article repays close study, as the conclusions are generalisable to all aspects of educational innovation and change.

Among the factors which indicate that a project is likely to fail are: a lukewarm or negative attitude from the head; lack of understanding and discussion among the staff; a sense that the project has been foisted on them from outside; lack of adequate knowledge and skills base among the staff; a sense of threat, suspicion or frustration; meagre material resources; a sense of low prestige for the project among pupils and teachers and so on. On the credit side, however, a project is likely to succeed if, for example:

1. The head and senior staff are clearly seen to be committed both formally, e.g. in meetings and statements, and also informally, in everyday conversations.
2. The staff most involved in the project:
   - feel that the project belongs to themselves, that it is home-grown
   - were involved from the start in diagnosing the problems to be solved, and in pondering and deciding what should be done
   - have an excellent grasp of aims and principles
   - clarify doubts, uncertainties and disagreements in discussion with each other
   - agree on the meanings of basic key terms.

Richardson goes on to examine the factors outside the school which affect failure and success of an initiative, including the LEA stance, inservice support, parental and community interest, additional resources, and so on.

There is an added complicating factor to innovation in multi-cultural education, subject as it is to tensions and pressures from within itself and from outside, in that it is perceived as a controversial issue. Thus, schools have a good excuse for inaction, for keeping a low profile, for not getting involved. It is time that more all-white schools began to address the issues with the same degree of courage that many multiracial schools have shown in facing up to their responsibilities (Mulvaney 1984).

If pupils raise concerns of injustice and inequality that they perceive, it must be educationally valid to follow them through, despite possible grousing from the armchair critics about 'political' education. The head of Cygnet was approached by a group of pupils who were disturbed that the local council appeared to have broken its promises with regard to a development on a neighbouring site that they had come to know and care about. The (perhaps conventional?) response of ordering them back to the classroom to get on with their work would not have been counted as 'political': it might be authoritarian, arbitrary, colluding with injustice, but not political!

In fact, the head sat down with them, and channelled their anxiety into the task of researching and documenting the evidence, identifying the appropriate officer, and preparing and arranging a deputation to present their point of view. This 'political' project turned out, in fact, to be a memorable and beneficial learning experience, probably because it was so fuelled by the interests of the children themselves. They also, incidentally, made a successful case.

The ability to accept and foster this independence of mind, this articulation of concern for justice and responsibility (whether the subsequent secondary schools like it or not) is important in current debates within multicultural education. It is relatively easy for a school, whether all-white or multiracial, to bring in some colourful aspect of other cultures or countries: an assembly on a festival like Chinese New Year, a wall-display, an international evening, the type of activities sometimes known as the three 'Ss': samosas, saris and steelbands. Because it is easy, it can be merely exotic and superficial, 'tokenist'. The story is told of a multiracial school where a group of white parents came to complain about their children's involvement in Divali celebrations; sensing prejudice, the teachers remonstrated with them. 'Nothing wrong with Divali' replied the parents, 'only why have you used the same theme and the same materials for the last five years? Is there nothing else from India our kids could do?'

Tinkering with pretty aspects of other cultures and countries does not constitute adequate preparation for children for multiracial Britain, although it may be the first, necessary, stage of opening up the issues (Grinter 1985). There must be facilities for moving on to, or incorporating, what has become known as an anti-racist approach, one that helps pupils identify and challenge the structural and institutional injustices and inequalities in the community, the society, the world economy, and so on. This would develop a critical awareness, not just in issues of race, but of gender and class, accent and dialect, difference and prejudice in general.

Clearly, the school itself must provide a foundation of genuine equality of opportunity: at Cygnet every effort is made to avoid reinforcing unhelpful stereotyping, such as in differential opportunities between the sexes in games, crafts, dance, and in roles within the classroom. Textbook and library materials are scrutinised, not by one decision-maker doing good, but by the collective efforts of staff, parents and pupils, with the opinions and sensitivities of black parents particularly sought. A group reading project is organised around a theme, using a variety of sources; differing opinions, conflicting facts emerge: which is right, which is valid, which is obviously biased? Practice in the ability to appraise and evaluate sources of information, images, the media, hidden messages, is an essential contribution to the young person's intellectual equipment and can be developed in any school in the land.

I began with the question of how we might recognise multicultural education in an all-white school, and have taken examples from a school where I have often had the opportunity to observe what I take to be multicultural education in action. This, of course, is a particular example of a marriage of theory and practice, and is not being proposed as a normative model to be replicated. It happens to work, within its own 'ecology' of staff, pupils and the community, with their particular qualities and relationships.

What I have tried to demonstrate is that our newly articulated statutory commitment to multicultural education has nothing to do with abandoning the core of good practice for the sake of some exotic marginalia. Cygnet's curriculum has all the necessary features of breadth and balance, differentiation and relevance. It starts where the pupils are, but sets clear goals, and seeks to assist all to achieve their potential. Without compromising this, it also manages actively to promote the skills, attitudes and concepts related to responsibility, interdependence and change.

The school prepares its pupils appropriately for society, because it is, in some respects, a scaled-down model of that society.

The curriculum of the school maintains the integrity of subject areas within an integrated project framework; the ethos of the school fosters the worth and self-awareness of each child within a corporate community. This reflects the view of society that acknowledges the access of ethnic minorities to social integration within an expanding common core of values, rights and duties, while preserving their integrity in terms of culture, background and lifestyles.

A sense that the school is designed for the pupils, not for the convenience of the administration, encourages a view of a society that is for its people, whatever their similarities or differences, where good relations are built not merely upon the concessions of tolerance and goodwill but on articulated standards of justice and equality.

A school community where accountability and involvement are paramount posits a world which is explicable and negotiable, not governed by dogma and prejudice.

Idealistic, possibly; but education without ideals reduces to the level of the conveyor-belt. As Robin Richardson further observes in his article:

> a map without utopia on it, it has been said, is not worth consulting. Admittedly, there are disadvantages, in dreams and ideals, the disadvantages of unreality and abstractions. But frequently, also it clears and strengthens your mind if you venture to dream for a while, as concretely and practically as possible, about the ideal situation to which all your current efforts are, you hope, directed. It may be very valuable, for example, in the present context of a school's planned response to the Swann Report, if head teachers and teachers write brief descriptions of what they hope their school will ideally be like in about ten years' time, and if they then compare and contrast these ideals in discussion with each other.

Discussion, the interplay of ideas, is paramount. Given a

pyramid diagram of power relationships, one would expect to place policy-making at the top, and the implementation of practice at the base. A genuinely effective policy in multicultural education or education in general, does not remain 'on high', but has to be absorbed by the intended beneficiaries of the policy, in this case, the very pupils themselves. Reciprocally, good practice: features like collaborative learning, empathy, ability to handle evidence and controversy, and so on, has to permeate back to the top, to the policy-makers. The success of a policy for multicultural education will be judged neither on the elegance of its phraseology or its exhaustiveness, nor on the colourfulness of the classroom displays, but on its outcomes in terms of equipping each and every future citizen appropriately and adequately for life together in a pluralist society in an interdependent world.

Nearly a decade on from Swann, to the surprise of many observers, the principles of multicultural education are alive and well and have been subsumed into equal opportunities, now a statutory obligation. Over a four-year cycle, every school will be independently inspected and reported on.

> The report should include evaluation of:
> - the school's policy and practice for equality of opportunity and the effects on the quality of learning and standards of achievement
> - how well the policy is understood, implemented and monitored...
> - key points for action in relation to equality of opportunity. (OFSTED 1993)

The curriculum framework for this was laid by the National Curriculum Council, which, says its Chairman, 'conscientiously sought to remove inequality and gender bias from each subject tackled', while adopting the motto 'minorities are a privilege not a problem'. He acknowledges the pressures on the status of multicultural education:

> There were demands from many quarters, and within NCC, for separate guidance. The debate raged as to whether the job of the NCC was to make equal opportunities an ever-present intrinsic aspect of its work, or to lead a crusade. Not without internal tension, it chose the former course. Others will judge if that was correct. (Graham 1993)

Moving the issue officially, and with statutory backing, from the margin to the main stream must be counted a success. The requirement cannot be ignored — a good summary of the legislation and the curriculum opportunities is available in *Equality Assurance in*

Schools (Runnymede Trust 1993).

A modular, accredited, study guide is now available enabling in-depth consideration of the issues for teachers and managers (NDCEMP Bristol 1993). The authors have more than an echo of Swann in this introduction, but it is an up-to-date reflection that we are not talking of 'optional extras' any more but of a basic entitlement:

> Curriculum guidance from the DES and from the National Curriculum Council has made clear that equal opportunities is not a discretionary matter dependent on the interests of particular schools or particular LEAs, but an integral aspect of curriculum development and implementation, and this has been underlined by the appearance of equal opportunities as a cross-curriculur dimenson, and in themes such as that of citizenship which emphasise equality issues in preparing young people for life beyond school. National Curriculum policy therefore points to the need for schools to strive to identify and counter barriers to achieving equal access and equitable outcomes for all in order to make the curriculum entitlement for all a reality.

References

AIMER (Access to Information on Multicultural Education Resources) (1993) *The Aimer Yearbook 1993*, Reading and Language Information Centre, University of Reading.

Button, J. (1989) *The Primary School in a Changing World* Centre for World Development Education.

DES (1985) *Education for All (The Swann Report)*, HMSO.

DES (1989) *Discipline in Schools (The Elton Report)*, HMSO.

Fisher, S. and Hicks, D. (1985) *World Studies 8–13: A Teacher's Handbook* Oliver and Boyd.

Graham, D. and Tyler, D. (1993) *A Lesson for Us All — The Making of the National Curriculum* Routledge.

Grinter, R. (1985) 'Bridging the gulf: the need for anti-racist multicultural education' in *Multicultural Teaching*, 3, (2).

HMSO (1988) *Report of the Committee of Inquiry into the Teaching of English Language (The Kingman Report)*

Klein, G. (1986) 'The best of British' in *Multicultural Teaching*, 4, (2).

Mulvaney, M. (1984) 'Multicultural education in the primary school', in Straker-Welds, M. (ed.) *Education for a Multicultural Society: Case Studies in ILEA Schools*, Bell and Hyman.

NCC (1989) *Circular Number 3: Implementing the National Curriculum in Primary Schools*, National Curriculum Council.

NDCEMP (1993) *Equal Opportunities in School Management* National Development Centre for Educational Management and Policy; University of Bristol.

Nixon, J. (1985) *A Teacher's Guide to Multicultural Education* Blackwell.

OFSTED (1993) *Handbook for the Inspection of Schools* HMSO.

Richardson, R. (1985) 'Each and every school: responding, reviewing, planning and doing' in *Multicultural Teaching*, 3, (2).

Runnymede Trust (1993) *Equality Assurance in Schools* Trentham Books.
Twitchin, J. and Demuth, C. (1985) *Multicultural Education: Views from the Classroom*
    BBC.

11 Behaviour management

C. Eric Spear

It is a common-place observation that children are more badly behaved than ever before, that there is not enough discipline in schools and that much of the trouble is caused by unco-operative parents.

My school log book records the following entries:

> Much annoyance — noise and running the shrubbery and flower bed — by town boys.
> Found many of the plants have been pulled up in the front borders; there has been more destruction of the premises of late than ever.

Another example of the rise of modern vandalism? Well no; actually these entries date from the 1880s! There are many more.

The master deplored the unco-operative and aggressive manner of some parents and often referred to pupil defiance. Corporal punishment was routine and hardly merited mention.

> Punished C.H. for absence without leave. It may be noted here that properly speaking only one case of 'corporal punishment' has occurred since this school opened: such an entry as the above merely denoting a stripe (or two) on the hand or back, of less severity than took place at the end of almost every lesson every day at Dr Birkbeck's school and at the National School at which the master himself taught and was a pupil teacher.

This historical perspective demonstrates that children have always been badly behaved at times but that modern teachers have to deal with the consequences of such behaviour without the major sanction which our forebears would have regarded as being essential. Since 1987, corporal punishment has been illegal in state schools. The legislation made no provision for supporting school discipline by alternative means. In 1989, the government published the Elton Report, on school discipline and, at the end of 1993, issued six draft circulars (published as circulars in May 1994) under the general title, *Pupils with Problems*, designed to advise teachers on how to deal with difficult children. In both cases there was little that was new, and no practical help or additional resources were forthcoming as a result.

Of course, things have changed considerably since Victorian times, and I am not suggesting, as some prominent politicians have done, that we need merely to return to Victorian values to solve our problems.

First we need to define the problem. Things are not as bad as the newspaper headlines would have you believe. Inspectors' reports regularly comment upon the quiet, well-disciplined atmosphere they encounter in schools.

> Most schools are successful in promoting good behaviour and discipline. The 1993 report from Her Majesty's Chief Inspector of Schools (HMCI) found that most schools were orderly and the overall standards of pupil behaviour were satisfactory or better. (*Pupils With Problems* Draft Circular on Pupil Behaviour and Discipline, DFE Dec 1993)

Riots in school are unknown, but they certainly aren't on the football terraces or inner-city streets. Yet these are the same youngsters, being contained by teachers during school-time but out of control of their parents and the police at other times. That, in itself, is a tribute to the fact that teachers manage pupil behaviour in school rather effectively.

Of course, schools are always the target of criticism when pupils misbehave out of school. Those with a nostalgic yearning for the past and its superior values will argue that pupils never behaved like that when they were at school. I am happy to concede that point, if only for the reason that in those days pupils left school at fourteen and so their subsequent misdeeds were a problem for society rather than for schools. Nowadays, those same pupils will be at school for between two and four years longer, so that it is schools which have to deal with the rebellious years of teenage life. A progressively earlier physical maturation of young people has brought down the age of puberty from post-school years, in Victorian times, to the top end of the primary school for many children today, with all the emotional and behavioural problems which that brings for the school to deal with.

Schools of today, therefore, face a much greater challenge than in even the recent past. The potential for behavioural problems within schools is greater and the major sanction of a previous generation has been withdrawn.

The problem is compounded by changed attitudes in modern society. Authority, of all sorts, is more regularly and successfully challenged now than ever before. Our population is more independently minded, less subservient and, some would say, less respectful and reverent towards traditional forms of authority and institutions, than in the past. Decisions do not have to be accepted unquestioningly. Indeed, the *Citizen's Charter* and its offspring, has elevated the right of the citizen to complain and to argue with the decisions and actions of 'authority' almost to the level of a routine obligation.

Clearly, in this climate of opinion and with the other variables just described, yesterday's solutions are not going to work, even if they were available, and what is needed now are solutions to today's and tomorrow's problems.

Creating a positive climate

On the whole, primary school children want to please and like to receive recognition for their effort to do so. This argues for a positive attitude on the part of the teacher in making it clear what is required of pupils and making it clear what is not allowed. Until the parameters are clear to all concerned, the teacher's reaction to pupil behaviour may appear inconsistent and arbitrary. Teacher responses must operate in the context of a clear, whole-school policy, applied consistently by everyone in the school.

Managing behaviour is all about re-enforcing right behaviour and penalising wrong behaviour, though of course there is more to good discipline than behaviour management. Behaviour management is interventionist. It implies that someone has a plan for someone else, and spends time and effort implementing it. Conceptually, we have to allow for the fact that behaviour management can be directed towards producing undesirable as well as good behaviour. Nazi youth indoctrination is an example of the former. Behaviour management is not an end in itself but a means to achieving a higher order of behaviour where the subject will become an autonomous, morally acting, self-disciplined being.

There is a sense in which people should want to do the right because it is right, not because of some extrinsic reason such as the fear of punishment or the hope of reward. This is a high-order level of morality achieved by a careful nurturing of the concept over a long period of time and by experiences which re-enforce this moral view. It, therefore, follows that, where children have not been subject to the sort of upbringing that re-enforces a desire to do the right, they may pose a problem when they enter school. The collective influence of the media has not always been positively beneficial, in the view of many. While it is true that television, in particular, has the potential for being a powerful influence for the good, the opposite is also true. The success of TV advertising is a powerful argument against those who say that TV does not influence the young.

When children enter school they have to adapt quickly to an environment where they are not, as individuals, the centre of attention. This is difficult enough. They are also presented with wider opportunities to secure that attention by exhibiting behaviour which demands the attention of teachers and other children. Often, unless the child already possesses outstanding social, physical or academic talents, the most effective way to gain attention will be by disruptive, anti-social behaviour.

It is at this point that behaviour management becomes necessary. The teacher must try to work out what motivates the child, what he is seeking to achieve and then try to devise ways in which the child can be guided, either to the achievement of these goals by positive and constructive behaviour, or guided towards different goals. There are some general principles to consider.

- It is more productive to reward good behaviour than to punish bad.
- Significant behaviour should receive immediate feedback. Praise and reward good behaviour as soon as possible after it happens, and clearly indicate displeasure at, and the consequences of, bad behaviour as soon as it happens.
- Aim to raise the child's self-esteem so that he has something to lose by inappropriate behaviour.
- Comment on the behaviour, not the person. Don't say, 'You are a bad boy!' say, 'Doing that upsets other people. It is not very pleasant behaviour.'
- Don't over-react. Keep a sense of proportion and know when it is politic to turn a blind eye. Over-correction of every minor infraction can quickly turn into a cycle of nagging, leading to a negative self-image, leading to bad behaviour, leading to more nagging.
- Be consistent and don't make threats which you cannot, or do not intend to carry out.
- Long-term promises are less effective than short-term or immediate ones. Reward systems should produce some immediate, tangible result, even if it is something as simple as a star on a chart.
- Sanctions, equally, should be immediately applicable with

young children. Children should be told what the wrong behaviour was, what they should have done and that, as a consequence, they will have some privilege withdrawn until they can demonstrate the correct behaviour. This can be something as simple as missing their turn in the sandpit or on the computer. However, the possibility of redemption must always be left open, otherwise there is no incentive to correct the behaviour.

- Place responsibility for making good or bad choices of behaviour on the child. Let the child know, clearly, the consequences of different courses of action and encourage him to make a reasoned choice.

A whole school policy

If rules are to be applied fairly and consistently, schools need to develop and implement policies which set out a shared set of values and attitides. The policy will need to set out the principles which should guide relationships between teachers, pupils and parents.

Pupils With Problems (ibid) states that:

'... schools are not value-free zones...' and that the ..., 'values they should be concerned to promote should include respect for others and property; honesty; trust and fairness; the virtues of self-respect and self-discipline.'

Few teachers would argue with the aim, or the view that:

Policies should be based on a clear and justifiable set of principles and values, and should be regularly reviewed.

The document distinguished between a code of conduct, which merely set out the rules to be followed, and the sanctions which will be applied to rule-breakers, and school policy which is intended to foster and maintain good behaviour.

Principles for a whole-school behaviour policy

- Underlying principles and values clearly stated.
- Positive encouragement to good behaviour rather than dwelling on the consequences of bad.
- Minimum rules, expressed positively — emphasis on personal responsibility.
- Involvement of every sector of the school community in its formulation, including children, and evaluation of its effectiveness periodically and review if necessary.

The teacher's role

The *Elton Report, Discipline in Schools* (DES 1989) placed great emphasis on the creation, by the classroom teacher, of a positive climate based on mutual respect. This is an important concept. If children feel that the teacher does not respect them they have less incentive to co-operate with what the teacher wants to happen in the classroom. The teacher sees the class as potentially hostile and the teaching style becomes more oppressive and formal. The *Elton Report* noted:

> They create a negative classroom atmosphere by frequent criticism and rare praise. They make use of loud public reprimands and threats. They are sometimes sarcastic. They tend to react aggressively to minor incidents. Their methods increase the danger of a major confrontation not only with individual pupils but with the whole class.

Faced with this kind of problem, what does the headteacher do? Contrary to the belief of some that discipline is a function of personality, you either have it or you haven't, group management is a skill which can be learned. The problem for teachers is that there has not been enough training available, either in initial teacher education or subsequently. It may be that, in the wake of the latest batch of circulars from the DFE, on *Pupils with Problems*, suitable training opportunities will become available, to address whatever problem there is perceived to be in this area, together with the GEST money to support it.

Personal responsibility

I cannot now remember the exact source, but I once heard the reported words of a well-respected, public boys' school teacher on the subject of developing a sense of personal responsibility. He said,

> If you trust boys they will let you down, but if you don't trust them they will do you down!

The important point about this is that children will only learn how to be responsible by exercising responsibility. Becoming responsible is not a function of the ageing process. There are plenty of irresponsible adults to prove that point! Equally, there are some very mature and responsible children, even in infant schools. Children who are given responsibility will not always get it right to begin with. It will be the teacher's job to manage the failures in positive ways, which encourage further attempts to improve, rather than to deny the opportunity of failure, or success, again.

Intractable discipline problems

It has to be conceded that, sometimes, just as society finds that it cannot cope with certain individuals and has to lock them up, so schools will have to admit that there are some children with whom it is not equipped to deal. Outside professionals, such as education welfare officers, or their equivalent, social services, child guidance and possibly the probation service may all be involved with some children, as well as the school. If, despite all their attention, a pupil remains intractably disruptive, the school has to consider its larger duty to the education of all the other pupils in the school. In the final analysis, and it will be only after every other avenue has been explored, the school may finally decide on exclusion. There has been a suggestion recently from the Secretary of State that schools are resorting to exclusion too readily. The evidence for this has not been adduced. It may be that there are some schools, driven by the expediency of the market-place and their position in various government compiled league tables for exams and 'truancy', who exclude pupils in order to maintain their image. It is also true that a number of other schools have become the LEA's final dumping ground for large numbers of excluded pupils. These are sometimes schools chosen because they have nothing to lose in terms of league tables because of their already disadvantaged catchment area, but there are also schools which pride themselves on giving such children a fresh start. Both sorts of school should be given extra help and support to allow them to manage these pupils.

One issue which must be faced up to is that the management of disruptive and disaffected pupils is costly in terms of personnel and time.

In many schools in the USA and Canada, for example, there are full-time counsellors who do nothing but deal with difficult children's problems. When a child becomes disruptive in class the class teacher is not expected to handle matters beyond a certain point. When the behaviour becomes unmanageable, the child is sent for a 'time out' session under the supervision of the specially trained counsellor. The counsellor will use behaviour management techniques to change the child's attitude to school, and may often be dealing with severe social and emotional problems brought from home. This is a very costly resource and one which British schools, especially primary schools, could not afford. There is scope for the headteacher and the special needs co-ordinator to play part of the role, but they both have other pressures on their time.

Trained classroom assistants are sometimes assigned as personal assistants to disruptive children, and have the time and the focus to build up a personal relationship which can benefit the child's attitude and behaviour and may help him with his work as well. Again, there is a cost involved and, if the government is really serious about these problems, additional resources are going to be needed.

References

HMSO (1989) *Discipline in Schools* Report of the Committee of Enquiry chaired by
    Lord Elton.
DFE (1994) *Pupils with Problems* (6 Circulars).

12 Early childhood education: managing to achieve quality

Geva M. Blenkin

There exists at the present time a ground swell of support for ensuring that a high-quality education is available for all young children in the United Kingdom. This signals an acceptance, nationally, of the world-wide evidence which is showing the significance and lasting impact that early experiences in group settings have, not only on children's educational success but also on their more general social development. Of particular interest is that evidence which shows that high-quality early education has a profound effect on the life chances of individuals, and on the consequent contributions they will be willing and able to make to society in the long term.

It is partly because this evidence concentrates on the effects of high-quality education on children's development, both intellectual and social, that the supporters of policies which will widen the availability of such experiences, not surprisingly, are turning to the teaching profession and to schools, rather than to other agencies which are concerned for the care of young children, to advise on the implementation of the policy.

In one sense, this is sensible and entirely appropriate. Professional teachers, after all, should be in the best position to know how to provide a high-quality education. This is not always the case, however, because education in the early years has been neglected for decades. Provision for our youngest children, as a result, is haphazard, and is often staffed by practitioners who tend to have a low status, even within the teaching profession, and whose morale, therefore, is low.

It is still commonplace, for example, to believe that anyone can teach little children, and that the early years is a soft option compared, say, to secondary teaching. This is even thought to be the case by some teachers, let alone parents and other interested lay people. It is often said that, because the content studied by a young child is easier than that required of a ten year-old, the task of educating the young child is less demanding.

As a result, it is also often thought that training levels can be less rigorous, because demands on the early years practitioner are seen as less intellectual. Witness, for example, the recent attempt to introduce a 'Mum's Army' of non-graduate teachers into early years' education.

However, quite contrary evidence is beginning to emerge from studies which show that high-quality education in the early years is very demanding of practitioners and not at all an easy option. Studies of four year-olds in infant classes, such as those made by Bennett and Kell (1989) and Pascal (1990) in the mid-1980s, for example, have revealed how fundamental issues related to the appropriateness of provision and adequacy of resourcing levels are often neglected, and poor-quality provision is usually the result.

If this is to be avoided, and the required standard of provision for young children is to be achieved, it must be planned and managed properly, and also resourced adequately and appropriately. And this is a major challenge for headteachers and senior managers in primary, infant and nursery schools. After all, if high-quality provision has been shown to have a profound effect for the good, we can assume confidently that poor-quality provision will have a similarly profound effect for the bad.

An appropriate response to this important initiative, therefore, needs to be thought through and costed very carefully at the level of top management. And, those responsible must also be prepared to act as advocates for young children, and to persuade school governors and parents to accept both the characteristics and the inevitable resource implications of establishing a developmentally appropriate curriculum.

My main aim in writing this chapter is to support headteachers in this process of advocacy and implementation. For, in my view, both are essential. And, I begin by offering a brief for the advocate, which falls into two main parts. The first of these relates to the research studies which have identified the profound effects of early education.

The evidence in support of high quality early education

It is self-evident that all parents want the very best for their young children. There is no doubt, therefore, that if they are shown the effects of high-quality early education on children's future life chances, they will want nothing less for their own children. Governors, interested lay people and politicians, too, are easily persuaded when faced with this evidence.

The long-term effects of high-quality provision are stark and far-reaching. For researchers have shown, in the longitudinal studies which cover more than two decades, that high-quality early education not only gives individual children a good start in their compulsory schooling, which has measurable benefits at least until the age of twelve years. It also helps them to adjust to society more readily, and, most significantly, enables them to make a more positive contribution to their communities and to society at large.

The 'High Scope' studies, for example, show that fewer of the boys who participated in the pre-school programme became involved in anti-social behaviour and crime during adolescence and early adulthood, and fewer of the girls became pregnant in their teens. (A useful summary of the findings of the high scope studies and other international studies which confirm these findings can be found in the Sylva article cited below.)

In the light of these findings, it is clear that it is easier at present to act as an advocate for high-quality early education than it has been for at least the last two decades. The economic and social arguments in favour of investment in this sector of schooling are as strong as the educational ones. David Weikart, the Director of the American High Scope Project, speaking at the recent opening of the High Scope Centre in London, for example, was widely quoted in the press as saying, 'We cannot afford not to make high-quality provision in the early years'. And this confident assertion was based on the finding from the US study that 'for every $1000 invested in the children who attended the pre-school programme, $4130 was returned to the tax payer (after controlling for inflation) by way of savings on educational or social provision required by the control group later in life' (quoted in Sylva 1982, p.685).

And a similar theme was picked up by Sir Claus Moser, again with much media interest and attention, at the launch of *Learning to Succeed*, the report of the National Commission on Education (1993). For he emphasised that the commission makes high quality nursery education its first goal. In the chapter of the Report entitled 'A good start in education', which contains a powerful argument in favour of high-quality early education, it is stated unequivocally that 'better provision for under-5s will yield benefits for the economy' (op.cit., p.120).

The advocate must not only persuade of the benefits, however. He or she must also be able to explain, in straightforward terms, what is meant by high-quality early education, and what are the essential features of a curriculum that is developmentally appropriate for young children.

The essential features of a high-quality curriculum for the early years

The first point to make here is that high-quality provision depends upon a curriculum which is, in essence, democratic. The approach adopted, therefore, must place the child and his or her development at the centre of planning, and all planning must focus on nurturing an active, independent and socially responsible young learner.

So, for example, in the most famous American version of this high-quality curriculum, the High Scope programme referred to above, the children are expected, each day, to 'plan, do and review'. And, in the more open European version, the children choose from a range of developmentally appropriate resources and activities, and are then encouraged to communicate and reflect upon ideas and interests which result, through conversations and a range of other modes. Thus, in both of these examples, even the youngest children are given responsibility for their own learning, supported of course by responsive adults.

Secondly, high-quality early education is holistic, rather than differentiated into school subjects, permitting subject study to emerge from experiences in a manner that makes sense to the individual child. This feature stems not only from a concern to help young children to make sense of the more academic demands of school subjects (which need to negotiate with the child the links between everyday understanding and the more formal demands made by school learning which was noted earlier in the chapter). It is also a response to the research which shows that young children can be put off school learning very early in their lives, if experiences are presented in a 'formal' or 'academic' manner too soon.

We had thought, in the past, that the problem of disaffection and alienation from school was one which emerged in adolescence and was an issue for our secondary colleagues. However, studies such as that of young children starting school, which was conducted by Gill Barrett on behalf of the Assistant Masters' and Mistresses' Association (AMMA) (Barrett 1986), provide us with powerful evidence that alienation occurs also among our four and five year-olds. And, these studies reveal how such alienation is widespread among our young children, especially when they are unable to make sense of the experiences that they meet in school, and are not helped effectively to do so. It can only be obviated by a curriculum which is framed in terms matched to the developmental level of the children themselves.

Hence, closely related to the holistic nature of a high quality early years curriculum is the emphasis which must be placed on development as the foremost consideration in planning. The content of the curriculum and the assessment of the children's performance are of vital importance, but they must be related to and, more importantly, they must promote development.

This requires that teachers who work with young children must understand children and how they develop. For teachers who have such an understanding, and, further, have learned how to use this understanding to inform their practice and make it more effective, are equipped to observe young children and to respond to the children appropriately in the light of these observations.

Finally, all high-quality educational provision for young children must not only be informal in style; it must also be playful in character. For the opportunity to play is essential to the young child because it is essential to the secure development of his or her understanding.

Most adults believe that schooling is a serious business, because it has such a profound effect on children's futures. Parents and teachers, therefore, have tended to push play to the fringes of school life, and have made school activities, even for our youngest children, serious and solemn.

This view has become even more entrenched since resources have been short and National Curriculum 'coverage' has been to the fore. Yet, well-resourced informal activities and play, both indoors and out-of-doors, are characteristic features of all of the high-quality programmes for young children which are featured in the research studies.

It is on the issue of playfulness in early education that the advocate for quality will need to be best informed and most persuasive. For the view that says we should go 'back to basics' and that 'earlier is better' for academic study is firmly entrenched in our folk culture. It is a position, however, that is contradicted by a growing body of literature deriving from research into effective early learning.

Fuller descriptions and analyses of the essential features of a high quality curriculum for the early years are readily available (see, for example, Blenkin and Kelly 1988). What must be emphasised here, however, is that all high-quality provision depends on the features listed above if it is to be developmentally appropriate.

All of the provision for under-8s that has been shown in the studies to have beneficial long-term effects on children has involved planning that is child-focused, has been informal, playful and interactive in style, has provided a richly resourced environment for learning, and has concentrated on helping young children to make sense of their experiences in school.

Being a well-informed advocate is one important role and responsibility for the headteacher who is determined to introduce high-quality into the early years' provision of the school. He or she must also, however, be able to manage the practical implementation of this policy commitment. And this must be done at a time when, on the one hand, the National Curriculum at Key Stage 1 is still relatively new, and is creating its own resource demands, and when, on the other hand, primary, infant and first schools are under pressure to admit children who are below statutory school age into their reception classes without any additional resources.

We must end, therefore, by considering what I would identify as important practical issues which must be addressed and problems which must be resolved if a high-quality education is to become a reality in schools.

Implementing high-quality provision

A first vital issue is to establish which children it is that the research in favour of high quality is referring to. This may seem an odd issue to highlight. It is important to emphasise, however, that most of the research is concerned with children under 8, and not only with the under-5s.

One of the worst effects of the National Curriculum on early childhood education has been to fracture the link between nursery and infant education, and to encourage many teachers to stop thinking about under-8s as 'infants'. For this has led some teachers to introduce children at Key Stage 1 to a highly academic curriculum far too early in their school careers. And yet it has been shown in the studies that young children up to the age of eight need adults to mediate between everyday experiences and school learning if they are to make sense of the more academic demands that school subjects make on them.

And we must not lose sight of the fact that the long tradition in western cultures of viewing early childhood as an especially sensitive period refers to the period defined for us by the Jesuits as from birth to seven. We need to remind ourselves, and the parents and governors in our schools, that children in the UK begin compulsory schooling at a very young and tender age, compared to those in almost any other nation. So, when the international research speaks of 'nursery education' or 'pre-school education' or of 'the early years', we need to be clear that it is speaking more often than not of education for children up to seven years of age.

I have emphasised this point because it becomes vital to the review and resourcing of early childhood education within a school context. For the provision of a high-quality curriculum, if it is to be effective in the ways described earlier, must be seen as essential to all children up to the age of seven, and not as applying only to those children who are of non-statutory school age. This means that any coherent strategy for the development of such a curriculum must involve all teachers and support staff who are working in the pre-school and Key Stage 1 phases and not just those working with nursery and reception classes.

This extension of concern for children up the age-range, of course, has the advantage of increasing the allocation of resources, both those that are financial and those relating to personnel. And this can be an important consideration when resources are short. For it must be understood that, if investment in early education is to have the effect of a fourfold saving at some stage in the future, that investment must be made in real terms in the present. It will be easier to make it if it is an initiative that involves, and is thus covered by, a significant proportion of the school's budget and staffing.

The quality, and quantity, of staffing is clearly a prime consideration, for, as the early years curriculum group points out,

> working with young children is a challenging and demanding task, requiring qualified nursery and infant staff.... [who] need appropriate child/adult ratios to enable them to talk to and work with young children (EYCG 1992, p.32).

They go on to point out that a quality curriculum is most likely to founder on inadequate numbers of staff, or on the employment of staff who are inadequately trained, or who are not supported with in-service professional training.

In order to achieve the appropriate quality of staffing, it is very likely that a substantial commitment to early years' in-service training for teachers, nursery nurses and other early years practitioners will be necessary. This is because the specialist training, especially for teachers, has been weakened in recent years. This has been a second unfortunate effect of the National Curriculum. For all initial training courses during the past decade or so have required student teachers, including those who intend to work in nurseries or with infants, to focus on the study of National Curriculum subjects and how to teach them.

This has encouraged teachers to concentrate their attention on subject content, defined in academic terms, and on what children are required to learn in those terms. And it has, as a consequence, weakened the ability of newly qualified teachers to participate in the mediation process which is so vital to young children's developing understanding, because it has deprived them of the study of child development and its influence on the framing of a developmentally appropriate curriculum.

This aspect of the early years' team's professional expertise may need to be strengthened and is, therefore, the second practical issue that will need to be addressed. The third issue concerns the establishment of a suitable environment for learning.

Again, high-quality resources are a significant factor in all of the successful early years' settings, and will need to be available if the children are to benefit from their early education. The members of the early years' curriculum group, in their guide for parents and governors which is referred to above, provide a useful checklist of children's practical resource needs. These include:

- equipment (including sand, clay and water) which is suited to their learning requirements
- equipment which is stored in such a way that they can see it, use it and put it away themselves
- access to a suitable outdoor environment
- a stimulating setting in which their own work is valued and attractively displayed
- easy access to washing and toilet facilities (EYCG 1992, p.22).

The group go on to show, in a very accessible way, how living in this carefully prepared environment, and using the resources that are made available, can promote learning and development in the early years.

Finally, high-quality education depends on the ability of the teacher to respond appropriately to the children. And this, in turn, depends on high-quality assessments and records of each individual child's progress within the group. Again, all high-quality provision for early learning has, for reference and support, effective studies and records of the children and their achievements.

Summary

I have outlined in this chapter the importance of high-quality provision in the early years of schooling. I have shown how research has highlighted the long-term and proven benefits of such a high quality education. I then identified the essential features of a curriculum which will deliver such high quality, and I ended by emphasising the essential resource commitments which must be made by a school which wishes to ensure the quality of its provision for the early years.

In conclusion, we need to remember that:

> young children are the most vulnerable and least powerful members of the community. They are also our greatest joy and asset (EYCG 1992, p.34).

The provision we make for them is thus a major responsibility which we should not take lightly.

References

Barrett, G. (1986) *Starting school: An Evaluation of the Experience* Report commissioned by the Assistant Masters' and Mistresses' Association (AMMA), AMMA and Centre for Applied Research, Norwich.

Bennett, N. and Kell, J. (1989) *Four Year Olds in School* Blackwell, Oxford.

Blenkin, G. M. and Kelly, A. V. (eds) (1988) *Early Childhood Education: A Developmental Curriculum* Chapman, London.

Early Years Curriculum Group (EYCG) (1992) *First Things First: Educating Young Children* Madeleine Lindley, Oldham.

National Commission on Education (1993) *Learning to Succeed: A Radical Look at Education Today and a Strategy for the Future* Heinemann, London.

Pascal, C. (1990) *Under Fives in Infant Classrooms* Trentham Books, Stoke.

Sylva, K. (1992) 'Quality care for the under fives: is it worth it?' in *RSA Journal*, **CXL**, (5433), 683–690.

13 Partnership with governors

David Hargrave

> I am very pleased to offer you the post of headteacher of the school, and hope that you will accept the governors' offer.

So speaks the chairman of the governors after a structured and lengthy process has been meticulously followed, determined by the governors' appointments policy.

The appointments committee will have agreed a job description, drawn up a person specification, decided on the form of advertisement and its best placement. Additionally, further details of the post, the school, the locality, will have been prepared, all to be sent out with application forms on request from prospective applicants. No doubt, at all stages the Chief Education Officer of the LEA or his representative will be involved in an advisory capacity. In employment terms, though, the governing body has the duties of an employer, and its recommendation for appointment must be accepted by the LEA, provided that the successful candidate satisfies the requirements of appropriate qualifications, health and physical capacity or fitness on educational grounds.

However, within the above legislated process is a hidden agenda which the chairman of governors and, indeed governors themselves, should acknowledge and guard against during the selection process. Consideration must be focused on the stage at which the school is in relation to its response to recent Education Acts. Is the governing body seeking to appoint a headteacher capable of and, needing to, initiate school development after a period of quiet and non-development? Is there a need to identify in the new headteacher high effectiveness qualities so that the current pace of development of the school can be maintained? The chairman of governors should consider, and guard against, possible governor intent to turn back the clock to a previous regime, or to appoint a facsimile of the resigning headteacher rather than acknowledge that headship appointments are infrequent opportunities to revitalise the school through bold pro-active leadership, if the right candidate can be identified. The advisability of the chairman's being influenced by the retiring headteacher is a further point for consideration.

The successful candidate will have gone through the onerous process of a considered, paper presentation of his planned and structured career progression. Carefully composed statements on the application form, and in the additional letter or curriculum vitae, will have been analyzed by the appointing governors. Candidates will have been observed minutely during visits to the school and questioned persistently and searchingly during the series of interviews that make up the selection process. The governors are all-powerful and hold the whip-hand. The candidates are pawns in the appointment game. No wonder the successful candidate feels at a considerable disadvantage, and rather daunted, at the moment of offer of the post of headteacher of the school. What is being taken on? How can one work with this group of governors? Can one cope with the problems facing the school? Is one going to be totally alone in the newly acquired situation?

Education acts of the past decade have changed radically the duties and responsibilities of governors. As a result, governors have been brought into a central forum to discuss their strengthened address of the conduct of the school, what is taught, general principles for school discipline, provision for pupils with special educational needs, policies on charging, staffing considerations, and decisions about the school's budget. Governors should carry out these responsibilities and service their duties as a governing body, and not as individual governors. They should act with knowledge and understanding of the school, and only on this basis can their decisions be based soundly and taken effectively.

The question can be asked: 'Where can such wide-ranging knowledge, awareness and understanding be accessed readily and quickly?' The question anticipates the vital relationship that must exist between the governors and the staff of the school. This crucial relationship is personified by the co-operative partnership that must exist between chairman and headteacher. The newly appointed headteacher will have served a professional apprenticeship as probationer, qualified teacher, teacher with various responsibilities (both curricular and managerial), head of department, head of year/lower school/upper school and, ultimately, deputy head. This profile of experience will have been gained in a number of varied schools under different management styles practised by a series of headteachers.

This on-the-job experience will have been enhanced by further academic study leading to diploma or higher degree, and broadened by attendance at a range of curriculum-based courses at local centres of training and development. Such a candidate for headship will have a professional profile of some considerable maturity and conviction, based on many years of accumulated experience.

Developing this scenario, the newly appointed headteacher must assume, immediately the interview and appointment process are completed, a position of confidence, leadership potential, and positivity. During the interviews, the governors rightly questioned, probed, analyzed and assessed the candidates, measuring experience and quality, the candidate feeling vulnerable, defensive and subservient to the imposing interviewing governing body. The metamorphosis following appointment must be instantaneous if the new headteacher is to grow into the leadership/managerial role essential in any in-post headteacher.

There is a further consideration which contributes to the headteacher–governor relationship. The new headteacher commences his contractual duties at a very real disadvantage. He is faced with the need to get to know the new school, its buildings, facilities, site, with all their shortcomings. He has inherited a staff, not of his own choosing and appointment, but each with a role and contribution representing the previous regime and being, to some degree, defensive of that position and resistant to change. He faces an unfamiliar body of pupils with the memory of the previous headteacher still firmly in their minds. He faces the parents of the children, apprehensive of the new face, and the possibility of innovation. He needs to establish lines of communication with the LEA over various matters, and meet and build up relationships with officers to the advantage of the school. The new head must face his new governing body, not as a vulnerable candidate, but now as leader, manager, supervisor, and organiser — a transformation requiring the utmost confidence and strength of character.

On the other hand, the chairman of governors can act from a position of confidence, of good knowledge of the school, the children, the parents, LEA, and members of the governing body. However, at the same time, the chair must wonder what innovations will stem from the new management, and what new directions will be proposed by the new occupant of the head's study.

The situation, so described, demands a dialogue, an extensive and wide-ranging dialogue so that each of these key people in the life and functioning of the school has an awareness and appreciation of what is required of the other. It is crucial that the chairman–headteacher relationship should be a close one and, initially, a series of meetings is essential to establish an effective working relationship based on a sharing of expertise, and on mutual confidence existing between them. Ideally, this relationship should be developed at a very early stage, so that the two functional teams involved in the school can start to work in harmony as soon as possible after the head's appointment.

The two teams referred to have quite distinct make-up, and this bears some analysis to clarify their differing modes of function. The headteacher, a committed and experienced professional, manages a group of trained, experienced, equally committed professionals who have seen educational change and responded to curricular innovation. They are career minded and have daily contact with pupils, colleagues and parents, sharing and shouldering the responsibility for the learning of children. The chairman of governors leads a team of voluntary people from very diverse backgrounds. They have contact with the school, but sporadically, and serve without remuneration on fixed-term contracts. Both teams have the same intent, to service the school but, obviously, from very different standpoints. The headteacher is in the unique position of having a precisely defined place in each team. He can choose not to be a member of the governing body but, even so, has the right to attend all meetings. As a governor, he enjoys all the rights and power accorded to all other governors, but he has both professional and legal responsibilities which no other governor shares. His membership as senior professional of the school charges him with the legal responsibility for the management and administration of the school, exercising the supervision of both the teaching and non-teaching staff. It would be an interesting scenario if the chairman of governors had a similar right of membership of the staff meeting so that the notion of partnership, certainly between the two team leaders, could become more of a reality. Hopefully, the mutual confidence ideal could be developed further through this reciprocal membership situation.

So, the two teams exist under their distinct leaderships; the natures of the teams are diverse; there is a parallelism and equality, but neither would exist or work without the other. The essentiality of a cross-fertilisation becomes evident, and deliberate and programmed information exchange should become an objective on both sides.

One vital link between school and governing body is the principal item on the governors' meeting agenda, namely the headteacher's report. This is the major vehicle of information which passes three times a year from the headteacher, staff and school to each and every governor. It is a vital updating, event-recording and advance notice-giving channel of information. The carefully composed and clearly presented, decimal notated paragraphed report should become the major focus of any governor as pre-meeting reading, highlighting, and question preparation. The agenda item should allow governors to obtain a lucid picture of the functioning of the school, both in retrospect since the last governors' meeting, and in prospect up to the next. Points of clarification should leave governors in no doubt as to the precise position pertaining to the school, and any unresolved points form the focus of an action plan.

Other items on the agenda will inform the governors of developing issues, quite often the LEA providing briefing notes for governors to guide governor discussion and inform of new legislation. Reports from committees of the governing body, plus various occasional items, compose a wide-ranging focus affecting the school. It is vital that the leaders of the two teams are fully cognisant with the agenda, have discussed each item and, as far as possible, anticipated issues likely to be raised. Such a dialogue, which may include the clerk to the governors, will be ongoing during composition of the agenda and at the pre-meeting between chairman and headteacher.

During the actual governors' meeting, assuming that each governor has completed the same preparations by reading thoroughly the agenda, reports and other relevant paperwork, opportunity for individuals' contribution must be assured through perceptive chairmanship. Although the headteacher has the paid responsibility for leadership, the governors, through the chairman, must feel that their contributions are valued and taken note of. Governors must feel part of the decision-making process, otherwise they can, and sadly often do, feel isolated and of no real value.

The involvement of each and every governor and the valuing of contribution through effective chairmanship confirms the principal function of the governing body as being to offer advice and support to the headteacher. As already stated, the headteacher has a responsibility in law for the day-to-day, term-to-term management of the school, its smooth running, effective delivery of the curriculum and learning of the pupils. In terms of budgeting, planning and staffing, it is clear that governors have a definite role to play considering proposals, monitoring implementations and progress, revising plans from the basis of their experience within education, and from outside in their business, commercial, and professional lives.

The chairman, working with the headteacher, must achieve and maintain a delicate balance between the opinions of the two teams. Sometimes this may be very easy when there is unanimity of purpose. However, on other occasions, there may be polarisation of opinion, and delicate negotiation may be necessary before resolution and agreement is reached. The headteacher's conviction, arising from his extensive experience prior to taking up his appointment or, indeed, from many years' service as a headteacher, may be at odds with governors' opinion over the curriculum, staffing, the school's budget, religious education and sex education. Long-serving governors, governors with a sound business/commercial background, governors retired from a civil service or educational background may have very definite opinions and ideas which they eloquently articulate. All the tact, diplomacy and mutual confidence and respect must be brought into play between headteacher and chairman. In relation to the curriculum, the pre-meeting discussions must have, as their guidelines, the requirement that the governors must have considered the LEA policy and guidelines on the curriculum. They must also have adopted or modified the policy statement and, thereafter, must monitor its delivery. The governors need to acknowledge that the headteacher, with the staff, has the responsibility for the organisation of the curriculum, including teaching methods and approaches. The headteacher must share the considered philosophies of himself and his staff with both the chairman and, indeed, all the governors, and opportunity should be made for members of staff to speak about their curricular enthusiasms at successive governors' meetings. Thereby, the governors will become better informed, get to know staff, and have a sounder basis for making far-reaching decisions during discussions on the curriculum and such other issues as budget, staffing, and buildings.

A further way that the chairman can work with the headteacher is to encourage and facilitate a much closer relationship with the day to day activities in the school. Governor visits, on a regular basis, can be a most rewarding information-gathering experience. Governors with little formal awareness of contemporary classroom activity can gain significantly by a well-prepared, paired visit to the school. Perceptive observation, questioning and clarification, explanation of methods and curricular activities can inform governors beneficially about the effectiveness of the teaching and the success of the learning in the school. Pairs of governors visiting a school can help to give confidence to each other in view of the fact that they are entering a professional world of work and, ultimately, ensure accuracy of observation of the functioning of the school in classroom terms. The chairman and headteacher must, together, produce guidelines for such visits as they can be daunting for both the governors and staff unless they are carefully planned and sensitively carried out. Through such visits, the chairman and headteacher can ensure that there is a productive exchange of information to the benefit of both groups of individuals.

The headteacher of a school can, at times, feel and be very lonely. To the pupils, parents, and local community he is a figurehead representing the philosophies and convictions reflected in the practices seen in the school. He represents the school in a public relations capacity, and must present a positive face, even in a crisis. However, he is not alone in this. The chairman of governors can be equally, or even more, isolated. He manages a team that is predominantly distinct from the school, but committed to the school. For the majority of the time he is distanced from his governor team with only occasional contact. The chairman, like the head, will have skills of leadership, be able to preside over and co-ordinate, be dominant in a relaxed non-aggressive way, be able to focus on what people can do best, be able to clarify objectives, set criteria and be a good communicator.

The relationship between headteacher and chairman is of vital importance. Each needs to be able to confide in the other. Each needs to be aware of his own strengths and weaknesses and be able to articulate them to the other. Such honesty and openness can lead to the existence of a vital, mutual respect, which will form the basis of sound co-operative function. Both the chairman and headteacher must demonstrate a professional trusting attitude towards the other, and be prepared to acknowledge the need to share both responsibility and workload.

Both the governors and the staff of the school have the opportunity of exerting a real impact on the development of the school. Where there is understanding and co-operation between the two groups, this impact is exciting, vital and of utmost benefit. Where there is unfamiliarity, mistrust and unilateralism, then only detriment can result. The positive impact, so described, will be realised only if the headteacher and chairman have co-operated over the definition of the complementary roles the two bodies possess and have striven to establish a real and identifiable working partnership, based on a mutual understanding of their distinct roles.

The extension of powers of the governing body as a whole has developed over the past decade. The *Education Act 1993*, regarded as the most significant piece of education legislation since the *1944 Act*, has far-reaching implications for schools and governing bodies. The working together of headteachers and chairmen is now of crucial importance. Every effort needs to be made to ensure that governors, staff, chairman and head strive to realise the unanimity of purpose for which all were appointed.

14   Marketing schools

Michael P. Brunt

Generally, educationalists resent the intrusion of the concepts of competition and marketing into their world otherwise untainted by such base considerations. For some, competition is considered *infra dignitatem*, while marketing is considered a bit of a joke, something to which really important, professional services do not demean themselves (McCloy 1985). For others, professional ethics demand that schools and teachers ought to eschew competition in favour of collaboration in the common interest. They see the profit motive as incompatible with a public service, dedicated to altruism. Some suspicion may be traced back to the days when the market was regarded as the place set aside for people to deceive each other (Frain 1981). The intellectual has never been kindly disposed towards the marketplace. For him/her it is a place of vulgar people and base motives (Stigler 1963). Others regard the analogies of industrial marketing as far-fetched and unhelpful in the context of a non-profit-making activity. Yet others argue that expert and trained professionals know what kind of education to provide and are unwilling to respond to the passing whims of governments, employers or the public. 'The professionals know best,' they say. Ironically, those same educationists who reject the notion of marketing in the context of schooling may see it as being perfectly legitimate for parents to exercise their rights and responsibilities for providing and obtaining the best possible educational experiences for their children by buying, for example, 'educational' toys. Indeed, this practice is widely applauded. Why, then, is it not recognised that those same parents are exercising their same market-place rights and responsibilities when 'buying in' schooling for their children?

It is the thesis of this chapter that concepts borrowed from the art and science of marketing may be adopted as analogies useful to our understanding of relationships between schools, children, their parents and society and in defining appropriate responses to the unabating demands made of schools and to the increasing competition among providing institutions.

An analogy may be drawn from the definition of marketing:

> Marketing involves balancing the company needs for profit against the benefits required by consumers so as to maximise long term earnings per share. Davidson 1975

There is a considerable resistance to treating children as a product to be finished off and to the equation of schooling to the activities of a porcelain factory: but it is not necessary to draw a strict equation, it is sufficient to draw a parallel.

> Marketing a school involves balancing society's needs for a cultured population against the immediate demands of parents, providers and consumers so as to maximise the school's contribution to the well-being of society at large.

The contribution of schools to society is made by means of the school's curriculum, defined as the sum of the experiences, directly or indirectly, overtly or discreetly, deliberately of fortuitously, presented by the school to the children.

Implicit in this parallel is the recognition of the difficulty of defining who is the client or customer or consumer of the education service (Douglas 1985). The primary consumers or clients are the pupils themselves who will eventually make direct use of their education for personal ends, the secondary consumers are their parents, future employers and society, who perceive the advantages of having a better behaved household, a more skilled workforce and more cultured neighbours. This chapter makes no attempt to define whose desires and interests should predominate in any conflict of values. Sometimes there will be irreconcilable differences. I have argued elsewhere that these should be mediated through the school's governing body (Brunt 1985a, b). It is central to the argument that the adoption of a marketing orientation and its attendant attitudes, value systems and management techniques is a necessary precondition for recognising such disputes and therefore for resolving them.

The marketing, orientation to education received its apotheosis during the 1980s by having two Education Acts devoted almost entirely to it, the *Education Act, 1980,* and the *Education Reform Act, 1988.* The former had as its *leitmotif,* its prevailing theme, the pursuit of the dominance of the consumer and the operation of free market economics within the education service. It established the conditions for greater competition among schools by strictly delimiting the circumstances in which admission to a school may be refused (*Education Act, 1980*, Sections 6 and 7). It also encouraged competition among neighbouring LEAs by allowing parents to send their children of compulsory school age across LEA boundaries (ibid, Section 31). It encouraged competition between the public and private sectors in the form of the assisted places scheme (ibid, Sections 17 and 18). This Act also obliges competing LEAs to describe their policies, their processes and their products in a prescribed form, in order that the potential consumer can make sounder judgements about the relative merits and demerits of the competing commodities (ibid, Section 8; the Education (School Information) (England) Regulations 1993, SI 1993/1502 and the Education (School Performance Information) (England) Regulations 1993, SI 1993/1503 as well as parallel Regulations for Wales). The *Education Act 1980*, was designed to meet growing pressure from parents for more involvement in school life. The vast majority of schools have responded to that pressure by opening to parents first their gates, then their doors and more recently by removing the palisades about the secret garden of the curriculum. The image of the interfering parent is being replaced by that of a parent as helper and partner in the education of his/her children. However, that there is still a resistance to parental involvement is evidenced by the demand made by the National Confederation of Parent Teacher Associations that parents be given a statutory right to establish a home-school association (Hammond 1985). The statutory framework of the 1980 Act would, of course, have been both ineffective and unnecessary, had not demographic change, falling enrolments, changed the seller's market of underprovision into the buyer's market of excess capacity, thus making competition among providers between and within the public and private sectors inevitable.

The 1980 Act has therefore created two of the classical conditions in which marketing can become important. It has provided the context for competition among schools and the requirement that the customer should be provided with the information on which to base a sound choice. When this is combined with reduced demand for places caused by a falling birth rate, we have the classic conditions necessary for competition.

The *Education Reform Act, 1988*, has taken the marketing orientation several logical strides further. Individual institutions are to become profit centres able to compete for trade, with the artificial barriers to competition (the planned admission limits of the *Education Act, 1980*) set aside so that schools must admit up to their building capacity, if there are sufficient applicants. Popular schools will become the (usually unwilling) agents of putting their neighbours out of business.

Another key strand is the breakdown of local government's virtual monopoly on the provision of schooling and its absolute monopoly on the provision of fee-free schooling. No longer (paraphrasing Ford's slogan 'You can have any colour car as long as it's black') will one be able to say of the education service: 'You can have any school as long as it's LEA-maintained'. City technology colleges, city technology colleges for the arts and grant-maintained (GM) schools, each established under the *Education Act, 1988*, were intended to provide alternative brands for customers to select. They are now to be joined, under the *Education Act, 1993* by a new type of grant-maintained school which will be 'sponsored' and which will not have had previous incarnation as an LEA-maintained school. None of these new brands has achieved a significant spread of availability and full customer choice remains illusory. Indeed, there is evidence that the providers are selecting their customers, not customers choosing their schools. In driving through Parliament the *Education Act, 1993*, with its new strategic authority for the GM sector, the funding agency for schools, ministers appear to have recognised that an entirely free market may not be able to react quickly enough to meet increased demand. The concept which underpins the legislation and continues to be embraced by Government, however, is that excellence is achieved, not by the intervention of governments, but by the combined effects of enlightened consumers exercising informed choice in a varied and competitive market place. It is also consistent with the prediction put forward by several commentators that the *Education Reform Act, 1988*, is but a staging post towards the introduction of a voucher system involving both the public and private sectors.

Another of the classical conditions necessary for competition is an increase in the opportunities for product differentiation. The abolition of the schools council and the introduction of the National Curriculum envisaged in the *Education Reform Act, 1988*, run counter to the free market mentality. The latter, however, offers a product specification with which all schools' provision may be compared and the national testing arrangements provide a yardstick against which the performance of schools will be measured.

It would be a mistake, however, to concentrate exclusively on the use of marketing as a means of promoting competition among educational institutions, marketing concepts can be useful in establishing strategies for improving the market standing of the education service generally in its competition for an increasing share of the public purse. Indeed, since the mid-1970s, the education service's public relations team has scored several own goals (William Tyndale, the Great Debate, disruption caused by successive pay disputes, the Honeyford Saga, Stratford Grant-Maintained School in

Newham) and has left the impression in the public mind that schools are inadequately equipped, understaffed, badly housed, indisciplined, incompetent in inculcating basic skills, irrelevant to the needs of the industrial and economic society and peopled by reactionary communist bureaucrats (Beare 1985). It follows from this disturbing summary of education's corporate image that schools do themselves and the service they represent inestimable damage if they base their competition with other schools on the demerits of their competitors rather than on their own merits.

Professor Ted Wragg (Wragg 1989) rightly emphasises the difficulties inherent in non-aggression pacts among neighbouring schools, as the silence leaves the press with only rumour and scandal on which to base its copy. Far better for heads in a locality to work in concert in providing, each in turn, press releases and features highlighting the excellence of the service provided in our schools.

To ensure that the analogy between the marketing of a school and the marketing of a product should not be extended beyond the bounds of reason, it is necessary to distinguish between social marketing and business marketing in three dimensions.

1. Business marketers try to meet the needs and wants of markets: social marketers try to change their attitudes or behaviours.
2. Business marketers aim to make a profit through serving the interests of the market; social marketers aim to serve the interests of the market without personal profit.
3. Business marketers market products and services through the medium of ideas: social marketers market the ideas themselves rather than products or services (Kotler 1975).

The first process undertaken by the marketing director is the four-step marketing planning process;

1(a). Gathering relevant information about the external environment and about the organisation's internal resources.
1(b). Identifying the organisational strengths and weaknesses vis-à-vis the external market and opportunities and competitive threats facing the organisation.
2. Laying down the marketing objectives of the organisation based on the results of the first two steps above.
3(a). Laying down strategies for achieving the objectives.
3(b). Laying down programmes for implementing the strategies to include timing, responsibilities and costs.
4. Measuring the progress towards achievement of the objectives, reviewing and amending the plan as necessary (Wills et al. 1975).

Phase one of the marketing planning process, therefore, will entail identifying the potential customers and defining the character-istics, educational background, attitude sets, etc, which enable them to be broken down into sub-groups. This 'market segmentation' can be useful when targeting any promotional activities. Since the school's offerings are unlikely to appeal equally to all people, segmentation of the market makes it possible for the school's characteristics to be presented accurately and attractively to people in ways which are relevant to them.

In many areas, the school's market has already been strictly delimited by geographical factors or the policy of the LEA, but it has been shown that parents are willing to move house to be in the catchment area of a favoured school (Guratsky 1982). The market is therefore not as rigorously delimited as might appear at first sight.

In order comprehensively to pursue the analysis of one's potential consumers, it should be remembered that consumers, when they purchase a commodity do not purchase the object *per se*, but the benefits, immediate or long term, which it potentially provides. Black and Decker, for example, made its fortune not because potential customers wanted 8 millimetre drills but because people wanted to have the wherewithal to make 8 millimetre holes; from which it follows that, if there had been developed a more cost-effective means of making holes, Black and Decker would develop that product or lose out on its market. Similarly, then, children do not want schooling, *per se*, but the benefits which it provides immediately or in the longer term. This distinction is helpful when schools decide what characteristics might make them more attractive to a potential client group. These characteristics are the criteria on the basis of which customers make their choices.

Choice criteria may be functional or non-functional. Functional criteria relate to the physical properties of a product, e.g. the number of miles to the gallon performed by a car. Non-functional criteria relate to the connotations evoked in the customer by the product, e.g. its style, image and tone. Functional criteria adopted in the selection of schools may vary widely from the perceived success rate of the school in achieving a desired educational outcome for its pupils, to the length of the school day. The market standing of a primary school serving an area with a large proportion of parents desiring selective secondary education for their children will clearly depend upon the school's success or otherwise in achieving that ambition, and a proportionate (or disproportionate) amount of time may therefore need to be devoted to the achievement of that aim. Some schools serve children a high proportion of whose parents are both away from home throughout the school day. In such cases, without abrogating their responsibilities for providing a curriculum suited to the long-term needs of the children and of society, schools will need to have regard to the advantages of extending the length of the school day, and their market standing will be disproportionately affected by any disruption of school dinners during an industrial dispute or by the abandonment or curtailment of after-school activities.

The more qualitative educational considerations are difficult to apply justly to schools as functional criteria of success. Nonetheless, parents continue to rely on such measures as selective school pass rates as a criterion for choosing a school. By contrast, parents who understand the shortcomings of that approach may be influenced to adopt a basically non-functional criterion such as the presence or absence of a uniform because of its associations with the school's style, tone or image. In the words of Curtis (1984):

> the less tangible the product, the more powerfully and persistently the judgement about it gets shaped by the packaging.

For this reason, headteachers may need to adopt visual symbols like logos, mottos, monograms and colour schemes to enhance the public image of the school.

Having identified one's potential customers and the criteria, functional or non-functional, which they may adopt in choosing the school, headteachers adopting the marketing approach should determine who are their potential competitors in the market-place. In a prosperous area, the local preparatory school may pose a real threat to the school's continued viability. In most areas, particularly in urban locations where schools are relatively accessible, the neighbouring school, with its newly appointed dynamic headteacher, is the potential competitor. In some areas of the inner cities, there may be a demand for provision sensitive to the tenets of different cultures and religions, and consequently education at home or at the local mosque may be considered by the potential clients (or their parents) to be a real alternative. In other cases, there may be a tradition of rejection of schooling, posing a real threat to the school's effectiveness. In all such cases, the headteacher should identify the characteristics of the potential competitor (be it the preparatory school, the neighbouring county school, the mosque or no school at all) which make it attractive to its clients or their parents. Those characteristics might be, in the case of the preparatory school, for example, its very separateness or its freedom from disruption during pay disputes or its perceived excellence in providing for gifted children or the range of extra-curricular activities or some combination of these and other factors. In the case of competition from the local mosque, there may well be a reluctance on the part of parents to allow girls and boys to be educated in the same school, or to take swimming lessons at the same time. The assessment of the competition is rarely as clear-cut, simple and starkly depicted as these few examples. Usually, there are more subtle nuances of choice in operation.

Having defined one's competitors in a certain market-place, one decides whether the school is able to compete in that sector, remembering that there may be some characteristics of the competition (for example, its selectivity, its separateness or its single-sex provision) which cannot be emulated.

Next, one makes a judgement about whether one wishes to compete for that sector of the market and risk alienating a different sector of the community. Stripped of its racial and emotional overtones, the Bradford, Drummond Middle School, Ray Honeyford affair could readily be viewed as a headteacher's conscious decision to concentrate on one sector of the market to the exclusion of the other.

This approach, the analysis of the potential consumers and competition and appropriate responses thereto, has been described as the SWOT (strengths, weaknesses, opportunities, threats) technique (Wills 1975). It involves an analysis of the school's internal strengths and weaknesses and the external opportunities and threats. The outcome of that analysis will be an initial position statement or marketing audit. It should include a strategy for building on the school's strengths, for eliminating its weaknesses, for taking advantage of the opportunities and for neutralising the threats.

The position statement or marketing audit is the first of four analyses which the marketing approach demands. It poses the question: 'Where is the school now?' it should be followed by:

- Question No. 2. 'where do you want to get to?': aims and objectives;
- Question No. 3. 'how do you propose to get there?': strategy and tactics;
- Question No. 4. 'how will you know when you have arrived?': performance appraisal.

The position statement is rather like the assessment of the product mix in the marketing context and it falls to the headteacher periodically in the light of assessments of the requirements of the potential consumers or in the light of increased competition or changes in the social or economic context to make subtle changes to the curriculum provided in order the better to cater for the special characteristics of the market in which the school is operating. For this purpose, the headteacher will need to engage in a continuing process of acquiring information on the consumers, their satisfaction with the provision, the changed provision which might better suit their needs and the size and share of the market for which the school is likely to be catering, so that the school will be able to take advantage of, and not be threatened by, environmental, social, economic and demographic change.

Aims and objectives

'Cheshire Puss, would you like to tell me which way I ought to walk from here?'
That depends on where you want to get to,' said the cat.
'I don't care where,' said Alice.
'Then it doesn't matter which way you walk,' said the cat.
'So long as I get somewhere,' said Alice as an explanation.
'Oh, you're bound to do that,' said the cat, 'if only you walk long enough.'

This quotation from *Alice in Wonderland* exemplifies as well as any the importance of defining the purpose of the school's activity and the destination for which it is heading. Too many schools are run on the principles of Christopher Columbus:

- when he set out, he did not know where he was going;
- when he arrived, he did not know where he was;
- when he got back, he did not know where he had been;
- and all this done on public money.

What is clear from the Peters and Waterman's (1982) study of excellent marketing practice in US industry as being an important facet of preparing a school for its market place is the adoption of a definite belief system and the commitment in practice to its implementation. The value system should not just be transmitted in writing but should pervade the whole culture of the institution, in its stories, anecdotes and activities. If good behaviour, consideration for others, academic achievement and the work ethic not only find reflection in the daily act of worship but pervade the school's daily dealings and sayings, then the spin-offs will percolate as far as the parents, whose commitment will, in turn, be enhanced. Peters and Austin (1985) in their analysis of the common characteristics of outstanding companies operating in the business market-place emphasise the importance of clarity and determination of purpose, advocating that businessmen, to be successful, have to know where they are going, have to have the ability to state that direction clearly and concisely and have to care about that purpose with passion. In short, they have to have a vision. The importance of the substance of that vision is a different issue from that of communicating it in all one's dealings with consistency and fervour.

According to Peters and Waterman, the value system is to be expressed in terms of qualitative rather than quantitative variables and should be underpinned by a firm belief in the dignity of individuals, be they workers or customers. Peters and Austin (1985), likewise, quoting Sara Lightfoot, show that these attitudes should be transmitted in practice throughout the organisation and that therefore attention should be paid to the need for teachers to have adult interaction, support, reward and criticism. If it is true in industry that only by treating people as adults can they in turn learn to treat their colleagues and customers with dignity in mature, selfless relationships, how much more apposite is that observation in the context of the school and its pupils.

When a school wholeheartedly adopts the marketing concept as a way of regulating its business, it bases its actions on the fundamental belief that, in every phase of its operations, the organisation must bring itself into mutually satisfactory relationships with the users of its services. The pattern of mutually satisfactory relationships is often termed user-orientation or market-orientation; that is the proposition that a school should face outwards towards the wants and needs of its users and not inwards towards what it likes doing or what it is experienced in doing (Frain 1981).

A further corollary of this marketing approach is the commitment to listen intently to, and act upon, customer requirements, suggestions and complaints. The excellent companies studied in Peters and Waterman (1982) and Peters and Austin (1985)

- provide structured opportunities for customers to complain
- expect the most senior members of staff to listen in to those complaints
- actively seek information on customer satisfaction
- put both compliments and complaints on public display
- disseminate and implement the recommendations.

Schools, like companies, therefore, break down into two groups. The first group, the more typical, views the complaint as an evil to be survived and forgotten. The second views the complaint as an opportunity to improve working practices and foster and improve public relations, working on the knowledge that each dissatisfied complainant has several scores of acquaintances, most of whom will, no doubt, hear of his or her disaffection, and pass it on, in a sensationalised form, to their neighbours. Unfortunately, the opposite attitude, that of excessive sensitivity to complaints, has traditionally been associated with the education service, which relies on a technician-like arrogance that the product will sell itself.

It is implicit in the advocacy of a marketing approach to managing schools that one is sensitive to the needs of children and the demands of parents and society, from which it follows that it is unnecessary, impossible and undesirable to lay down a single rigid definition of the curriculum applicable to the widely differing social, economic and cultural environments and to children with widely disparate abilities, aptitudes and motivations. Such rigidity is incompatible with the increasing necessity for responsiveness to change and flexibility of delivery required of schools. In defining curricular aims and objectives, it is also implicit in the marketing approach that the school should give extensive consideration to the needs of the direct and indirect consumers, pupils, parents, potential employers and future neighbours. Relevant changes which need to be taken into account include declining enrolments, new technology, changes in the structure of the family, the growth of leisure, the decline of heavy industry, the rise of high-technology industry and the multi-ethnic nature of society. Consequently, the curriculum should provide pupils with the knowledge, conceptual understanding, skills, attitudes and personal qualities necessary for the individual's future effective participation in and contribution towards his home, his work, his leisure, the social, economic and political environment and personal relationships. These considerations should be a direct and primary focus of the school's aims and purposes, rather than a casual indirect spin-off of the academic curriculum (Hewlett 1985).

Strategy and tactics

The third strand to the marketing approach has to do with resources, obtaining them and deploying them. For a headteacher, obtaining from a council-tax-capped LEA an adequate budget share is a primary activity. In the words of Charles Tandy, founder of the Tandy Corporation (quoted in Peters and Austin 1985): 'You can't sell goods from an empty wagon.'

However, the headteacher must avoid leaving the impression that the school is failing for want of resources or that it will fail if it does not receive more resources. Parents will not send their children to a failing school, LEA members and officers will not wish to invest in failure. Who wants to shop with an organisation of which one requires a long-term service, if its proprietors dress it up as bordering on bankruptcy? Far better to base one's arguments for increased resources on evidence of previous success with limited means.

Resource acquisition may be an important consideration, but resource disposition is crucial — it is the equivalent of the product mix in the marketing context. If the school's aims and objectives speak loftily of positive discrimination and in practice the remedial class is perpetually banished to the mobile hut, all the senior staff are men and English as a second language is first to be withdrawn whenever any member of staff is absent, the whole ostensible value system is discovered as a sham, with disastrous consequences for morale. The balance of resource disposition is a policy issue which requires to be clearly laid down and must accord with the thrust of the school's belief system.

There are four key variables in the strategy and tactics of marketing, namely product, place, price and promotion. An analysis of the nature of the product or service which is to be provided will give insight into the additional specialist qualifications and personal attributes, recruitment methods and training requirements of the personnel to be employed. An analysis of the place in the context of marketing a school would appear at first sight to be redundant, as the location of the school is a given fact over which the headteacher has no control; but on closer examination it can be imagined that some marketing activities located other than at the school — community-based charitable ventures, surveys conducted in the locality, displays and exhibitions in local museums and shopping centres and the activities of home–school liaison teachers — are both valid and relevant educational activities and have spin-offs for the market standing of the school. It must be recognised that headteachers are not often provided with the figures on which to base an analysis of the price (in, for example, teacher or other staffing time) of entering certain markets. The assessment of the opportunity costs of one course of action as against another is usually addressed superficially and intuitively, if at all. Although local management of schools under the *Education Reform Act, 1988,* has already been in operation in primary schools for several years, continuing downward pressure on public expenditure has created a climate in which the flexible use of resources which was presaged in 1988 has in practice been realised only to a limited degree. As to promotion, schools continue to be coy about adopting strategies for selling themselves or their services to their potential customers, an attitude which is founded on a professional ethic now abandoned by the legal profession. If the analogy of schools competing in the market-place continues to be valid, it will not be long before headteachers need to examine the choice of communications media for an active promotion strategy together with the nature of the message to be transmitted. For the time being at least, the message will probably continue to be rather indiscriminately targeted and based on a public relations type of strategy as described below.

Performance appraisal

The fourth strand to the marketing approach is performance appraisal — how do we know when we have arrived? The difficulty with answering this question is probably founded in the fact that education is both the journey and the arrival, both a process and a product. The usual thrust of school performance measures has been to concentrate on the latter to the exclusion of the former. Pupil achievement, concentrating solely on areas in which outcomes can be measured, has been paramount. In the secondary domain, the average number of 'O' level passes per pupil, sometimes crudely related to the nature of the pupil intake of the school, has been king. The fact that these examinations were devised to measure pupil performance and not school effectiveness has largely been overlooked. In the primary sector, the use of National Curriculum assessment levels has now been embraced by central government, but the factors over which the school has no control, e.g. the nature of its intake continues to be ignored, as is the fact that, for numbers around 30 (the average cohort of a primary school), percentage scores are largely meaningless and too much prone to substantial variation because of the performance of just one pupil. The testing arrangements incorporated into the 1988 Act attempt to make good the absence of agreed measures of output, but make no attempt to account for differences in the nature of the schools' inputs.

Academics invent a new measure of school effectiveness every week using the most sophisticated statistical techniques of multiple linear regression analysis, cluster analysis and analysis of variance, with the result that most of the debate and discussion surrounds the validity of the measures rather than the excellence of the children's performance which is what one is attempting to monitor.

Such measures of school effectiveness as are used should be few in number and simple of application: their shortcomings should be recognised from the outset. The word 'satisficing' has been used to describe the real world process of reaching a satisfactory but avowedly imperfact solution to a complex issue. Much more satisfactory than pupil performance measures as a yardstick of school success, despite being often disparaged as 'soft' data not validated by quasi-scientific enquiry, are measures of customer satisfaction. It matters but little if Johnny has achieved scores of 130s throughout on standardised tests, if the range of his experiences at primary school has totally alienated him from any future committed participation in secondary education. Fortunately, such cases are extremely rare, but their absence is not born of any commitment on the part of the education service to the measurement of consumer satisfaction. One 'soft' source of data on the strength (or absence) of consumer satisfaction is for the headteacher to spend a substantial part of the school day with one (randomly selected) child. It will not be altogether difficult for the headteacher's sensitive observation to discern the whole range of pupil emotion from joy through puzzlement, boredom, frustration, loneliness and fear to anger at receiving less than the 10 minutes of individual attention from the teacher which is the most that the average child in a primary school can hope for in a day. A range of carefully constructed questions will soon reveal that the 'customer' has constructive remarks to make about the quality of the fare provided for him/her. This technique is widely used by school inspectors. Even a small number of such visits, if rigorously acted upon and used as the basis of small but significant improvements in the quality of the child's working day, can make a substantial contribution to the teachers' performance and the children's self-esteem. Peters and Waterman (op cit) and Peters and Austin (op cit) both refer to this technique as 'Management by Walking About'. It can be, in the school setting, as fruitful a source of small items of potential improvement and as creative of a climate of respect for the pursuit of the objective of consumer satisfaction as it has been shown to be in the pursuit of excellence in the industrial setting. However, it is recognised that teachers vest a great measure of professional pride in their classroom performance. It would therefore be an essential preliminary to such an approach that there should have been created within the school a climate of trust, collegiality, self-confidence and commitment to excellence.

The measures which could readily be used may not be perfect, but most of them have the distinct advantage of having been available for years, so that real comparison of progress over time can be made, for example:

- attendance rates
- proportion of the children in the immediate area opting for the school
- proportion of parents involved in school activities
- proportion of children smiling
- number of letters of appreciation received.

Among the several excellent practical suggestions in Sullivan's handbook *Marketing your Primary School* (1991) is an extract from the National Primary Centre's pamphlet designed to assist parents to make a judgement about their child's school. Twenty questions focus parents' attention on relationships. The same twenty questions can help headteachers to focus on the most important issues.

1. Were you able to make an appointment to meet the headteacher?

2. Is there a school prospectus?
3. Were you able to find your way in easily?
4. Was your welcome friendly from all the staff?
5. Were you shown all around the school including the classrooms?
6. Was there a sense of calm and order in the classroom and corridors?
7. Did you feel impressed by the standard of work displayed on the walls?
8. Was there a sense of industry among the children?
9. Was the noise level acceptable to you?
10. Were you aware of many aspects of the curriculum taking place, e.g. science, maths, computer?
11. Was equipment easily available and set out for children?
12. Does the school promote an interest in music and/or sport?
13. Are parents actively encouraged to help in the classrooms?
14. Is there a PTA or parent association?
15. Is there a parents' room?
16. Is there a feeder nursery or playgroup?
17. Are school policy documents on curriculum matters available for you to read and take home?
18. Do you feel that the school will value the contribution you make to your child's education?
19. Do you think, knowing your child, that he/she will be happy coming to this school?
20. If you were a child again, would you like to be a pupil at this school?

It should be noted:

1. That these measures have largely to do with 'customer satisfaction' rather than pupil performance.
2. That they cannot reasonably be used as a basis for comparison with other schools in different circumstances but can be used to monitor one school's progress over the years.
3. That no attempt has been made to find the best possible measures, but, in the context of a real-world complex environment, they may be the best measures possible.

These measures are to be contrasted with the highly sophisticated measuring tools which academics attempt to devise to measure pupil or school performance and to which they attribute spurious statistical validity, which process has been equated elsewhere with the weighing of mules in Texas.

If they want to weigh a mule in Texas, first they tie the back legs together, then they tie the front legs together, then they tie the front legs to the back legs. Then they look around for a big plank which they balance on a fulcrum, then they place the mule on one end of the plank before looking high and low for a boulder that will exactly balance the mule. When at last they have found such a boulder, they guess the weight of the boulder.

Readers whose patience has permitted them to read thus far will probably be surprised that advertising has not featured more prominently in the discussion. They will be more surprised to learn that advertising has nothing to do with marketing. Advertising is a subset of selling, which is a product-led activity, whereas marketing is a consumer-dominated approach. It is attempting to assume that a product which has been so excellently honed by the processes described above will, in effect, advertise and sell itself. In the words of Ralph Waldo Emerson:

> If a man write a better book, preach a better sermon or make a better mousetrap, though he build his house in the woods, the world will make a beaten path to his door.

But it is never safe to assume that you are providing a service with inbuilt acceptability. For this reason, proper attention must be given to marketing communications, which is not the same as advertising. Generally, the information booklets available for parents prior to their children's admission are attractively presented and give, in language readily accessible to the average parent, simple information about practical considerations like admission arrangements, school hours and holiday dates, dinner money, dress requirements and sickness arrangements. Other documents provide the technical curricular information required by the *Education Act, 1980* (Section 8).

An effective school brochure should have regard to the following factors.

- What are the benefits of attending your school as they might be seen from the viewpoint of the potential customer? What are his/her needs?
- What sector of the market is the leaflet aimed at? It may be necessary to provide different leaflets for different market segments.
- Attract attention, adopt a house style and/or logo.
- Arouse interest and create a desire for the benefits promised by the school; be enthusiastic.
- Promote action on the part of the reader by getting him/her to seek more information or enrol his/her child.
- Layouts should be simple and attractive.

The booklet's contents should embrace:

1. a description of the benefits provided by the school
2. a description, in layman's terms, of what pupils will learn
3. a statement of the teaching and learning methods
4. an indication of the later progression available as a result of the benefits to be obtained at the school
5. the school's credentials and the quality of the staff
6. a re-statement of the important benefits of attending the school.

Public relations practice is the deliberate, planned and sustained effort to establish and maintain mutual understanding between the schools and its public. The key word here is 'mutual'. Too many of the communications emanating from schools are one-sided. Prize days, open days, parents' evenings, information on curricular aims and objectives, school reports, brochures and letters contain a welter of information for, instructions to and requests for money from parents. If the marketing mentality is adopted, however, then there will pervade these documents and meetings a sense of openness and willingness to listen to and act upon the views and aspirations of individual parents.

Despite the best preparation and preventative action, unfortunate incidents beyond the control of the headteacher and his or her staff can occasionally do untold harm to the market standing of the school by being recounted in lurid detail in the press. The damage will be minimised if sound relationships have been established in advance by providing regular positive copy and invitations to social events. Any items which then appear in the local press should serve as free publicity and marketing material. Local and national newspapers, radio and television welcome ready-made news items, particularly those with a distinct personal interest line. Consequently, the focus should not be on the advertisement of a particular course but on using a personal storyline, the particular success of an individual pupil, for example, as a means of obtaining for the school an association with that success. Care should be taken to obtain the agreement of parents for their children to be mentioned by name, and guidance from the local education authority should be respected, particularly when issues of a party political nature are involved. The local Council's press office can sometimes serve as a useful circulation route for material.

A good press release will have the following characteristics:

- a good headline attracting immediate interest
- a local people-centred angle
- a first paragraph stating who the story is about, what it is

about and why, when and where it has happened or will happen (the five Ws)
- brevity
- one or more quotable quotes from a named individual
- a photograph showing relevant (local or well-known) people, and
- a contact telephone number.

Its layout should include wide margins, double spacing, a dateline and explanatory notes. Other useful forms of publicity for the school include letters to the press, calls to local phone-in programmes, interviews and feature articles.

The school's communications should reflect its marketing strategy. In defining it, the headteacher will need to address the following questions which serve as a summary of the main points of this chapter.

1. How accurate is the school's position statement?
2. How lucid and visionary is the school's document of aims and objectives?
3. How relevant are those aims to the needs and demands of the various consumer groups?
4. Does the school have a value system which pervades its very ethos?
5. Does the concept of the worth and dignity of the individual pervade the value system?
6. Are all the school's personnel committed to the development of those aims and objectives?
7. How accepting of, and responsive to, criticism is the school's staff?
8. How attractive and inviting is the school building?
9. Does the school have a house style, logo, motto, image?
10. How easy or difficult is it to make contact with the school?
11. What criteria has the school adopted in measuring its effectiveness in achieving its own objectives?
12. Are the measurements in terms of consumer satisfaction?
13. Are the school brochures effectively designed for each of the market segments and written in terms readily comprehensible to the layman?
14. What arrangements have been made to provide the media with frequent and positive copy about the school?

References

Beare, H. (1985) 'Education's corporate image', in *Educational Management and Administration* **14** (2).

Brunt, M. P. (1985a) 'Marketing the primary school: working through the governors: Part I', in *Education* **13** (1), 3–13.

Brunt, M. P. (1985b) 'Marketing the primary school: working through the governors: Part II', in *Education* **13** (2), 3–13.

Curtis, J. H. R. (1984) 'Marketing further education'. Coombe Lodge Working Paper.

Davidson, J. H. (1975) *Offensive Marketing: Or How to Make Your Competitors Followers* Penguin.

Davies, P. & Scribbins, K. (1985) *Marketing Further and Higher Education* Longman.

Douglas, B. (1985) 'Consumerism, control and the evaluation of the professional' in *Educational Management and Administration* **14** (2).

Frain, J. (1981) *Introduction to Marketing* Macdonald and Evans.

Guratsky, S. P. (1982) *Owner-occupation and the Allocation of Comprehensive School Places: the case of Walsall* Centre for Urban and Regional Studies.

Hammond, J. (1985) 'Re-assessing roles — teachers, parents and governors', in *Educational Management and Administration* **14** (2).

Hewlett, M. (1985) 'A curriculum for consumers' in *Educational Management and Administration* **14** (2).

Knight, B. A. A. (1977) *The Cost of Running a School* Scottish Centre for Studies in School Administration.

Kotler, P. (1975) *Marketing for Non-Profit Organisations* Prentice Hall.

McCloy, R. (1985) 'Week by week' in *Education* **166** (6).

Peters, T. J. & Austin, N. (1985) *A Passion for Excellence: The Leadership Difference* Collins.

Peters, T. J. & Waterman, R. H. (1982) *In Search of Excellence: Lessons from America's Best-Run Companies* Harper and Row.

Stigler, G. S. (1963) *The Intellectual and the Market Place* Institute of Economic Affairs Occasional Paper.

Sullivan, M. (1991) *Marketing your Primary School* Longman.

Wills, G. et al. (1975) *Introducing Marketing* Pan.

Wragg, E. (1989) 'The hot dinner ladies' in *The Teacher* 20 March 1988.

Further reading

Cawthray, B. (1982) *Putting it Together: Marketing and Advertising* Bristol Polytechnic Management Learning Productions.

Cuthbert, R. (1979) *The Marketing Function in Education Management* Further Education Staff College.

Kotler, P. (1980) *Marketing Management — Analysis, Planning and Control* Prentice Hall.

15 Caring, curriculum and choice: managing continuity in the education market-place

John Thorp

Introduction

Earlier versions of this chapter (Thorp 1987 and 1989) sought to trace the development of an 'official rhetoric of continuity' alongside what was depicted as the teacher's 'conventional wisdom' of continuity in practice. The version presented here, as we look forward and beyond the fundamental changes in education of the last five years or so towards what our schools may be like at the turn of the century, re-presents this twofold analysis. Its relevance appears undiminished, and serves to remind us once again of the useful distinction made by Elizabeth Richardson (1973) between 'the "caring" and "demanding" sides of the educational task'. It is concerned, on the one hand, with what happens to *children* as they face various changes in their educational lives, whether it be teachers, classes or schools and, on the other, with what happens to children's *learning* as they experience those changes. As before, therefore, the focus here is on both caring *and* curriculum.

The manager of continuity must acknowledge that the context in which we as educators now all operate, presents him with a situation of sharp discontinuity. Recent legislation has served to impose an 'official' version of continuity in some respects quite different in focus from previously accepted and desirable professional practice. The 'official' focus now is most clearly on the 'demanding' side of our task and from this point of view continuity encapsulates common-sense notions of progress and development. In this light, those who would consider the management of continuity in education must consider how planning and preparation may build on what a child has already experienced, and ask questions about whether or not the various parts of the educational experience fit together to make a coherent whole. This is not always an easy task, for children make progress at different rates and in different directions, and so those concerned to manage continuity must also ask how to prevent arbitrary divisions in the total organisation of the education system from cutting across or destroying the continuous educational progress of each child. As Dean (1980) puts it:

> ... we need to make the curve of continuity a smooth one from teacher to teacher, class to class and school to school.

An examination of notions of 'continuity' poses interesting questions about the nature of educational provision in the new context. It raises the sometimes thorny question of the relationship between 'policy' and 'practice' which leads in the end to the issue of 'control'. Very quickly we begin to ask about the implications for our practice as we move swiftly towards an increasingly centralised system of education. This newer kind of centralised policy-making leads us initially to identify what is called here *'the official rhetoric of continuity'* as the changes envisaged took shape, and then to consider the reality of *'an imposed continuity'* as the legal requirements have been made clear.

The other side of this issue of control though, and one which we must not lose sight of, is of course what happens in practice. The points at which curriculum continuity is most seriously threatened are where children change teachers, classes or perhaps most importantly, change schools. How teachers manage these changes becomes generalised in what we might call their *'conventional wisdom of continuity'*. However, the focus of this conventional wisdom seems at first glance to be not the curriculum but rather *children's welfare*. Those who would manage continuity may well be led to ask how this conventional wisdom will adapt itself to the newer requirements.

Managing then is about getting things done, making things happen, things you want to happen. However, good management is also about evaluating what actually happens, because sometimes other things happen which you don't want to happen. This enables the manager to identify some of the barriers to what he is trying to achieve. Later in this chapter then, we shall consider continuity in practice first of all by asking questions about the teacher's conventional wisdom of continuity: is it just about children's welfare? Evaluating continuity in practice also involves looking critically at interprofessional relationships, for this is its very basis and we will seek to identify those barriers to real professional co-operation which, in turn, create curriculum discontinuity. And what about those who experience discontinuity? Evaluating practice, it is believed here, involves taking seriously the views of our pupils, those who inhabit the management–instructional interface and who, through constant interaction and negotiation, in no small part shape it.

Together, these elements: the official rhetoric and conventional wisdom of continuity and the issues raised by the evaluation of practice, it is suggested, form the baseline from which any consideration of the management of continuity must begin.

The official rhetoric of continuity

Official statements about 'continuity' go back a long way. The Hadow Report (1931) asserted that:

> ...the process of education from the age of 5 to the end of the secondary stage should be envisaged as a coherent whole, that there should be no sharp division between infant, junior and post primary stages, and that the transition from any one stage to the succeeding stage should be as smooth and gradual as possible.

This encompassing view hints at a duality in the notion of continuity that in later versions becomes even more apparent. By the time of the *Plowden Report* (DES 1967) it was seen fit to assert that 'learning is a continuous process from birth', whilst also pointing out the need to avoid strain at the points of transfer from one class to another and from one school to another. It is here that we see emerging the duality which reflects the 'caring — demanding' dimensions or 'tutorial — teaching' functions noted by Richardson above. However, as I shall show in this chapter, it is the latter of these, embodied in notions of *curriculum continuity* that became by far the most prominent concern in the multitude of official documents published during the 1980s and which made increasingly insistent 'demands' for professional consideration. In a sense, these have now been overtaken as we have moved into a new era, one which requires us to face squarely the challenging and far reaching implications of legislative change in the late 1980s and 1990s.

The 'caring' dimension though has not always been absent from the official rhetoric of continuity. Perhaps its epitome is embodied in that familiar sentence from the *Plowden Report* (DES 1967) 'At the heart of the educational process lies the child.' Our 'caring' as teachers begins with the very first educational change the child encounters, the entry into school. The *Plowden Report* sees continuity here in terms of:

> It ought not to be just a matter of bringing a child to school, but of placing him in a *co-operative undertaking* in which mother and teacher both have parts to play. (my emphasis)

and indicates how this caring for the child makes real demands on teachers:

> ... welcoming a child is more than a matter of reserving proper time to attend to him. It is the *quality of the welcome and the imaginative insight given to it which counts.* (my emphasis)

Similarly 'caring' about children as they move on to secondary school, the report suggests must ensure that

> ... if change is to stimulate and not dishearten, it must be *carefully prepared and not too sudden.* (my emphasis)

Without question, however, the last two decades of the century have seen a much more direct 'official' focus on the *demanding* side of the educational task, particularly on curriculum continuity. Perhaps since the great debate brought issues of curriculum into public debate, but certainly since the *HMI Primary Survey* (DES 1978) identified the differential success of the 'considerable efforts...made to ease children's *transition* from one school to the next' with the fact that *curriculum continuity* was 'largely overlooked', has this trend gained in momentum. The report on local authority arrangements for the school curriculum (DES 1979) remarked on the great variety of ways in which schools were tackling issues of continuity, but also noticed too the discrepancy between what the LEAs said was going on and what the primary survey the year before had found was going on. Again, the distinction is made between 'transition' and 'continuity'. In the HMI discussion paper *A View of the Curriculum* (DES 1980) the concern was being made increasingly explicit:

> The variety of age ranges found in schools and the numerous points of transfer which now co-exist argue urgently for more thought to be given to curricular continuity and progression.

and so too its focus:

> ... schools as a whole need to shape their policies and to plan the content of work with awareness of what has preceded.

But this document also makes the vital distinction between a *vertical continuity*, that between different ages and stages, and a *horizontal continuity*, between schools in the same stage:

> Between primary schools and the schools which receive their pupils there needs to be not only communication about individuals but also consultation about aspects of the curriculum. Similar consultation is also necessary between the primary schools of an area ... It is ... important to try to ensure that comparable expectations are being established about the range of experience and performance of pupils at a given stage.

The message is restated in *The School Curriculum* (DES 1981):

> Authorities and schools need to ensure continuity in pupils' programmes both within and between the primary and secondary phases, whether this involves direct transfer from primary to secondary schools or transition through middle schools.

and then extended:

> Records should be kept and transmitted with this end in view.

This message is repeated again and again in the various publications of the *Curriculum Matters* series. Incidentally, each one in the series on *Aspects of the Curriculum 5–16* is prefaced with the remark: 'It is essential that this document should be read as a whole.'

Each of these documents emphasises that 'continuity and progression should be ensured from one class or teacher to another and from one school to another' (DES 1985c) and that to ensure it requires 'adequate curricular liaison between contributory and receiving schools' (DES 1984). The authors of *Science 5–16: A Statement of Policy* (DES 1985d) can state that:

> Under present circumstances few secondary schools can rely on any degree of common experience in science on the part of their new pupils. Continuity between schools is, in practice, far too often ignored.

whilst those of *English from 5–16* (DES 1984) are much more explicitly prescriptive:

> There should be agreement between the schools about what pupils should be expected to have learnt and experienced by the time they transfer.

In *Better Schools* (DES 1985b) it is noted that, not only is there no agreement *between* schools, but also within them for as they say

> ... there is little evidence of agreed curriculum policies directly influencing the school as a whole.

The message can be no more easily found than neatly packaged in this paragraph from *The Curriculum from 5–16* (DES 1985a):

> There is, therefore, a need for *unity of purpose* throughout the 5–16 span. That unity needs also to apply across the school system as a whole if the desired range and quality of experience and learning are to have a more assured place than they do now across the country, in LEAs, in individual schools and above all, in what is offered to individual pupils.

A National Curriculum: from rhetoric to reality?

A brief examination of DES/HMI publications through the 1980s reveals the emerging elements of the official rhetoric of continuity. Since this chapter was first written, we have of course witnessed further significant pieces of legislation, the *Education Acts* of 1986, 1988, 1992 and 1993, each of which have served to strengthen considerably the curricular focus of the official view of continuity. The first of these (*Education No. 2 Act*, 1986) provided a framework of responsibility for the curriculum involving the LEAs, school governors and headteachers, with each given a clearly defined role. Although advances were made at this stage towards enhancing the possibility of continuity between the schools within authorities by requiring each LEA to formulate a written curriculum policy and send it to all their schools and governors who, in the light of which, were in turn required to formulate and make public their school curriculum policy, clearly, the Government had in mind a rather less casual or 'localised' approach.

This 'nationalised' approach was revealed first in the *National Curriculum 5–16* consultation document (DES 1987a) and has been made ever more clear for us in the National Curriculum document-ation which has appeared since then. It is embedded in statute, the *Education Reform Act 1988*. The consultation document (DES 1987a) had acknowledged that:

> Many LEAs and schools have made important advances towards achieving a good curriculum for pupils aged 5–16, which offers progression, continuity and coherence between its different stages.

but then complained that progress had been, 'variable, uncertain and slow' and indicated that the Government wished 'to move ahead at a faster pace'. This document also clearly indicated their aims:

> Pupils should be entitled to the same opportunities wherever

they go to school and standards of attainment must be raised throughout England and Wales.

The achievement of these aims, it was thought, would be reached by a 'national curriculum' which would, on the one hand, ensure that:

> ... all pupils, regardless of sex, ethnic origin and geographical location, (should) have access to broadly the same good and relevant curriculum and programmes of study which include the key content, skills and processes which they need to learn...

while at the same time:

> It will also help children's progression within and between primary and secondary education (and on to further and higher education) and will help to secure the continuity and coherence which is too often lacking in what they are taught.

Above all, the move away from possible localised solutions was emphasised as the Government's conclusions were stressed:

> ... *consistent improvement in standards can be guaranteed only within a national framework for the secular curriculum.*

The official view of the current position is no better summarised than in this statement from the National Curriculum Council (NCC 1989):

> The National Curriculum will provide teachers with clear objectives for their teaching; children with identifiable targets for their learning; parents with accurate, accessible information about what their children can be expected to know, understand and be able to do, and what they actually achieve. The result will be higher expectations and more effective progression and continuity throughout the years of full-time education.

The *Education Reform Act* has ensured that we have in place a National Curriculum comprising specified foundation subjects, attainment targets and programmes of study. A pivotal strategy in the attempt to raise standards within this national framework has been the setting up of assessment arrangements for each of the four key stages. According to the *Task Group on Assessment and Testing Report* (DES 1987b) such assessment drives the promotion of children's learning. The outcomes of such an arrangement, it was claimed, would be threefold: first, in terms of the identification of specific learning goals and the measurement of their achievement; secondly, in providing a real basis for planning for progression; and thirdly, in supplying teachers with a framework for communication and a vocabulary of continuity. Of course the realisation of each of these outcomes requires detailed systems of recording and reporting.

In 1992 the *Education (Schools) Act* introduced a system of regular inspections to monitor the operation of this new system. In the *Handbook for the Inspection of Schools* (OFSTED 1993) the criteria by which the quality of 'assessment, recording and reporting' will be judged are set out:

- the school's arrangements result in accurate and comprehensive records of the achievements of individual pupils in relation to National Curriculum attainment targets and against other objectives

- the school's arrangements for assessment are manageable

- the outcomes are constructive and helpful to pupils, teachers, parents and employers

- the outcomes inform subsequent work.

Inspectors are instructed to report on the quality of a school's liaison arrangements and, in particular, to focus on 'the extent to which these are used to improve standards of achievement and quality of learning'.

This now poses huge questions for those who would consider the *management of continuity* at whatever level of the system. The reality to be found out there in the real world of schools, it would seem, has been quite different in the past from the one now 'legally' defined. Those of us who are, or have been, practitioners know from experience how much thought and effort, time and activity is directed at helping children move smoothly and successfully from one school to another. But this is our 'caring' function which can itself present us with a stiff managerial task. When we consider the implications of the newer rhetoric which asserts how much better we have been as practitioners at addressing the 'welfare' aspects of continuity than the curricular ones (DES 1985a) and the newly imposed 'reality' requiring our focus on the 'demanding' side of our task, i.e. the curriculum, it would seem that we are facing a situation of genuine hysteresis. The management task has become monumental.

The following sections of this chapter will look at the management of continuity from these two perspectives, considering how we may move towards bridging the gap between a rhetoric which now requires the focus on curriculum and the reality it acknowledges of the effective caring for pupils as they undergo traumatic changes in their educational lives.

Managing continuity 1: towards a conventional wisdom

The distinction noted in the official rhetoric of continuity between 'transition' and 'continuity' instructs us to look carefully at what happens in schools. If asked, most teachers would, of course, display considerable agreement about what would consist of good practice in managing continuity: how it should be organised and who should benefit, so much so that we may refer to it as the practitioner's 'conventional wisdom' of continuity. In this conventional wisdom, certain changes the child must go through in the course of his educational life are considered to be events of such importance and the source of so much possible trauma that they have to be carefully managed. Each change of class, change of teacher, the move into the juniors, may represent such an event, but for the primary teacher the two most critical changes are those the child undergoes when first entering the school and then transferring to secondary school.

The entry into school is perhaps the single most stressful event of the life of each child up to age five, and parents, teachers and schools work very hard to alleviate the stress. Ghaye and Pascal (1988), reporting on a pilot research project, suggest a threefold differentiation of potentially stressful activities as children start school. They refer to these as *'separations'*, when children have to leave parents, family, and the familiarity of home as part of a new daily routine; *'transitions'*, as children move from one activity to another, one part of the classroom or school to another during the day; and *'incorporations'*, as children are engaged in those activities which lead them to become part of a new and less familiar social group. This differentiation can help us to think carefully about particular strategies for overcoming possible difficulties, and how the continuity from home to school might be successfully managed. A brief consideration of the ways in which this is accomplished reveals that there are both problems and strategies for overcoming them which are general problems of 'continuity' rather than being age-specific. In thinking about these, I want to consider what we may think of as three 'management' strategies in particular: *'liaison'*, *'transition'* and *'induction'*. The first of these: *'liaison'* might be thought of as the stage of *communication* where first contacts are made, and the exchange of information about the school and teachers and the child and his or her home takes place. The various activities which may result from this kind of strategy would go a long way to meeting the need for what Blatchford et al. (1982) call 'the continuity of environmental demands' ensuring that, '...the demands of one stage must be compatible with those of the next'.

When I was working in school, we tried to meet this most

important requirement by sending out to parents of children approaching school age, along with a letter of welcome, a booklet of ideas and suggestions about appropriate ways to help prepare children for school, but which also incorporated information about the school and its ways of going about its business. This was also supplemented by an invitation to parents to come into school for an informal chat with me and the child's first teacher, when we encouraged parents to tell us as much as possible about their children. We tried to establish, as early as possible, a relationship which we saw as a 'partnership', working together to do the utmost for the good of the child. In this respect our intentions and our practice reflected these comments in the *Rumbold Report* (1990):

> The one constant element in the child's experience of these transition processes is the parent, and not surprisingly it is the quality of involvement or partnership between parents and educators which is likely to determine the effectiveness of continuity. It is only by drawing on parents' detailed knowledge of their children that educators can begin to gain an understanding of the range of their previous experiences together with an indication of their social and intellectual skills and competencies.

There is a danger, however, that sometimes the arrangements we make as we attempt to manage the transition from home to school can become part of what Ghaye and Pascal (1988) have called a 'child–school incorporation process', a one-way process in which the child adjusts to the school. Looking back, ours was perhaps too much a one-sided arrangement. As a true 'partnership', it might have been much more, enabling us to overcome more speedily some of those inevitable difficulties which can occur as parents sometimes try to help their children in ways not always entirely appropriate. As the *House of Commons Education, Science and Arts Committee Report* (1988) suggests: parents should be made perfectly clear of 'the dangers of trying to introduce a formal kind of teaching and learning at too early an age'. We've all encountered this, haven't we?

One way in which problems of this kind may come to light at an early stage might be through home visiting. Reception teachers may find out a great deal more about the children they are about to welcome into school by visiting them at home and, just as importantly, in the same way, parents might more effectively understand what the school was trying to achieve and its preferred teaching methods. How much better if communication with parents as partners can sometimes be accomplished on their own ground rather than always that of the teachers. As Cleave et al. (1982) recommend:

... gaps in understanding might be bridged if parents and staff could have more insights into each other's worlds, both of which are inhabited by the child.

Activities to prepare the way and ease the *transition* from home to school may constitute a second management strategy. There is, of course, in many areas, institutionally organised 'transition' in the form of nursery schools or classes, which must be the ideal we should aim for, whereas in other places, playgroups or other voluntary self-help groups fulfil this valuable function more informally. These first pre-school contacts outside the home are vitally important and we should not underestimate the contribution made by those who have the responsibility for guiding the child through this stage, for as Blatchford et al. (1982) put it:

This is a serious responsibility, not least because first experiences may set up an enduring pattern that will structure the child's reactions to settings he will encounter later in his life.

The informally organised playgroup serves another very valuable function, too, in that it encourages parental participation in the transition from home to school. Parents can be involved in planning, preparing and supervising relevant activities for children, which may help them to understand and appreciate the constraints under which teachers also operate once their child is at school. At the playgroup too, parents are in control, they decide on when, and how often, their own children will attend, perhaps increasing attendance as the time for school approaches. Teachers can overcome the lack of formal contact that may exist between the school and the nursery by visiting the children in the playgroup before they come into school. Some schools find that they have the space for the playgroup children approaching school age to spend time in a spare room on a number of occasions before they actually start school.

As children actually enter school, and how this is made easier and smoother, enables us to consider a third strategy, the management of *induction*. Many schools make very great efforts to ensure that children coming to school for the first time are made welcome, feel secure and happy. There are many ways of doing this. During my time as headteacher, we evolved our practice over a period of twelve months, during which time we involved parents in discussion and practical trial of ways for children to enter school. Each intake of children during three terms had a slightly different induction period, each one modified after parents were invited into school to consider successes and failures. Together we arrived at our school policy. As part of the gradual process of taking children into school, we tried to engage their parents, establishing a relationship based on trust, a partnership caring for the child in an atmosphere where parents were always welcome and teachers always interested.

An important way of thinking about minimising the difference between home and school is that referred to by Cleave et al. (1982) as 'continuity of scale'. These writers make practical suggestions about the ways in which the environment the child first encounters at school can be managed. They recommend:

- a secure base of appropriate scale ... a child-orientated setting
- a gradual extension of the range of new territory
- the careful organisation of space the young child needs
- familiarity with the school before he starts will give the child an idea of what to expect...

This concern with 'scale', and the kinds of 'relationships' tied up with it, have therefore significant implications for the way in which daily events like assembly, playtime and dinner-time are organised, and we should consider them carefully if 'induction' is to be managed effectively.

If we now turn to the other end of children's primary school experience, we find them facing transfer to secondary school, and here we may see similar strategies used to manage the changeover from one stage to the next. In many ways these strategies have already been 'rehearsed' at the point of entry into the primary school and, as I shall try to show initially, their focus is ostensibly children's 'welfare'. Later in this chapter I shall discuss the view that this is perhaps not, in fact, the case and the implications this has for the management of continuity. I don't want to dwell on it here but when we consider the first of the strategies noted above, liaison, we perhaps get a hint of later arguments. Any successful *liaison* is about good communication and obviously this occurs at the teacher level. It may be that communication passes only between headteachers, or between headteachers and heads of year, or alternatively schools may have teachers with specially designated responsibility for primary–secondary liaison. Liaison might operate formally through specifically organised meetings or informally through a telephone call. The essence of its success as a management strategy lies in the establishment of effective lines of communication. Liaison between primary and secondary schools over the transfer of pupils then will involve the *communication of information* about those pupils. However, as we shall see later on, it is the content of this information which is crucial, whether, in fact, it contains only personal details, with perhaps the odd test result thrown in, or whether it contains a more useful curriculum profile. Liaison, as the communication of information, also occurs as the secondary school makes itself known to parents through meetings and open evenings in both feeder primary schools and in the secondary schools themselves, through publicity materials and brochures, and as the secondary school teachers make themselves and their ways known to their future pupils in their final year in primary school. The *Secondary Transfer Project* (ILEA 1987, 1988), however, found that many schools were not making the most of the opportunity of transfer to secondary school to build a positive relationship between parents and their children's new teachers, and recommended that schools give more attention to finding ways of welcoming parents into the process of their children's secondary education.

Activities organised to ease the *transition* from primary school to secondary school may seem more immediately concerned with children's welfare in the way that it is seen as a preparation for things to come. This may take the form of anything from a range of joint activities for fourth-year junior and first-year secondary pupils to short preliminary visits to the secondary school for new entrants to have a look around. There may be a succession of planned visits or even a full working day actually in the secondary school for future pupils. Writers such as Dutch and McCall (1974) have described the possibility of a transition department within the secondary school, while David (1988) reports on how one secondary school actually went some way towards this by converting two spare rooms into primary style classrooms with noted benefits not only for the children coming into the school who found something familiar but also for the teachers involved who found themselves with an opportunity to explore different ways of working. In their interesting final report to the Social Science Research Council (SSRC) on *The Adaptation of Pupils to Secondary Schools*, Woods and Measor (1982) describe a particular scheme they had observed in which children made two visits to their new secondary school during which they experienced some lesson situations. They were treated to a play by teachers in the English department, and magical experiments in the science laboratory, both of which, as they were intended to, helped create a certain excitement and expectancy.

In this rural and relatively isolated part of North Yorkshire, where children face a lengthy train and coach journey to their new secondary school, their primary school teachers try to ensure that part of the transition the children make is that they become much more familiar with other children from neighbouring villages who will also be transferring to the secondary school. Preliminary visits are made to the new school in order to familiarise the children with their new surroundings, and these are made at the same time as the other children of the same age from neighbouring villages. To further this familiarisation process, a range of 'cluster' activities are planned, throughout their time in primary school, to involve the children from a number of small schools in joint activities.

The management of *induction* or 'getting them in' is now extensively covered in a growing literature on pastoral care: a fact in itself, which emphasises its 'welfare' focus (Hamblin 1978; Baldwin and Wells 1979). For instance, Leslie Button (1981) in his book on *Group Tutoring for the Form Teacher* suggests a detailed programme covering the whole first year in secondary school. His programme would include a fair amount of time: the first day, all day during the first week, 35 minutes or one period on each day, and then 35 minutes or one period each week + 15 minutes on each of two other days. He goes on to suggest a number of themes which might be covered in this time:

- the pupil's place in school
- building up a caring community
- relationships, the self and social skills
- communication skills
- school work and study skills
- academic guidance and careers education
- health and hygiene education
- personal interests.

This kind of tutorial programme is designed, of course, to enable the tutor responsible time and opportunity to get to know, so very much better, the children in his group, in fact, in a way rather more like the primary school teachers the children have just left. Woods and Measor (1982) are also convinced of the value of 'careful devised and programmed induction schemes'. Although their emphasis is slightly different to that of Button, they too make recommendations which we would do well to note. Among them are:

> *a sponsorship scheme* in which 2nd (or 5th/6th) year pupils take responsibility for new first year pupils during the first day, especially in informal periods of the day
> *homework skills* should be taught
> *rules and the rationality behind them* should be made very clear

Other writers, like Cox (1984), have noted that, in general, too little time is given over to implementing effective schemes, largely because of the demands of other priorities during the year, while the rather different approach reported by Brice (1984) goes some way to overcome this. Known as *The Gateway Project*, it involves an induction period during the first week of the summer holidays when new first-year pupils are given the opportunity of a week in the school on their own with their new teachers affording them the opportunity to settle into the school on their own. However, we would also do well to heed the advice of Walton (1983) who suggests that '*induction demands extremely careful and skilled management*'.

This focus on two major changes the child undergoes in his educational life, the entry into primary school and the transfer to secondary school, enables us to examine activities which support what were suggested as three possible management strategies: liaison, transition and induction. Taken together, these activities shape what we might refer to as the teacher's conventional wisdom of continuity and, as we can see, its basis seems to a large extent to be about children's welfare. In other words, it seems to concentrate on the caring side of the educational task. In a subsequent section, I want to examine this rather more carefully, and ask questions about its implications for the management of continuity and the purposes it serves, but first I want to consider the other demanding side of the educational task and, in particular, to ask if the possible strategies we have identified in a 'welfare' contect can be applied to the management of curriculum continuity.

Managing continuity 2: towards curriculum continuity

It is appropriate to look back to a report as significant as the Cockcroft Report (DES 1982) and to notice how it saw fit to comment on much of what was accepted as good practice in terms of the transfer of children from one school to another, that:

> ... while making a major contribution to ease of transfer from a pastoral and social point of view, we do not always pay as much attention as we would wish to ensuring continuity of mathematical development.

A similar conclusion was reached more recently by HMI (1989):

> The substantial majority of the primary and secondary schools in the sample work hard to ensure that the pupils transfer without ill-effects at the age of eleven. Care is taken to prepare the children and they are received with sympathy at their new schools. Much is achieved for all in the pastoral sense.... The general picture regarding curriculum continuity at the age of transfer is rather less satisfactory. No school achieved effective links in all aspects of the curriculum though every group of schools had some good practice on which to build.

This is the nettle which those who would manage continuity perhaps never quite grasped, and which, in no small measure, contributed to the seeming desire of central government to overlay a framework of continuity in the form of a National Curriculum.

True, it was a task which, over recent years, had grown in complexity with the increasing number of possible transfers a child may have to make during his or her educational career. These may include playgroup, nursery, infant school, first school, junior school, middle school, lower school, upper school, high school, sixth-form college. It was a situation which had led HMI (1980) to comment that:

> The variety of age ranges found in schools and the numerous points of transfer which now coexist argue urgently for more thought to be given to curricular continuity and progression.... (and) more effort to establish and maintain continuity and coherence in what children learn and are expected to achieve.

In a further publication (DES 1985b) HMI indicated possible ways of achieving this continuity *within* schools they say, by 'clear curricular policies which all the staff have been involved in developing' and while accepting that, between schools, continuity was more difficult to achieve, they insisted that it was nevertheless possible 'to arrive at some important agreed objectives' made easier by the existence of LEA policies. The importance of clear policies for continuity is restated in the more recent HMI study of curriculum continuity (HMI 1989):

> To be effective, curriculum continuity both within and between schools requires a clearly formulated policy and efficient administrative routines.

and,

> In attempting to improve curriculum continuity it is important that aims and objectives are established for the transfer procedure and that they are clearly set out in a policy document.

We might consider how our three strategies may yet help us towards the effective management of continuity. In the final report of an LEA development centre project on *Continuity in Education (Junior to Secondary)*, Neal (1975) suggests that continuity in the curriculum is dependent on effective liaison between schools. This report also identifies some of the difficulties in establishing such effective liaison procedures, like staffing ratios, distances between schools, the large number of feeder primary schools to each secondary school and the general lack of sympathy between primary and secondary school but then goes on to make a number of recommendations to overcome them. Its view is similar to that of the *Bullock Report* (1975) of the same year, that '*effective liaison is a priority need.*' Marland (1977) however, warned that exhortations to create closer liaison can be 'romantic vaguenesses' in reality difficult to achieve. He too acknowledged that much liaison between schools has a pastoral focus and that little is achieved to establish a 'functional continuity'. How then might this be achieved?

The manager of continuity might consider two ways forward. The first involves keeping *effective records*, until recently a much neglected aspect of our professionalism when compared with other comparable groups like social workers or doctors. Teachers have tended to carry around in their heads a great store of information about their pupils but the real test came, of course, when others needed to take over, whether it be in the same school, in the next class or in another school. For the teacher taking a child for the first time, as the *Bullock Report* (DES 1975) put it:

> There is no substitute for first hand knowledge of the children and of the kind of learning situation in which they have been involved.

But, as the *Cockcroft Report* (DES 1982) acknowledged, it is not an easy task 'to record concisely on paper'. All too often it resulted in what Bullock referred to as 'shadowy assessments' containing no more than an 'intimation of a child's earlier education'. The demand for more detailed record keeping then has been with us for some time. In the area of language, for instance, Marland (1977) listed four clear requirements:

1. a language 'profile', that is a description of each pupil's language use
2. standardised reading data, measured by the same tests throughout the group of schools, preferably in the form of informal reading inventories or diagnostic test data
3. titles of books read
4. samples of various kinds of writing by the pupil.

This kind of detail could be similarly replicated for other areas of the curriculum. As we have sought to work out the implications of implementing the requirements of the National Curriculum, we have become increasingly aware that it is this area of record keeping which has required our most urgent attention.

However, the crucial point for the manager of continuity is contained in what Marland (1977) went on to say about records, that 'knowledge of schools or of individual pupils is not in itself enough unless it leads to *action*'. This indicates a second possible way forward, for a prerequisite of action according to HMI (DES 1980) is 'not only communication about individuals, but also *consultation* about aspects of the curriculum'. In this way then, groups of schools, through effective liaison procedures involving consultation about curriculum and detailed records of each child's work, could create a broadly agreed policy addressing problems of continuity.

Such an agreed policy would have implications for the management of transition since it would have to acknowledge what the Schools Council (1972) in a much more recently sounding turn of phrase once referred to as 'the single sweep of total education'. Such a policy would also have to address some of the pedagogical as well as curricular implications of continuity as teachers begin to tackle the requirements of the recent changes. In the also distant words of the *Plowden Report* (DES 1967), teachers would 'need to know each others' work', and in so doing may then be more able to translate into action the kind of *philosophy of continuity* embodied in the National Curriculum. Curriculum planning and schemes of work would then have to take into full account both previous and future stages in the child's development. Teaching methods and learning materials may then be selected with careful reference to what had gone before and to what would follow as children's real needs are identified and tackled at each stage of their development.

Examples of how this might work out in practice occurred in this part of North Yorkshire when a working group of primary headteachers, along with the secondary school head of art, organised an exhibition of examples of children's artwork from all the feeder primary schools, the two lower schools and the upper school in the Whitby area. The aim was not to display samples of excellence but rather to show *stages of development*. The display, which filled the upper school hall, was open to the public and aroused much interest. The organisers eventually produced a booklet describing these stages of development which was distributed among all the participating schools. The teachers involved were so pleased with the idea that it was repeated in the area of science. The real success of the projects though is reflected in the working together of teachers of all age-groups in the common purpose of investigating the stages of development, in particular curriculum areas, of children from the age of 4 to 18. This may be a useful way to develop what many more teachers are now doing within the more limited scope of single key stages as they draw up cluster portfolios of children's work in the core subjects for moderation purposes.

Cleave et al. (1982) suggest other strategies which may help to minimise curricular discontinuity for the child:

- recognise readiness for more complex tasks
- supply appropriate resources
- allow for changing physical demands of a new school
- organise activities in the new setting which are already familiar
- gradually expand new materials and activities
- encourage parental support.

Although these writers were considering in particular the child's move from home to school, I think these sensible strategies could have application over every transition between stages in the child's educational life. A focus on these might enable us to avoid what Midgley and Urdan (1992) have called 'developmental mismatch' in the arrangements we make for children as they move from one stage in their education to another. Their focus is on transfer in the middle years but the warning they give us about this transition might equally be applied to others:

> Think for a moment about developing children. As they move through early adolescence they are becoming more knowledgeable and skilful and are developing cognitively. They are growing in their ability to use critical thinking to explore open-ended questions or moral dilemmas. They begin to understand that there is a limit on an individual's ability rather than believing that if they try hard they can do anything. They express a desire for more control over their personal and academic lives. They go through a period of increasing self-focus, self-consciousness and concern about their status relative to their peers. Relationships with friends and adults outside the home become especially important in their lives. Yet there is evidence that the middle grades learning environment, compared to the elementary environment, is less demanding cognitively, is more evaluative and focused on comparing students' ability, provides fewer opportunities for student self-management and choice, and is more formal and impersonal. We see this as evidence of the lack of fit between children at this stage of life and the environment they experience in many middle-level schools.

The acceptance of a philosophy of continuity would also have implications for the management of induction. There would be less repetition of work already done as children move into the secondary school, less of the tendency to 'start again'. This would, of course, be more likely to be the case where groups of feeder primary schools and their secondary school had got together to consider common approaches and to identify broadly agreed goals. Such an approach would go some way towards meeting the need for what Richards (1982) calls 'curriculum consistency' by which he means:

> ... the opportunity for *all* pupils to be introduced to some of the major concepts, skills, rules and underlying generalisations associated with established ways of knowing (both theoretical and practical) in our society.

The National Curriculum now provides the framework of what

every child can expect to experience but it does still require the variety of teachers involved in each child's journey through school to be involved in discussion *at every level* aimed at establishing a broad common understanding about content and the pedagogical implications of its delivery at the various stages. Induction then involves building on the experiences children have already had and also making headway to overcome those other external or subcultural factors which may mitigate against successful continuity, for example, the deep-seated gender differences noted by Woods and Measor (1982) in attitudes towards maths and science and by Catton (1985) towards craft design technology (CDT). The *Education Reform Act* goes some way to providing more equality of opportunity for previously disadvantaged groups, like girls in these areas, but this opportunity now needs careful management if these gains are not to be lost. The agenda has been set for us, we need now to act on it.

Although it is therefore possible to identify to a certain degree 'liaison', 'transition' and 'induction' as possible components of planned curriculum continuity, we must also be aware of the rather more limited success in the implementation of these as management strategies. Legislation requires a curriculum that is 'balanced and broadly based' and this is already in place. It also sets out a series of attainment targets and programmes of study which span the years of compulsory education. The management of continuity over these years as children pass through the various institutionalised stages could certainly be enhanced if those involved had clearly articulated strategies with which to approach their task. The fact that they haven't in the past leads us to look at those hidden or unintentional consequences of action, what Stillman (1985) refers to as 'resulting transitions' and consider the evaluation of continuity in practice.

Managing continuity 3: towards an evaluation of practice

A not so conventional wisdom

One of the immediate effects of looking at aspects of the organisation of transfer, like the welfare of children or curriculum continuity, is that it can deflect attention away from what Galton (1983a) suggests is a much more important concern, 'the effect on pupils of teachers'. For, despite the very considerable efforts which go into caring for children as they transfer from one school to another, such changes can be seriously traumatic. Galton asks as to look for reasons within ourselves as to why we treat children in schools the way we do, for, as he says:

... only when we do this will we make the discovery that the gap between what we ideally would like to do and what in practice we actually do has similar origins whether we are primary, secondary or teachers in higher education.

Galton (1983b) suggests that, rather than teachers changing their particular teaching styles to suit the needs of children, as might be inferred from the welfare focus of the teacher's conventional wisdom, it is rather more the case of children having to adapt themselves to meet the demands made on them by new teachers. Moreover, it is a situation which starts early. In her excellent study, Willes (1983) shows how children from their very first days in school learn how to become pupils:

> It seems beyond dispute that teachers start with a thoroughly internalised set of expectations about the interaction in classrooms and the role relations that the interaction reflects and reinforces.

In reporting a small empirical study, Ribbins (1981) uncovers other intentions behind pastoral arrangements, clear indication that transfer could be managed 'to serve other functions than those of the needs of children'. He found that programmes of induction in secondary schools were seen by some teachers as the opportunity first of all to attract 'really good children' to the school, a blatant kind of impression management, and secondly to identify both children with problems *and* problem children. Willes (1983) sees this kind of activity deriving from the teacher's 'custodial' rather than 'educative' function, that which is often overlooked in educational discussion, 'the obligation to control a number of pupils'. Ribbins (1981) concludes of some induction activities:

> ... that the main interests being served by these events are often those of the school and its teachers rather than those of the child.

This conclusion directs the manager of continuity to consider the context of activities or strategies designed to promote such continuity with great care because it may be that the situation is much more complex than 'conventional wisdom' might at first indicate. In particular, it demands a very careful consideration of whose interests are being served by such activities and strategies.

Professionalism and curriculum discontinuity

Curriculum continuity coupled with effective record-keeping is also often discussed from the teachers' perspective, usually in terms of the way in which it enhances their claim to professionalism. One of

the very real barriers to such professionalism and thus to real
continuity is seen as the difficulty encountered in getting teachers to
work co-operatively. But, this shows the confusion which surrounds
the use of the term 'professionalism', for real barriers to continuity
may be erected by teachers seeking to defend what they see as the
basis of their professionalism, the maintenance of autonomy. Within
schools, this autonomy can be a difficult task for the manager to
tackle given the preponderance of class teaching reinforced as it is by
architectural determinism, while between schools the difficulties are
even greater.

This is especially the case between primary and secondary
school, where significant differences between teachers' views of
professionalism may be found. The term 'profession' encompasses
the notion that the basis of practice is a body of knowledge about
that practice acquired through professional training. The class
teacher–subject teacher differentiation may thus point up the
contrasting focus of the professionalism of primary and secondary
teachers, the former rooted in pedagogical relationships with
children, the latter in subject specialism. Reporting his research a
decade ago Stillman (1984) pointed out the extent of the difficulties
for the manager of continuity:

> In essence the research suggested that not only are teachers'
> current attitudes to colleagues in other sectors unlikely to
> encourage the appropriate initiatives for successful liaison, but
> also that where teachers come together to try to set up
> curriculum linking, there are still many difficult techniques
> involved in getting people to work together. It seems quite
> possible for linking initiatives to fail long before the actual
> educational issues ever arise.

Achieving continuity requires that we cut through this bifurcation,
as Hargreaves and Earl (1990) put it:

> A sense of vision, of scope, of seeing the whole picture is
> important here. So too is a sense of self, of the things one holds
> most sacred and that must now be questioned. The elementary
> teacher's protectiveness of his or her own class and the
> secondary teacher's loyalty to, and identification with, the
> subject — educators must now subject these sacred norms to
> critical review.

According to Gorwood (1991) recent change has had little impact:

> Although the Education Reform Act heralded significant
> changes in schools .... it could do little to influence what has
> been seen in all recent research as the main cause of lack of

continuity: ineffective teacher communication. Teachers in associated schools seldom come into contact with relevant colleagues and there is mutual distrust.

Of course, to take this argument too far may be to oversimplify it and the problem runs much too deep for us to allow that but it does cut across another important issue for the manager of continuity to consider. He must be careful not to confuse continuity in the curriculum with *progression*. In certain senses, parts of the curriculum may seem to be continuous like a historical project, elements appear to follow on as part of a seemingly logical framework. The National Curriculum may seem to provide both the framework and a vocabulary for progression in its programmes of study (PoS), attainment targets (ATs) and statements of attainment (SoA). Managing progression, however, directs attention much more sharply at the level of children, those who *experience* the curriculum. The class teacher seems to be in a good position to ensure continuity, both in a horizontal or integrative sense, like language or maths across the curriculum *and* progression, whereas this has to be more carefully managed when the child is taught by a number of subject specialists.

In some areas of the curriculum there exists a fairly clearly defined hierarchy of skills which some children master more quickly than others. Perhaps we should also consider then whether the organisation of individual learning found in many primary classrooms enables the teacher to manage progression more effectively compared with specialist subject teaching, which might be dictated more by organisational constraints, resulting in children having mastered certain skills being forced into needless repetition waiting for others to catch up. This can be especially true as children move into secondary school from a number of contributory primary schools. It is the ineffectiveness of recent change in addressing this problem which Gorwood (1991) finds most depressing. He suggests that, despite the specifications in National Curriculum documentation, these will do little to eradicate what he sees as the major causes of discontinuity:

> There will still be unnecessary repetition and pupils will become bored; there will still be bewilderment from pupils who have missed out on previous essential learning; schools will still find it difficult to find a common starting point for pupils with different kinds of educational background. There is no legislation requiring schools to adopt particular kinds of curriculum organisation or teaching style. Yet it is these aspects of their education that cause pupils significant difficulties at the time of transition. Continuity is best achieved when teachers take

congisance of what and how their pupils learned before coming to them. It is still very much an optional issue whether primary and secondary teachers communicate about the pupils in whom they have a common interest.

This is the nettle which must be grasped. It requires tackling the sensitive question of teacher attitudes and, for those who would more effectively manage continuity, it is important that limiting ideas about professionalism are not allowed to get in the way of real continuity and progression for individual children, particularly as we have seen, when they move from primary to secondary school.

For Ginnever (1986), the way forward is perhaps best initiated at headteacher level, for as he says:

> ...discussions between headteachers across the sectors is a minefield... Yet it is at headteacher level that discussions have to begin... They have the power to bring about change, but for it to work they must see it as desirable.

While for Hargreaves and Earl (1990), the way forward is in *managing* appropriate relationships between primary and secondary school teachers achieved by,

> ...encouraging and facilitating communication, joint planning and joint work among teachers from different school levels through meetings, visits, exchanges, and by establishing norms of collaboration and collegiality.

Responding to practice: children's views

An important aspect of any evaluation of practice must be the inclusion of the views of the participants. However, the recent study of continuity in practice by HMI (1989) pointed out that:

> ...the opinions of pupils were largely overlooked, which is disappointing as the majority of pupils were thoughtful, informative and articulate when discussing their transfer from primary to secondary school.

Although there appears a grave imbalance in the significance attached to the views of children compared with teachers in most writing about evaluation, for Meighan (1978) it is perhaps surprising in this case, given the identified focus here of the teachers' conventional wisdom of transfer. He points out:

> ...existing definitions of the situation appear to take teaching as more important than learning, the teacher's activity as more central than the pupil's... *despite the official rhetoric of educational*

writing and debate that makes claims for the pupil's welfare as the central focus.

Despite the fact that the experience of the participants is often formally neglected, the transfer of children from primary to secondary school provides those who work in schools with a most instructive example of the contrast between the formal (or intended) and informal (or unintended) consequences of organisation. Measor and Woods (1983) stress the importance of this informal aspect saying:

> Above all, it is in the interaction between identities and formal and informal cultures, that pupil transfer and other status passages have to be understood.

Those who would consider continuity in educational contexts would therefore do well to heed Hargreaves (1982) advice:

> Teachers and adults become blind to the hidden curriculum because that is not what schooling is officially supposed to be about. We believe our own grown-up propaganda. One needs the eyes of a child or a stranger to see.

A number of studies now exist which begin to detail the pupil's view of transfer, particularly to secondary school. Brown and Armstrong (1986) reveal how surprised they were by the range of worries that children expressed before transfer while Walton (1983) comments how so often these problems that children experience go unrecognised by teachers. Smith (1985) suggests that thinking about the size of the secondary school is what causes most problems for children, and their parents, and he is led to make twenty-one recommendations to ease their worries in the lead up to transfer. The ILEA Secondary Transfer Project (1987) found that difficulties in adapting to secondary school had a curricular dimension, in particular they found that poor readers settled less well than others. Similarly, my own study of children's views of primary–secondary transfer (Thorp 1980 and 1983) revealed that the most significant cause for concern among children was the threat to existing identities of imposed banding labels. Woods and Measor's (1982) larger scale study led them to see the threat to identity or self image in more general terms:

> All the paraphernalia supporting one's conception of self would have to be constructed anew — private spaces, reputations (for example as a fighter) appearances, and, most importantly, friends.

Another dimension to continuity is of course as children enter a new school other than at normal points of transfer. In reporting their study of 'newcomers' to schools in Australia, Elliott and Punch (1991) report that children, on entering a new school, have to make accommodation in three major areas: 'the curriculum of the school; the teachers and the other students'. Similarly, they conclude that it is the informal or social aspects of the transfer which appear uppermost among the concerns of the children:

> Newcomers realised very early that their happiness in the new school would be heavily influenced by how well they fitted in with other students.

Elsewhere Woods (1987) also attempts to consider the child's experience of transfer from infants to junior school, and in comparison indicates how at this younger age, children's anxieties are on the whole 'more immediate and more localised' and significantly, 'more susceptible to conventional treatment'. Observing how a group of seven year-olds adapted to their junior school Woods (1987) notes:

> The move from infant to junior is a considerable transition for young children to make. They have experience of only a small range of teaching approaches. Their adaptability, as yet, is limited. It is not surprising that, at the beginning of their junior career when first exposed to this new approach they were, for a time, in a kind of limbo. They had lost the stern external controls of the old... without, as yet, having developed the internal ones of the new. At the beginning of the year, therefore, this class was a noisy, rather undisciplined group, its members bursting and vying with each other at times for individual attention and with very limited powers of application.

Their activity at this stage is mostly directed towards the teacher but it is not, according to Woods, 'attended by the same kind of developments as in puberty', as in the later secondary school transfer.

It is that relationship between formally organised structures within schools and the informal groups or subcultures which either respond to, or are created and sustained by them, which we find at the transfer to secondary school stage, that I find most disturbing. Here, we find the activity surrounding the ideas of liaison, transition and induction in a quite different light and which we might describe as the 'informal management of continuity'. Liaison at this informal level would include communication among children about the impending change of school, the spread of rumours, myths and exaggerated scare-mongering about new teachers and older children. According to Measor and Woods (1983), these activities are functional in that they 'prepare the pupil emotionally as well as socially for a quite profound change to the new world of the upper school'. Transition is seen as a distinct phase overlapping both primary and secondary schools, a pre-adolescent state of flux, the ritual preparation for teenage, and the passage through it as a 'status passage'. Delamont (1983), for instance, indicates how pupils seem to select roles for themselves during this passage and adopt strategies to accomplish them. And induction then involves the ceremonies of initiation into a variety of subcultures, either pro- or anti-school, and the appropriation of associated 'styles'.

Those who have looked closely at this informal level of activity are left with no doubts that it is a passage of some vitality and significance, which, in a sense, both teachers and older pupils are competing to define for the passagees. Teachers might say they are anxious to avert the possible discontinuity that some subcultural values might inflict, while children might see it rather as the natural continuity of growth towards adolescence. It is most sympathetically described by Measor and Woods (1984):

> The root difficulty for teachers is that while they accept their roles as elders witnessing the pupils' ritual progress through the transition, some of the progress interferes with the continuities thought desirable in the formal passage...

and the dilemma for the management of continuity made clear.

Managing continuity 4: a new era?

The first section of this chapter traces the development of thinking about 'continuity' and tries to show how the framework provided by the National Curriculum grew out of an earlier official rhetoric and into legislation in the *1988 Education Reform Act*. The consequences of this Act have indeed been far reaching, effecting fundamental changes in the way the children of this country are educated.

The principles embodied in that legislation were more recently re-affirmed in the White Paper *Choice and Diversity: a New Framework for Schools* (DFE 1992) and placed on statute the following year. This legislation has firmly established what is now commonly referred to as an 'education market' (see, for example: Ball, 1993). The basic elements of this so-called market are identified for us in the White Paper: namely choice, diversity, open-enrolment and competition.

Extending parental *choice* has been a fundamental policy

objective of the present Government since its first administration began in 1979. The principle of parental choice was firmly established in the *Education Acts* of 1980 and 1986 while the scope of such choice has been successively extended in the *Education Acts* of 1988 and 1993. A necessary *diversity* in the range of educational provision supposedly now makes real parental choice a possibility. This is further reinforced with the removal of the power of LEAs to manage the distribution of admission numbers to individual schools within a geographical area. *Open-enrolement* now enables schools to recruit children to their capacity. The simple 'market' principle adopted is one in which 'good' schools are intended to prosper at the expense of 'less good' schools. In other words, schools now find themselves in open *competition* with each other to attract parents and children as 'customers', in a situation in which funding follows the child. Such market competition, it is assumed, will serve to drive up standards.

However, the introduction of this new educational market-place in which all schools have now to operate has also resulted in a number of perhaps unintended consequences which the manager of continuity must consider. The root of this is strangely dichotomous: on the one hand, the National Curriculum provides a more clearly defined framework for continuity and progression; while on the other, the choice and diversity of the educational market creates a context in which such continuity is all the more difficult to manage and achieve.

Choice and continuity

Open enrolment appears to facilitate parental choice: we might consider the extent of the possible discontinuity which could result from the exercise of such choice. Freedom to choose, in theory at least, means that parents can enter or move their children to whichever school they want, provided there are places available. In a situation as fluid and uncertain as this, continuity becomes a real problem. How is curriculum continuity and progression to be achieved for the child who is moved frequently between schools? Such movement would almost certainly result in an unbalanced curriculum experience. For example, a 'mobile' individual child could quite easily encounter Victorian Britain three or four times and Invaders and Settlers not at all! In such cases, a National Curriculum makes little difference to what children actually experience: the framework it provides for continuity and progression also requires a measure of stability. How does choice then cut across entitlement?

Diversity and continuity

Diversity of provision makes the education market a reality: without a range of different types of school for parents to choose from then there is no market. Such diversity was introduced in the *Education Reform Act* of 1988 even if, since then, progress towards establishing the grant maintained (GM) option has been somewhat faltering. However, in addition to schools provided by local education authorities, or receiving 'grant aid' from the churches, there are now some grant maintained schools which have 'opted out' of local authority control and receive their funding direct from the DFE. There are also city technical colleges (CTC) and one city college for the technology of the arts (CCTA) besides a substantial number of independent schools. In one sense, real choice now exists for parents, although there are also implications here for who is actually able to make such choice, given the constraints of transport and finance.

However, such diversity may also serve to complicate the management of continuity. Relationships between 'opted-out' schools and the local authorities are not very warm to say the least, and we might expect co-operation between schools in the different sectors to be minimal. This is particularly disappointing, given the fact that HMI (1989) had identified the significance of the support provided by LEAs where continuity was seen to be more successfully achieved. Of this kind of support, HMI comment:

> In-service courses have been provided, and supply teachers made available to promote liaison work and to allow the attendance of teachers at meetings of working parties. In three of the authorities substantial financial support has been given to assist promising initiatives.

The removal of schools from under the umbrella of LEA control therefore removes them from a possible network of supportive relationships.

Competition and continuity

If it succeeds, open-enrolment driving the operation of this market will inevitably mean that some 'popular' schools will be full, others will be less full and, when the effects of per capita funding are felt, some very 'unpopular' ones likely to close. As a result, schools appear to have been forced into a situation in which they have to 'compete' for pupils. The effects of this may be twofold. First, we need to ask about the management of continuity within the school itself as rolls fall, income is reduced, staffing is cut and teachers have to struggle to maintain and deliver a broadly based and balanced curriculum. Similarly, curriculum management problems may also arise for schools as numbers of children increase. For the manager of continuity, in both instances, the task is to manage the changing circumstances. And, secondly, we need to consider how competition between schools may serve to disrupt the kind of co-operation required to ensure continuity between schools. Indeed, how far does the need to compete with other schools in the market-place inhibit thinking about continuity which is so essentially co-operative? And how far will the 'insularity' which such competition between schools will inevitably bring, lead to real disincentives to exercising choice as parents continue to be frustrated by the absence of guarantees against the kinds of unnecessary repetition of work or missing out of important key steps in learning as children actually make the move from one school to another.

There is a further aspect to this which is worth noting if the operation of the education market successfully closes some schools. The full implications of the kinds of restrictions on choice this would lead to is still unclear. What is clear, however, is that such a market can only operate with at least some surplus places in the schools, and maintaining surplus places is also costly. This leads us to ask whether the introduction of such market forces into the school system has another purpose.

The Audit Commission (1990) recently drew attention to the cost of approximately 0.9 million surplus places, cautiously estimated to be in the region of £140 million a year. As a result, there appear to be grounds for believing that the Government may be hoping that the operation of the education market might yet be a successful strategy for removing surplus places, while at the same time proving to be an effective mechanism to control what the schools are doing.

Testing and discontinuity

If market choice is to operate effectively, then parents as consumers must have appropriate information on which to base their decision-making. One of the central ways of doing this, it is thought, is to provide parents with information about the standards of children's academic achievements in the school. In order to do this, all children are now tested at certain points in their school career.

One of the central features of the National Curriculum is therefore the testing arrangements it introduced at the end of each key stage. Perhaps more than any other, it is this aspect of the legislation which attracted most criticism from educators who might have wondered how much notice was taken of the substantial research evidence which demonstrates the destructive results of 'labelling' children. After all, it was an understanding of the effects of streaming, informed by this research, which had led to the removal of the old 11 + test. Typical of the objections to the kind of competition between children which the present arrangements have brought back were those of the British Association for Counselling (see Havilland, 1988):

> We question the atmosphere of competition that will be engendered by national testing. Competition can be helpful, it can motivate, but competition where a large number of our children will be less than average (statistically this has to be the case) will lead to young people who believe themselves to be less than average people. It will demotivate them and lead to a withdrawal and lessened confidence.

It seems that all those in-school processes which contribute to pupil disaffection, particularly the labelling effects of streaming, were thought likely to be intensified as a result of the new testing arrangements.

An equally disturbing warning is found in the comments of Midgley and Urdan (1992) as they consider differences between what they call 'ability-focused' and task-focused' students. They suggest that ability-focused students believe the purpose of schooling is to judge them, to enable them 'to demonstrate their ability relative to others'. Task-focused students on the other hand, believe the purpose of schooling is individual development, to enable them 'to make progress, learn something new, to master a task'. In comparison, they say:

> Years of research have provided us with consistent evidence that task-focused students, as compared to ability-focused students, try harder, persist longer, are more eager for challenge, use more effective learning strategies, and are generally more engaged in learning.... We now know that the classroom and school learning environments are an important influence.

Midgley and Urdan believe there is evidence to show that learning environments for younger children tend to be more 'task-focused' and for older children more 'ability focused'. On the one hand this is an issue for the manager of continuity to address as children move from one learning environment to another, and in particular between primary and secondary school, but on the other it is also an issue for all teachers as they seek ways to manage arrangements for testing their children sensitively.

These questions arising from thinking about some of the implications of the introduction of market values to education provide the context in which any consideration of continuity must now be considered. On the one hand, the imposition of a centrally controlled National Curriculum and the desire to give choice to parents over their children's schooling seems somewhat paradoxical, a case of giving more choice about less. It has, however, weakened professional control over the curriculum and provided a crude mechanism for accountability. What is more, giving choice to parents-as-consumers, forces schools into the kind of competitive market-place situation which compels them to abandon the kind of co-operation so essential to the achievement of real continuity, itself embedded in the idea of a national curriculum framework. And, on the other hand, the return to mass testing, one of the ways in which it is intended to both inform parental choice and impose a kind of continuity on the system brings with it the now well-documented detrimental side-effects on children.

The new context is by no means a straightforward one and is further complicated by the seeming unfairness which characterises the way in which it is likely to work out in practice. This poses a number of difficult questions for those who would now consider continuity, among the most fundamental of them is that of Sallis (1988) who asks:

> How can we reconcile choice for parents with equal opportunity for children, given that the desire for choice arises from, feeds on and perpetuates inequality?

How, indeed, might the needs of our children in terms of continuity be served by such competition both within and between schools?

Conclusion

In this chapter I have tried to show that thinking about 'continuity' occurs at different levels which involves the indentification of an 'official rhetoric/reality' and a 'teacher's conventional wisdom' of continuity. However, a consideration of 'continuity in practice' reveals the significant differences of emphasis between them. The official rhetoric was thought to be mainly concerned with 'curriculum continuity' or what might be called the 'demanding' side of the educational task. This is further strengthened by the official 'framework of continuity' contained in the National Curriculum. The teacher's conventional wisdom, on the other hand, seemed to be about children's welfare, or the 'caring' side of the educational task. For whatever reason, a critical look at practice seems to indicate how much better teachers have been at the caring side than the demanding one. The experience of recent change seems to indicate that, if the detrimental effects of a market approach to educational provision are to be avoided, there is now perhaps even more urgent need for teachers to rediscover and retain their traditional area of expertise.

In looking at issues of continuity, there are marked differences in emphases as children get older. For younger children, continuity would seem to be less of a problem. The predominant classteacher role might embody both the caring and demanding side of the educational task, and movement between classes may very often be in one primary school under the management of one headteacher. As children get older, the functions of caring and demanding diversify and after the crossing of the 'great divide' between primary and secondary schools they are very often shared between complementary roles of 'academic' and 'pastoral' staff. There are those who argue that such a differentiation is a useful one, for they argue that as children grow towards adolescence then *discontinuity* can serve a useful function. Measor and Woods (1984) for instance, suggest that

> ...it would be a mistake to aim for an entirely smooth continuous transition... the trauma associated with a sharp break is functional.

Another part of this discontinuity which may also be functional is the 'split' of the caring and demanding or pastoral and academic roles as children enter the secondary school. Best and Ribbins (1983) take issue with those who argue that these two functions should be combined by showing how the needs of the child, the development of 'autonomy, rationality, sensitivity and the like', must be considered alongside the differences in *relationships* between 'the child and the teacher as instructor, carer and disciplinarian'. As children grow and need *different* relationships with adults in school, so too should schools seek to develop those appropriate relationships, a situation not always possible, suggest Best and Ribbins, 'where teachers are wearing more than one hat'. This becomes especially important to remember for as children grow in their need for greater *independence*, the increasingly 'product' orientated curriculum of the later years seems to demand greater *dependency*.

As we arrive at the stage where we begin to appreciate that children need these different kinds of relationships as they develop, we find that our attention is being focused for us very much more sharply on just the one, the demanding or the curriculum side of our task. It would seem that the requirements embodied in the *1988 Education Act* are an attempt to replace our conventional wisdom, to change the common-sense way in which we think about our job. The changes that this has brought has meant a shift in the balance of educational power with the result that, as teachers, we have been removed from certain levels of decision-making about the curriculum. The need now is for us to resist being deflected from our other professional responsibility, that of 'caring' for children. This has become even more important as we enter an era which promises a far greater emphasis on the 'product' of our enterprise and we must therefore not allow ourselves to become what Apple and Teitelbaum (1986) call 'de-skilled' in this area of 'care'. It is here that those who would manage continuity may find their greatest task, because now we must learn how to manage both the worst excesses of 'choice' and their effects on already disadvantaged groups and the worst excesses of 'testing' and their effects on children.

However, the manager of continuity who wishes to retain a view of the child at the centre of the educational stage will remember the words of Richardson (1973) who insists that:

> Being an educator — in the broadest sense of the term — involves both making demands on and caring about the person.

and realise that 'continuity' is not about one thing or the other, but a *unity of both caring and curriculum*. It is a view which has been clearly expressed again recently in the Rumbold Report (DES 1990):

> We believe it to be of critical importance for healthy and productive living and learning that teachers do not lose sight of the child's all-round development in pursuit of detailed inform-ation exclusively about what children know and can do in the subjects of the curriculum.

For above all, as Dean (1980) so rightly points out:

> Continuity is what is or is not experienced by the individual child

and it is the totality of that experience which should be considered by the manager of continuity as he strives for the fine balance between the demands of a rhetoric which sees children as human resources and his commitment to practice which insists on treating children as human beings.

References

Apple, M. and Teitelbaum, K. (1986) 'Are teachers losing control of their skills and curriculum' *Journal of Curriculum Studies* **18** (2).

Baldwin, J. and Wells, H. (1979) *Active Tutorial Work: The First Year* Blackwell.

Ball, S. J. (1993) 'Education markets, choice and social class; the market as a class strategy in the UK and USA'. *British Journal of Sociology*, **14** (1).

Best, R. and Ribbins, P. (1983) 'Rethinking the pastoral–academic split' *Pastoral Care* **1** (1).

Blatchford, P., Battle, S. and Mays, J (1982) *The First Transition: Home to Pre-school* NFER/Nelson.

Blythe, A. and Derricott, R. (1985) 'Continuities and discontinuities in the primary curriculum' *Curriculum* **6** (2).

Board of Education (1931) *The Primary School: The Hadow Report* HMSO.
Brown, J. and Armstrong, M. (1986) 'Transfer from junior to secondary: the child's perspective' in Youngman, M. (ed.) *Mid-schooling Transfer: Problems and Proposals* NFER/Nelson.
Brice, C. (1984) The Gateway Project at Holloway School, Islington in Gorwood, B. (ed.) *Intermediate Schooling*, Aspects of Education No. 32.
Button, L. (1981) *Group Tutoring for the Form Teacher 1. Lower Secondary School* Hodder & Stoughton.
Catton, J. (1985) *Ways and Means: the Craft Design and Technology Education of Girls* SCDC/Longman.
Cleave, S., Jowett, J. and Bate, M. (1982) *And So to School: a Study of Continuity from Pre-School to Infant School.* NFER/Nelson.
Cox, T. (1984) Transfer from primary to secondary school — a primary school view in Gorwood, B. (ed.) *Intermediate Schooling*, Aspects of Education No. 32.
David, H. (1988) 'Junior partners: bridging the secondary transfer gap' *Times Education Supplement* 14 October.
Dean, J. (1980) 'Continuity' in Richards, C. (ed.) *Primary Education: Issues for the Eighties* A. & C. Black.
Delamont, S. (1983) The ethnography of transfer in Galton, M. and Willcocks, J. (eds) *Moving from the Primary Classroom* RKP.
DES (1967) *Children and their Primary Schools, The Plowden Report* HMSO.
DES (1975) *A Language for Life, The Bullock Report* HMSO.
DES (1978) *Primary Education in England, A Survey by HMI* HMSO.
DES (1979) *Local Authority Arrangements for the School Curriculum* Report on Circular 14/77 HMSO.
DES (1980) *A View of the Curriculum* HMI Series: Matters for Discussion, HMSO.
DES (1981) *The School Curriculum* HMSO.
DES (1982) *Mathematics Counts, The Cockcroft Report* HMSO.
DES (1984) *English from 5 to 16* Curriculum Matters 1 HMSO.
DES (1985a) *The Curriculum from 5 to 16* Curriculum Matters 2 HMSO.
DES (1985b) *Better Schools* HMSO.
DES (1985c) *Mathematics from 5 to 16* Curriculum Matters 3 HMSO.
DES (1985d) *Science: a Statement of Policy* HMSO.
DES (1987a) *The National Curriculum 5–16 a consultation document* HMSO.
DES (1987b) *National Curriculum Task Group on Assessment and Testing* A Report, HMSO.
DES (1989) *National Curriculum: from Policy to Practice* HMSO.
DES (1990) *Starting with Quality, The Rumbold Report* HMSO.
DFE (1992) *Choice and Diversity: a New Framework for Schools* HMSO.
Dutch, R. D. and McCall, J. (1974) 'Transition to secondary: an experiment in a Scottish comprehensive school' *British Journal of Educational Psychology* No. 44.
Elliott, J. and Punch, K. F. (1991) 'The social adjustment of newcomers in secondary school' *British Journal of Guidance and Counselling* **19** (2).
Galton, M. (1983a) 'Changing schools — changing teachers' in Smith, L. A. (ed.) *Changing Schools: The Problem of Transition* Report of the proceedings of the March Education Conference, Goldsmiths College.
Galton, M. (1983b) 'Problems of transition' in Galton, M. and Willcocks, S. (eds) *Moving from the Primary Classroom* RKP.
Galton, M. and Willcocks, J. (1983) *Moving from the Primary Classroom* RKP.
Ghaye, A. and Pascal, C. (1988) 'Four year-old children in reception classrooms: participant perceptions and practice' *Educational Studies* **14** (2).
Ginnever, S. (1986) 'Liaison and curriculum continuity' in Youngman, M. (ed.) *Mid-schooling Transfer: Problems and Proposals* NFER/Nelson.
Gorwood, B. (1984) 'Intermediate schooling' *Aspects of Education No. 32* University of Hull.

Gorwood, B. (1991) 'Primary–secondary transfer after the National Curriculum' *School Organisation* **11** (3).

Gorwood, B. (1986) *School Transfer and Curriculum Continuity* Croom Helm.

Hamblin, D. (1978) *The Teacher and Pastoral Care* Blackwell.

Hargreaves, A. and Earl, L. (1990) *Rights of Passage: a Review of Selected Research about Schooling in the Transition Years* Ontario Dept. of Education, Queens Printer.

Hargreaves, D. (1982) *The Challenge for the Comprehensive School* RKP.

Havilland, J. (ed.) (1988) *Take Care Mr Baker* Fourth Estate.

HMI (1989) '*Curriculum continuity at 11-plus*' Education Observed 10, DES.

Hobbs, S., Kerr, J., Sylvester, A. and Williams, G. (1988) 'What happens to children when they go to the big school?' SED Research Project 1986/7 *School Organisation* **8** (1).

House of Commons (1988) *Educational provision for the Under Fives* First Report of Education, Science and Arts Committee. HMSO.

ILEA (1987) 'The first year at secondary school: general curricular and pastoral' *Secondary Transfer Project Bulletin 11.*

ILEA (1988) 'Pupils adjustment to secondary school' *Secondary Transfer Project Bulletin 16.*

Marland, M. (1977) *Language Across the Curriculum* Heinemann.

Measor, L. and Woods, P. (1983) 'The interpretation of pupil myths' in Hammersley, M. (ed.) *The Ethnography of Schooling* Nafferton.

Measor, L. and Woods, P. (1984) *Changing Schools: Pupils Perspectives on Transfer to a Comprehensive* Open University Press.

Meighan, R. (1978) 'A pupil's eye view of teaching performance' *Educational Review* **30** (2).

Midgley, C. and Urdan, T. (1992) 'The transition to middle level schools: making it a good experience for all students' *Middle School Journal* November.

NCC (1989) *An Introduction to the National Curriculum* National Curriculum Council.

Neal, P. D. (1975) *Continuity in Education: Junior to Secondary* EDC Project 5 Final Report, City of Birmingham Education Dept.

Ribbins, P. (1981) 'What kinds of conferences do teachers really need to help them meet their pastoral responsibilities?' *West Midlands Journal of Pastoral Care* **1** (2).

Richards, C. (1982) 'Curriculum consistency' in Richards, C. (ed.) *New Directions on Primary Education* Falmer.

Richardson, E. (1973) *The Teacher, the School and the Task of Management* Heinemann.

Sallis, J. (1988) *Schools, Parents and Governors a New Approach to Accountability* Routledge.

Schools Council (1972) *Education in the Middle Years* Working Paper No. 42. Evans.

Smith, J. (1985) *Transferring to Secondary School* Home and School Council.

Stillman, A. (1984) 'Transfer from school to school' *Educational Research* **26** (3).

Stillman, A. (1985) 'Curriculum continuity: some problems and solutions from a research perspective' in Castle, J. and Lawrence, I. (eds) *Policies for Curricular Continuity* West London Institute of Higher Education.

Thorp, J. (1980) 'From primary school to secondary school: the sub-cultural context of a status passage Unpublished BPhil Dissertation' University of Birmingham.

Thorp, J. (1983) 'Evaluating practice: pupils' views of transfer from the primary school to the secondary school' *Pastoral Care* **1** (1).

Thorp, J. (1987) 'Caring and curriculum: the management of continuity' in Craig, I. (ed.) *Primary School Management in Action* Longman.

Thorp, J. (1988) 'Starting school: thinking about our practice' *Rumpus* No. 22 Winter.

Thorp, J. (1989) 'Caring and curriculum: the management of continuity' in Craig, I. (ed.) (1989) *Primary School Management in Action* (2nd edn.), Longman.

Walton, S. (1983) 'Junior to secondary: towards an easy transition' *School Organisation* **3** (1).

Willes, M. (1983) *Children into Pupils: a Study of Language in Early Schooling* RKP.

Woods, P. (1987) 'Becoming a junior: pupil development following transfer from infants' in Pollard, A. (ed.) *Children and their Primary Schools, A New Perspective* Falmer.

Woods, P. and Measor, L. (1982) *'The adaptation of pupils to secondary school'* Final Report SSRC.

Youngman, M. (ed.) (1986) *Mid-schooling Transfer: Problems and Proposals* NFER/ Nelson.

16 Preparing for an OFSTED primary school inspection

Mike Aylen

If to do were as easy as to know what were good to do...

This chapter is intended to help primary schools to use inspection effectively and reduce stress upon staff through careful preparation.

The *Handbook for the Inspection of Schools* produced by the Office for Standards in Education (OFSTED) states that the purpose of inspection is to identify strengths and weaknesses in schools so that this may improve the quality of education offered and raise the standard achieved by their pupils.

The purposes of inspection, set out in the *Education (Schools) Act 1992*, are to report on:

- the quality of education provided by schools
- the educational standards achieved in schools
- whether the financial resources made available are managed efficiently
- the spiritual, moral, social and cultural development of pupils and schools.

Publication of the handbook represents an important development in the openness of inspection procedures. It sets out in detail the reporting headings, provides information about the way inspections are to be organised, and includes criteria against which judgements are to be made. The range of information required from schools prior to inspection is specified, together with the responsibilities of governors and a code of conduct for inspectors. As well as giving a comprehensive basis for inspection, the framework also provides a useful structure for school self-review. It has much to offer schools seeking to develop their own approach to systematic quality assurance beyond the immediate demands of the external inspection cycle.

Information required before inspection

Effective inspection requires procedures for the exchange of accurate information. Following announcement by OFSTED that a school is to be inspected, governors are invited to provide information about its recent history and stage of development. Such detail is used to inform the inspection contract, and provides a chance for the school to supply early data about its context.

Once the inspection contract has been awarded, and the registered inspector appointed, there are two broad categories of preliminary information required from schools. The first involves the completion of headteacher forms, copies of which are contained in the handbook. For schools wishing to do so, arrangements are in hand enabling these to be processed using computer software. Data required includes basic information about the school, its community, pupils, summary data about attendance and exclusions, results of National Curriculum assessment, disapplication and teaching time, staffing composition and deployment, teaching group organisation, financial details and use of educational resources. There is an opportunity for the headteacher to make a personal statement about the development and recent history of the school and to bring particular matters to the attention of the inspection team. It can be helpful for staff as well as governors to contribute their views to these statements. This reinforces a collegiate approach in preparing for inspection and helps to develop a sense of shared ownership from the outset. There is also a questionnaire to be completed on school financial administration and an additional form for schools with nursery classes or units.

The second category of information relates principally to school documentation, some of which is a statutory requirement. The registered inspector is responsible for ensuring that the school knows what information is necessary, and will discuss how best this can be made available. For primary schools this currently includes: a copy of the school development plan; the school prospectus, normally with a statement of its aims and objectives; the most recent headteacher's report to the governing body and governors' annual report to parents; statements of the governing body's policies; other policy statements, for example any relating to behaviour and discipline, marking and assessment; where appropriate school's articles of government; copies of schemes of work; the staff handbook where one exists; class and teacher timetables; attendance records for the previous school year; staff job descriptions; staff development policy; the latest financial audit report; links with support services for pupils with special educational needs; extra-curricular activities with the age group and numbers of pupils involved; links with contributory and receiving schools and colleges, parents, the community and other outside agencies; joint teaching with other schools; pupils attainments on admission; staff and working group meetings; relevant local education authority policies.

In preparing for inspection a careful review of the full range of pre-inspection information required is necessary. While much of this may be readily available, an action plan is useful to ensure that appropriate documentation is built up over time and that there are procedures for keeping it updated to reflect the latest statutory requirements and school developments. Evidence of this planning can be incorporated in the school development plan which will be made available to the inspection team. It may be the case that some documentation is in the process of rewriting, or that some has yet to be completed: evidence that the process is being managed will support the school in explaining its position.

The existence of careful documentation can serve as an indicator of efficient management. For members of an inspection team it provides a helpful insight into the school's intentions and will support their formulation of pre-inspection hypotheses. What will be tested, however, is whether policies are sound, understood and implemented. With this in mind, there is a particular need to ensure that all who need to know are familiar with, and understand the content of, policy statements and that they reflect as accurately as possible the day to day practices of the school. Key issues are: compliance with statutory requirements; consistency of one school policy with another; clarity of practical procedures including who is responsible for what, when and to whom; and procedures for disseminating information. The section of the *Inspection Handbook* which outlines the statutory basis for education is an informative guide, while indicators, within the 'guidance: inspection schedule' can also be used to inform the requirements of policy document-ation.

Inspection procedures

Much of the apprehension and stress associated with inspection can arise from uncertainty about procedures, the scope of personal responsibilities before, during and after the inspection, and the range of issues which are to be reported. It is therefore useful for schools to familiarise themselves with such details well in advance of an inspection. A proactive approach strengthens morale and encourages the view that inspection is a shared enterprise, over which the school can rightly exercise important elements of control, rather than a process 'done to it' in which the school can be perceived as a passive 'victim'.

Governors of primary schools are responsible for notifying all parents of registered pupils, the local education authority in the case of LEA maintained schools, and the foundation governors where applicable that an inspection is to take place. They also have the responsibility to arrange the pre-inspection meeting for parents, having agreed a suitable date with the registered inspector. There is a draft letter in the handbook for this purpose. The meeting is for parents of registered pupils. Some schools have arranged for the headteacher, other members of staff, or representatives of the governing body to be present to introduce the registered inspector beforehand. This also enables them to confirm that those attending are entitled to do so. Following the meeting the registered inspector should inform the headteacher and the chair of the governing body of the parents' views.

It will be beneficial for governors and members of the teaching staff to read several inspection reports of other schools, including those within the handbook. This helps to establish an understanding of the reporting framework, of the style of writing and to place into context terms such as 'satisfactory' when used in inspection reports.

Headteachers will be aware of the need to keep school governors systematically informed over a period of time about all aspects of the life and work of the school. One strategy is to organise this information flow around OFSTED reporting headings. Of particular importance is information relating to pupils' standards of achievement. This approach helps to ensure that any specific areas of developmental need are drawn to governors' attention well in advance of inspection so that appropriate action can be planned and that inspection findings related to them do not come as a surprise.

Methods for gathering evidence

It is important for teachers to have a clear understanding of the methods used by inspectors to gather evidence. There have been historical differences in approaches to inspection by different LEAs. Some have placed strong emphasis upon their advisory role in schools while others have adopted systematic inspection procedures leading to published reports. Even in these cases, however, approaches to inspection will have varied. Members of OFSTED inspection teams each have a cluster of reporting responsibilities which will frequently include one or more subjects. In order to build a secure evidence, base inspectors will seek to observe teaching across a variety of age-groups involving different aspects of learning. Time will also be spent talking with pupils about their work. Primary teachers and pupils are becoming increasingly accustomed to the presence of supporting adults, including class assistants and parents in classrooms. Many teachers are therefore used to other adults observing their professional practice and sharing the day to day life of the classroom. Nevertheless the prospect of different inspectors visiting a classroom for varying and sometimes unpredictable periods of time over several days is not without stress, even for the most experienced.

A useful step towards acclimatisation is for the headteacher to work with members of the teaching staff and to undertake periods of structured observation in the classroom. It will be of value for the focus of such observation to be identified in advance. The OFSTED handbook includes copies of the lesson observation proforma used in inspection with headings such as content of lesson, standards of achievement, quality of learning, quality of teaching and contribution to achievements in other areas. The handbook also provides detailed criteria to inform evaluations which are made against a five point scale. Carefully structured observation which recognises positive aspects of teaching and learning as well as providing developmental feedback can be a powerful means of validating the professional contribution made by teachers, of building confidence and a developing awareness of the criteria which inform inspection judgements. A number of schools will already be familiar with processes of structured classroom observation associated with teacher appraisal.

Evidence will also be gathered through scrutiny of teachers' written plans. Where these are shared between staff there is a useful opportunity for co-ordinators to obtain an overview of the development of their subject throughout the school and to identify emergent development and resource needs. Where a common approach to planning is adopted it is easier for the headteacher to monitor overall breadth, balance and continuity throughout the curriculum, matters which will be evaluated during the course of inspection.

Careful review of samples of pupils' work from each class will also form part of the inspection procedure together with an evaluation of pupil records. Consideration might therefore usefully be given to ways in which the response of individual teachers to work helps to enhance pupils' achievement, to consistency of approach in marking and criteria used for assessment, and the potential value of systems to moderate judgements of standards.

In the pursuit of evidence to inform particular reporting responsibilities, inspectors will need to interview the head and other members of staff with regard to roles and responsibilities, management and planning. With this in mind, it will be profitable to spend some time analysing details of information requirements linked to individual sections of the OFSTED framework. There is much truth in the saying that, if you chop your own wood, it will warm you twice. Accordingly, time invested in understanding the reporting framework enables the school both to take stock of its present stage of development, and also to anticipate specific questions, ensuring that the necessary information is to hand enabling an effective response during the inspection week.

For example, the subject evidence form, in addition to recording details of standards of achievement, quality of learning and quality of teaching, also requires evidence and judgements about assessment, recording and reporting, curriculum content, provision for pupils with special educational needs, management and administration of the subject, and resources and their management. This includes details about teaching and non-teaching staff, resources for learning and accommodation. It would therefore be a valuable exercise in its own right, regardless of inspection, for subject co-ordinators to use the detail within the handbook to build up a series of self-review questions against each heading and to check whether all teaching and other appropriate members of staff share a common understanding about the issues they raise. Inconsistencies in such matters are likely to become evident during the inspection process. Procedures of this kind are, however, time-consuming, and schools may feel that external support would be more efficient. In this case a careful analysis of priorities will be important as part of the school development plan. This will include targeted support requirements over time, and a specific brief to which a consultant or adviser can respond.

Some questions would be common to a number of subject areas. Many are obvious or can be developed from statements in part 4 of the handbook, which offers guidance on the inspection schedule, or from relevant technical papers. Examples are outlined in Appendix A.

Individual subjects will lead to more specifically targeted questions. A similar procedure might be adopted for reporting headings within the framework sections relating to efficiency of the school, pupils' personal development and behaviour and sub-headings within factors contributing to these findings. Again technical papers in the handbook may contain relevant information.

Planning the use of time

Part of the information sought by the registered inspector some five weeks prior to the inspection will be the timetables for the programme of learning activity in each class during the inspection week. Such detail enables individual members of the inspection team to plan the most effective use of their time in order to achieve a balance of evidence, both across different aspects of their reporting subject(s) and also across different year groups. It is not always the easiest task for primary teachers to predict accurately the pattern of future activities. Nevertheless, a general move towards detailed daily planning well in advance of inspection can help individual teachers and the school generally to analyze more effectively the way in which time is used during the teaching day. It may also enable identification of areas of overlap where one aspect of the National Curriculum programme of study for a particular subject is delivered through another. Obvious examples arise in English where, for example, reporting and recording may be linked to science investigations; in reading, used to research information for a geographical topic; or where dramatic activity may involve enacting an historic event with important opportunities for pupils to develop speaking and listening skills. Similarly music may have a role in dance activity. Awareness of the way time is used during the teaching day enables the school to manage and articulate more confidently its coverage of the National Curriculum. OFSTED lesson observation proformas include a section requiring inspectors to record 'contribution to achievements in other areas'. Observations will therefore be passed to the inspector with responsibility for that curriculum area, enabling a broader picture to be formed of the range of learning activity during the inspection week. This helps to ensure effective evaluation where a structured topic or thematic approach is used to deliver the curriculum. In preparing class timetables, teachers will make their own judgement about the principal subject focus of a lesson. Care is needed, however, to ensure that the session to be observed actually reflects the subject recorded and planned. If, for any reason, an alteration has been necessary it should be noted on a teacher's plans and the matter drawn to the attention of the inspector involved.

Another important element in planning the use of time during the inspection week is for staff to indicate clearly at the outset their availability to receive feedback information or to discuss their specific responsibilities with inspectors. In spite of pressures upon inspectors' time, there will be occasions, where, for example, preparation time is needed for a forthcoming session, when it will not be in the best interests of pupils, or the quality of an ensuing lesson, for time to be given in responding to an inspector's questions or engaging in discussion. Nevertheless, if the school is to benefit fully from the substantial financial investment and developmental opportunity which an inspection represents, and to capitalise upon the opportunity to explain details of its practice, time invested in such activity during the inspection week is likely to be time well spent. It may also be useful for teachers to make brief notes during or immediately after the exchange of information for later reflection or reference.

Reporting and discussion of findings

The amount of information reported by inspectors to staff generally during the inspection week will of necessity be limited by the amount of time available, although it would not be unusual for co-ordinators to receive information about developmental needs within their subject or specific area of responsibility. The registered inspector, however, must offer to discuss the main findings of the inspection with the governing body, and separately with the headteacher and other members of the senior management team, as soon as possible after the end of the inspection, and before the report is finalised.

The oral report to the headteacher immediately after the inspection will be both formal and detailed. Its length will vary with individual circumstance but three hours is by no means unknown. Careful thought therefore needs to be given to note-taking during this session. A common procedure is for the deputy head or a senior member of staff to attend to this so that the headteacher is free to give full attention to the detail of information provided. This also ensures that a professional colleague is present with whom the head can subsequently discuss and check perceptions of the oral report at an early opportunity. While this is not an occasion to dispute inspection judgements, it is nevertheless of vital importance for the head to challenge any factual inaccuracies and to seek clarification about any details which are unclear. Despite the inevitable demands of the inspection week and the possible build-up of other pressures, it would therefore be wise for headteachers to prepare themselves carefully and to ensure that they are free of distractions beforehand, during and immediately following this session. Apart from the oral report to the school governors, it is the only summary of inspection findings given prior to the receipt of the written report and will contain useful additional information.

While the subsequent oral report to the school governors will focus more broadly upon the main inspection findings and key issues for action, arrangements for careful note-taking are also required.

Whatever the individual reaction of governors to aspects of the report, there will no doubt be a wish for rigour in maintaining the discipline and professional courtesies of this meeting. An appropriate climate to ensure that the clearest possible communication takes place within the time available enables governors to capitalise upon every opportunity to seek clarification where necessary. Where there are serious residual errors of factual accuracy which have a significant bearing on the findings of the inspection, inspectors will reconsider the relevant judgements. In other cases, there can be no modification of the judgements to be included in the report. The reporting meeting can be challenging for all involved and the role of the chairperson is therefore of paramount importance in planning and regulating this session. A brief discussion with the registered inspector beforehand about customary patterns of procedure is likely to be helpful.

Responding to the report

Under normal circumstances the written report and summary for parents will be received within five weeks from the end of the inspection. Governors are responsible for sending a copy of the summary free of charge to all parents: both the report and summary must be available for inspection at the school. Copies of the reports must be provided to anyone who asks: no charge may be made for a single copy of the summary, but a charge may be made not exceeding the cost of supply for copies of the full report and multiples of the summary. Consideration may also need to be given in advance to arrangements for its translation into other languages where necessary. Within forty working days of receiving the report, governors are also responsible for preparing an action plan and, within a further five working days, for sending a copy to all parents, all staff employed at the school, OFSTED, the local education authority (or Secretary of State in the case of grant maintained schools) and those responsible for the appointment of foundation governors where applicable.

Preparation of the action plan can usefully be started before receipt of the final written report. Again guidance from the LEA or an external agent may be helpful or necessary. While it would be inappropriate for the headteacher, staff or governors to be drawn into a premature response, consideration needs to be given to ways in which the governing body is to manage its communications about the report to parents, the public, in particular to the press and other media if required. Unless there are those familiar with such matters, it would be wise to seek professional advice, especially where it is known that the inspection report will be of a particularly critical nature.

Financial costs

While the actual cost of the inspection will be met by OFSTED, the process is not without expense to individual schools. It would therefore be prudent to make some budgetary provision for this. Some costs will be tangential. For example, copies of some of the documentation required in advance of the inspection will already be available since it is a statutory requirement. Nevertheless, collating the necessary materials and preparing the headteacher forms prior to inspection can prove time-consuming and support for this may need to be costed. There may also be reprographic costs involved, for example, in copying the summary report and governors' action plan to parents and others who need to know. As already indicated, costs for making individual copies of the full report available to individuals can be charged to them within prescribed rates. Additional advisory support may well be considered a worthwhile investment. This will hopefully be of benefit to the school beyond the immediate scope of the inspection, but some provision may be needed to meet costs involved. Additional meetings, such as the pre-inspection parents' meeting and post-inspection meeting with governors, may usefully be combined with other purposes but are likely to incur some expenditure.

In conclusion, the words of John Ford, over 250 years ago, in spite of their possibly over-cautious tone are still relevant today, both for inspector and inspected.

> Undertake no more than you can manage,
> Perform with delight and a kind of unweariness,
> Be watchful over strangers,
> Trust not your memory, but immediately make entries in proper books,
> At proper times inspect your affairs;
> He who observes the rules laid down will be likely to thrive and prosper in the world.

Appendix A

Assessment, recording and reporting

Is there a school marking policy? How does it work and how was it established?

What procedures exist/are planned for teachers to moderate their assessments of pupils' work?
What records are kept of pupil achievement? How are they used?

Quality and range of curriculum

How does school planning ensure pupils' entitlement to a full and balanced range of National Curriculum subjects?
How does planning cater for pupils' individual levels of development and more than one age group in individual classes?
What links are planned with learning related to other areas of the curriculum?

Provision for pupils with SEN

What proportion of pupils have special needs in relation to this area of the curriculum?
What are they and how are they met?
What particular arrangements are made for pupils of special ability?
What role do support or external staff play in supporting pupils' needs?

Management and co-ordination of a subject

Who is responsible for maintaining an overview of teachers' planning?
Is planning shared between staff? For what purpose and in what way? What are their procedures for updating the scheme of work: who is involved in this: when was it last undertaken?

Resources and their management

What procedures are there for sharing staff expertise in this subject?
What role do people other than teachers play in supporting pupils' learning?
How are resource needs identified?
In what way are decisions reached about priorities for expenditure?

Figure 16.1 Inspection schedule

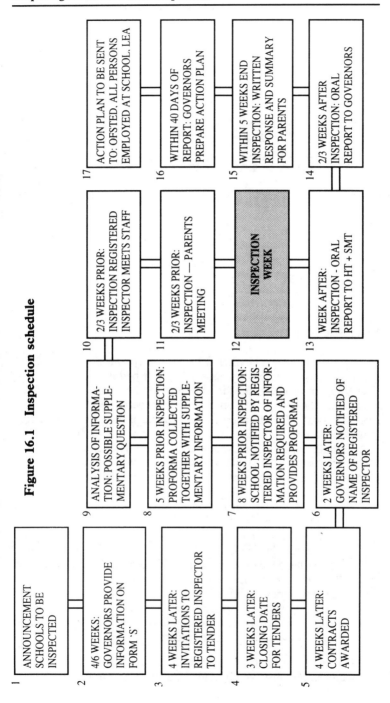

1 ANNOUNCEMENT SCHOOLS TO BE INSPECTED

2 4/6 WEEKS: GOVERNORS PROVIDE INFORMATION ON FORM 'S'

3 4 WEEKS LATER: INVITATIONS TO REGISTERED INSPECTOR TO TENDER

4 3 WEEKS LATER: CLOSING DATE FOR TENDERS

5 4 WEEKS LATER: CONTRACTS AWARDED

6 2 WEEKS LATER: GOVERNORS NOTIFIED OF NAME OF REGISTERED INSPECTOR

7 8 WEEKS PRIOR INSPECTION: SCHOOL NOTIFIED BY REGISTERED INSPECTOR OF INFORMATION REQUIRED AND PROVIDES PROFORMA

8 5 WEEKS PRIOR INSPECTION: PROFORMA COLLECTED TOGETHER WITH SUPPLEMENTARY INFORMATION

9 ANALYSIS OF INFORMATION: POSSIBLE SUPPLEMENTARY QUESTION

10 2/3 WEEKS PRIOR: INSPECTION REGISTERED INSPECTOR MEETS STAFF

11 2/3 WEEKS PRIOR: INSPECTION — PARENTS MEETING

12 INSPECTION WEEK

13 WEEK AFTER: INSPECTION - ORAL REPORT TO HT + SMT

14 2/3 WEEKS AFTER INSPECTION: ORAL REPORT TO GOVERNORS

15 WITHIN 5 WEEKS END INSPECTION: WRITTEN RESPONSE AND SUMMARY FOR PARENTS

16 WITHIN 40 DAYS OF REPORT: GOVERNORS PREPARE ACTION PLAN

17 ACTION PLAN TO BE SENT TO: OFSTED. ALL PERSONS EMPLOYED AT SCHOOL. LEA

17 Employer/employee relationships: employer viewpoints

Derek Esp

Introduction

I was asked to write a chapter from the viewpoint of a former CEO when the forerunner of this book was published in 1987. Since that time there have been considerable developments nationally which have been reflected in my own diversified experience as an employer. I am a former CEO belonging to the 'jurassic park generation' of pre-*Education Reform Act* chief officers. I am also a director (governor) of a city technology college and a county councillor. It is difficult therefore to speak of a single 'employer' viewpoint. I complicate my perspective further through my work as an inspector under the OFSTED arrangements. My main specialism is to look at school management, i.e. the performance of heads and governors as managers and employers.

Since 1987, considerable changes and constant reform and revision of reforms have dominated the work of schools and the time and energy of heads. There are more 'official' guidelines available to heads than in 1987. The National Curriculum revised and the OFSTED guidelines on inspection, although subject to 'revision permanente', do spell out public expectations. The *Better Schools* paper (DES 1985) articulated the public concerns and hopes which these reforms were intended to address:

> The quality of school education concerns everyone. What is achieved by those who provide it, and by the pupils for whom it

is provided, has lasting effects on the prosperity and well-being of each individual citizen and of the whole nation

This lays a heavy burden on the head of Much Rumbling in the Bog Primary School but also promises continuing public interest and support.

Monitoring and support systems themselves are in a state of flux. LEAs display a greater diversity of practice than they did before the *Education Act of 1988*. Some have separated out their services to schools, and schools have the freedom to 'buy' services where they will. Other LEAs have tried to retain a more traditional relationship with schools, although this becomes increasingly difficult. The governors of grant-maintained schools are developing a variety of approaches to school management, as are the governors of the small number of city technology colleges. The new funding agency for schools, which, in some respects, will share the same responsibilities as LEAs, has yet to demonstrate how it will advise and support schools in difficulty. The DFE may expect it to take on board the current budget and other problems experienced by some GM schools.

In this chapter, I shall attempt to analyse the characteristics of the 'good' employer, outline the employer's expectations of the head as 'employee' and reflect on the support that heads will need now that there is a greater diversity of employers and support systems. I shall also consider the more fluid state of employer and employee roles as we move into the next century.

The employer

The effect of legislation in the late 1980s, and the early 1990s, has been to give greater autonomy to schools. This legislation has also increased the powers of the Secretary of State, putting a squeeze on the traditional role of the LEA. We have a National Curriculum, and an increasingly standardised common funding formula for schools. Schools are now inspected on a four-yearly cycle by independent inspectors commissioned and monitored by another new organisation — OFSTED.

Power and authority in education is distributed to many 'players'. It is exercised by heads, school governors, The local education authorities, the funding agency for schools, OFSTED, the new school curriculum and assessment authority, the Secretary of State for Education and Parliament. Within the local education authorities, elected members and officers have a much diminished role. They are responsible for setting frameworks within which schools manage their own affairs and for monitoring the educational and financial performance of schools. The *1993 Education Act* has the potential to damage even this strategic role. Where local education authorities choose to appoint a chief education officer, he or she will be less of a team captain and more of a referee, monitoring the performance of the real players — the headteachers. But the alternative referee, in the form of the funding agency will also share a review and monitoring role. The LEA should have released schools from petty-fogging restrictions once inherent in the working practices of a minority of LEAs. It is hoped that the funding agency for schools will not re-impose restrictions and administrative demands on schools. The style of management in LEAs and the funding agency will be critical to the Government's stated intention to give more autonomy to schools.

The school can only be relatively autonomous because it has to work within the regulations and guidelines laid down by external authority. However, the increased autonomy for schools, whether LEA or grant maintained will require competent self management which has to be encouraged and nurtured by the employer. Schools will be providing learning opportunities for pupils without access to a unified, comprehensive support structure. Like the 'learning company', the school will need to be 'an organisation which facilitates the learning of all its members and continuously transforms itself' (Pedlar, Boydell and Burgoyne 1989).

Heads and their immediate employers, the governors, need the guidance and support of external agencies. In 1985, a report (Audit Commission 1985) provided a checklist for employees and others to assess the local authority in terms of its public image and responsiveness. You and your governors might use this to assess the usefulness of the support received from the LEA, the funding agency, OFSTED and all those other external organisations impinging on the life of your school (see Figure 17.1).

What impression is gained by people who try to contact the authority? Rate the authority on each of the following:

Difficult to find the right person						Easy to find the right person
Unhelpful						Helpful
Bueaucratic						Flexible
Inefficient, slow service						Efficient, quick service
Poorly informed staff						Well-informed staff

Figure 17.1

The employer, whether LEA officer or member, school governor or the head as manager, can assess their approach to employees with the checklist originally designed to check LEA responsiveness.

- Do employees have pride in their Authority (or school) and enjoy working for it?
- How satisfactory are working conditions?
- Do staff feel well informed and appreciated?
- Is delegation accompanied by greater accountability and recognition?
- Do staff respect chief officers (the head) and have their own opinions listened to and respected?

External problems such as national disputes will have an impact on morale. However, employers must ensure that their own attitudes and actions provide a positive climate in which employer and employees can work together to the benefit of the children, whatever the external situation.

An employer's view of the role of the headteacher in the 1990s

Competent school management is essential for the new demands being made on schools. In his annual report for 1990, the senior chief inspector (SCI) (DES 1990) reported that the management of schools left much to be desired. In only about a third of those inspected was senior management considered to be particularly effective. At the time of writing, it is not possible to hear the verdict on school management arising from the first OFSTED primary school inspections in 1994. The situation has not changed greatly in secondary schools, and the same may be true for primary schools.

The weakened role of the LEA and the increased opportunities for self-management will develop the role of the head as leading professional and chief executive. It is important to consider the impact of current changes on the competences required for headship. The school effectiveness movement has debated the changed nature of leadership and management tasks in schools in the 1990s. Some of these changes have been described by Reynolds (1991):

- a heightened public relations or marketing orientation and an ability to sell the product
- the capacity to relate to parents
- the capacity to find sources of support in the community
- the capacity to manage rapid change, not to manage a steady state orientation

- the capacity to motivate staff in times when instrumental rewards like promotion and advancement are rare
- the capacity to relate to pupils, since the wave of future consumerism will ... increasingly involve consumer opinion surveys with pupils.

This analysis is in accord with the findings of the School Management Task Force (ED/SMTI) (DES 1990). The comments in that report about effective schools provide a checklist for the governors and the headteachers. Effective schools are described as follows:

- good leadership offering breadth of vision and the ability to motivate others
- appropriate delegation with involvement in policy-making by staff other than the head
- clearly established and purposeful staffing structures well-qualified staff with an appropriate blend of experience and expertise
- clear aims and associated objectives applied with care and consistency
- effective communications and clear systems of record-keeping and assessment
- the means to identify and develop pupils' particular strengths, promoting high expectations by both teachers and pupils
- a coherent curriculum which considers pupils' experience as a whole and demonstrates a concern for their development in society
- a positive ethos: an orderly yet relaxed atmosphere of work
- a suitable working environment
- skills of deploying and managing material resources
- good relationships with parents, the local community and sources of external support
- the capacity to manage change, to solve problems and to develop organically.

These studies echo the findings of earlier work undertaken in the USA where 'behaviours characteristic of effective leadership in schools' included: demonstration of commitment to academic goals, creating a climate of high expectations, functioning as a leader in teaching and learning methodology, consulting effectively with others, creating order and discipline, marshalling resources, using time well and evaluating results (NASSP 1982).

These various prescriptions for effectiveness imply that there is more to the job than just managing change. Recent legislation has laid down detailed requirements for the National Curriculum, assessment and testing. Implementation of even a scaled-down and modified National Curriculum requires meticulous recording and organisation, i.e. good bureaucratic skills! Effective financial planning, control and review are a requirement if educational priorities are to be implemented effectively. New skills of buying in services from the LEA or elsewhere require much more understanding of contract procedures. I hold to my view expressed in a recent book on management competences in schools: 'All schools will have to display some of the characteristics of bureaucratic organisations simply because of the increased requirements to plan, organise and monitor what they are doing.... Schools will be hybrid organisations — bureaucracies complying with national prescriptions, and dynamic organisations, recruiting pupils and seeking community support in a competitive quasi-market' (Esp 1993).

The controlling and monitoring authority (LEA or funding agency) will be more distant from the school. Governors and headteachers will have to decide on sources of training and support and strive to improve their effectiveness. A natural framework for this will be the four-yearly inspection cycle. The *Handbook of Guidance* for inspection (OFSTED 1993) offers a useful springboard for school based development. Rather than waiting for an OFSTED inspection to demand an action plan from the governors it will be better to study the criteria used to assess effective school management. The framework and associated guidance is available to all schools and all teachers. It provides useful descriptions, e.g. 'where a school is well managed, pupils learn effectively and efficiently. The leadership of the governing body and headteacher gives a clear direction to the school's work. The school's aims are well publicised and translated into clear objectives with attainable targets. Priorities for development are based on sound evaluation and are reflected in the organisation of the school. The development and training of staff are clearly linked to their responsibilities. Pupils and staff understand what is expected of them, are well motivated and have high aspirations. The structures and systems which enable staff to work effectively are in place and regularly monitored. Lines of communication are clear. The school community is orderly, has positive attitudes to work, and sound relationships. Parents are well informed and confident about the school and their child's progress. Finance is efficiently managed and focused on clear priorities for the provision of resources'. The framework and associated guidance also encourages the positive management, deployment and development of staff:

The extent to which there are adequate arrangements for

recruitment, retention, motivation and reward of staff members ... the effectiveness of support staff and the extent to which they enhance the work of teachers... the extent to which there are effective arrangements to extend the knowledge and skills of teachers, and other staff where appropriate, and appraisal arrangements to provide a realistic picture of the effectiveness of their work and to support their professional development.

The employer: creating the right conditions for effective schools

All employers, including local education authorities and school governors can make life difficult if the right conditions are not created for the workforce. For two years I was adviser to a new school where the governors had freedom to establish their own arrangements for management. A decision was taken to keep the governing body out of day to day management and allow the headteacher and staff to have considerable freedom within broad policy guidelines and an annual review of educational priorities and budget requirements. Some of the basic requirements outlined below were put in place.

A clear job description for the head

This was required for selection purposes, but also provided essential ground rules for the head and governors in terms of their respective responsibilities. In this case, for a large secondary school, the governors were prepared to leave professional appointments to the head and senior staff. The only exceptions were Deputy Head posts where the candidates would have to stand in for the head in the case of his absence or untimely demise.

Provision of a 'personnel specification' for the job

If someone is required to be proactive, develop teamwork, create a positive climate and manage well, then these school effectiveness 'preferred behaviours' need to be stated. This was done for the new school. Governors benefit from a clear statement of the style of management required for success. They can be encouraged to provide freedom and flexibility. The governors can then concentrate on helping and supporting the school staff, perhaps volunteering their own professional advice and individual skills. They can concentrate on the key tasks of agreeing policies, establishing key priorities year-by-year in the school development plan, and acting as an important link with the local community.

Delegation to the head

In the new school, the head was given extensive delegated powers. The governors should be prepared to delegate management of the budget to the head. With delegation comes accountability and a responsibility to consult governors and parents on key issues. Consultation will enable the head to make decisions on the numbers of teaching and non-teaching staff within an overall staffing budget and obtain freedom to approve expenditure and exercise virements of funds within the total budget without constant reference back to the governors. I would put in one word of caution here. Governors, as well as heads, are exercising new powers and are taking their responsibilities seriously. I came across a potential problem in a series of national seminars on the OFSTED inspection arrangements. Many chairs of governing bodies accepted the OFSTED assumption that the inspectors would report formally to the head and senior staff before reporting to governors. Some governors held the view that management, i.e. the head, should receive the inspector's comments after it had been considered by the 'board'. They expected normal commercial practice, where the board of directors hears the bad news and the good news first from the external consultant or the auditor. I leave this problem with you. It will be less of a problem if such processes and procedures are included in the general 'rules of engagement' for the head and the governors.

Reduction of the administrative load

The main load these days comes from national legislation. The local education authority can still help, however, by offering simple guidelines, appropriate information technology and effective support and advisory services. Some of these will be 'core' services available free of charge, others may be optional support available on payment. The Somerset LEA offers schools the option of platinum, gold and silver levels of support, giving the school the option of how much help it requires, for example, with budget management and control.

Governors

They need help as well. Local education authorities and other providers are endeavouring to provide support to governors. Provision is still patchy, and more needs to be done for governors at or near their school or home base.

Procedures

Governors and heads need clear procedures for employee relations issues. Governors should have these procedures in place, using overall guidelines from the local education authority or other sources of support.

For example, the aim of a disciplinary procedure is to improve performance. It provides a formal framework within which individual employees know what they have to do specifically in order to improve their performance. The procedure provides a timetable for review and various graded levels of employer response. The disciplinary procedure replaces the furtive, underhand methods still used in a minority of schools where everyone (except Mr X and Ms Y) knows that Mr X and Ms Y are considered to be failures! Grievance procedures can also be helpful. They solve nothing, but provide a proper framework for serious grievances, individual and collective, to be heard by independent adjudication.

Appraisal

This is now a requirement. The head benefits from a proper appraisal system where positive answers are given to questions such as:

- How am I doing?
- How can I improve?
- What am I doing well?
- What are you going to do to help me to improve?

Supporting the head of the self-managing school

Local education authorities and other support services have the task of empowering individual heads and their schools. This is so that the school can develop a positive climate which encourages individual and institutional development, and therefore better teaching and learning, (Esp op cit). Local education authorities and LEA consortia have provided documentation, information about sources of help, training opportunities, advisory services, networking opportunities and other forms of support. A similar role has been developed by the grant maintained schools centre and their consultants. Other external sources can provide some of these services too. LEAs will vary in their ability to provide such services directly. Others may fill the gap, but in some instances the school may find it difficult to access support when it is needed unless it begins to build up its own directory of support services, and equally importantly, its assessment of the capacity and competence of those services which it purchases from the LEA or elsewhere.

There are a variety of ways in which external support can assist the school. These include:

Mentoring

This can support individual development. A mentor can be a valuable critical friend who can help the individual's professional development. It has been said that self-development requires someone who can give feedback, question, share, discuss, challenge, comfort and guide one through the learning and development cycle (Kirkham 1992).

Coaching

This focuses upon skills and competences in action. In the primary school, the head may wish to play a part as coach for colleagues. From time to time, the school may wish to call on special skills and expertise for the development of individuals, teams or the whole staff.

External evaluation of the school

The four-yearly cycle of OFSTED inspections will provide a systematic means of review. Schools may need to seek external support from the LEA or elsewhere in order to implement part of the action plan prepared by governors in response to key issues raised by the inspection team.

Tutoring

Some aspects of individual or team development will benefit from tutor support. Higher education institutions have developed courses which allow for accreditation of workplace experience and make such opportunities a realistic option for the individual teacher.

Supporting the school's own internal trainers and developers

The self-managing school will wish to build up its own expertise. In some LEA areas, governing bodies also have a governor charged specifically with the task of identifying training needs and seeking external help for governor development. External services should be able to offer a range of services for training and development. The training and development lead body (TDLB) has established national standards for matters such as identification of training and development needs, provision of learning opportunities and support, and evaluation of the effectiveness of training and development.

Providing support materials

Self-managing schools will seek increasingly to use external materials to nurture individual, team and whole school development. Good self-study materials are now available for those wanting to improve their competence as managers in schools.

The school management task force was established to work with the public and private sector providers to ensure that adequate provision was available; to help local authorities to establish practicable strategies and to set timetables for training of existing heads and senior staff. However, the position seems as patchy now as it was when the task force was set up. Higher education institutions, professional associations and private consultants are making provision for management training and development alongside local education authorities but there is not yet sufficient provision to meet the requirements of schools, whether self-managed in the local education authority or the grant-maintained schools sectors

The proactive employee

There are few signs that a national scheme of effective training and development for heads is likely to be established. The initiative must be taken therefore by heads and staff in schools. It is good for personal and professional development if a head contributes locally, regionally or nationally to educational developments. Local education authorities and other support services will be more effective if they include people with present or immediate past experience of headship. As the squeeze continues on local education authority budgets, there will be an increasing tendency to keep only a small 'core' staff at HQ and depend on more flexible use of serving heads on short term secondments. There are few such opportunities available to primary heads at present.

There are a number of formal mechanisms that local education authorities can use to engage the active participation of heads in policy development and service review. Professional associations provide opportunities for some heads to participate in policy discussions with elected members and officers. Heads may serve on education committees as added members. Regular meetings between the chief education officer and heads may continue to be a valuable opportunity to share ideas. Because of changes in the traditional CEO role this may not continue. Some local education authorities may retain a CEO but separate out their services under another officer in order to separate out the local education authority's 'client' and 'contractor' roles. This could give a further opportunity for involvement as local education authority services are run by charitable trusts, friendly societies or commercial companies at some distance from the 'core' LEA's management control. This may be the effect of competition legislation. In this case, the head will have the opportunity of having a key client role on a 'user' or 'consumer' group where there will be a chance to influence the nature and quality of services offered to schools.

The core LEA itself will need to consult heads concernng the services that need to be made available to schools. The LEA may act as representative for client schools in order to secure best provision at reasonable cost. The LEA will need to have feedback from school about its policies and relationships with schools if it is to remain responsive, or if it is to survive, given the alternative of grant maintained status.

The new school inspection arrangements provide heads and other teachers with a chance to serve other schools. If it were possible for teachers to qualify for inspector status through development and assessment of inspection skills in the workplace this would do much for individual professional development and performance. It would also guarantee a continuing supply of independent inspectors as people retire. This is a viable career progression for the head who retires early.

Conclusion: who is the employer and who is employed?

The forward-looking title to this book is a reminder that the context in which the head works is still evolving. Whatever changes are to come, the success of the service will depend upon the key leaders. The 1977 HMI paper on good schools observed that the most important single factor is the quality of the leadership of the head. HMI saw heads of good schools as having:

> qualities of imagination and vision, tempered by realism which enabled them to sum up not only their present situations but also future attainable goals.

Such heads had appreciated the need for specific educational aims, both social and intellectual, and had

the capacity to communicate these to staff, pupils and parents,
to win their assent and to put their own policies into practice.
Their sympathetic understanding of staff and pupils, their
accessibility, good humour and sense of proportion, and their
dedication to their task had won them the respect of parents,
teachers and pupils.

In the constantly changing scene of education management and
administration, the head is likely to remain the one person whose
leadership position is most likely to influence the development of
improved educational standards and effective schools. Although a
few heads are now on fixed-term contracts, the role of head is likely
to remain a stable and fixed element in the next few decades. This
may not be so for other people. The post of CEO is likely to
disappear in several local education authorities. In one instance, the
responsibilities for education and social services have been merged
for a chief officer who has 'lost' a number of schools to the grant
maintained sector. If smaller unitary local authorities develop, then
there will be a tendency for more schools to go grant maintained.
Smaller LEAs will probably chose to combine education responsibilities for a chief officer with leisure services or other responsibilities. The division of the client and contractor roles forced by
competition legislation will also put pressure on the traditional
appointment of a CEO responsible for all aspects of education.

Yet more changes may come about. Ten years ago it was
unthinkable that a substantial number of people would now earn a
living as self-employed education consultants. The new inspection
arrangements may encourage some teachers to opt for self-employed
status, spending some time on part-time teaching contracts, and the
rest of their working time as independent registered and team
inspectors. They, in turn, may employ other people in their
inspection teams. Others will serve as self-employed associates of the
provider 'arm' of LEAs, working in a company, for a charitable trust
or for a friendly society. This blurring of employer/employee
boundaries may encourage a greater variety of contracts. As well as
managing the permanent teaching and non teaching staff the head
may also, as client, employ contractors to provide some of the
teaching and other services to the school. Education officers in the
new post-1993 Education Act climate are having to make similar
adjustments to their traditional role as employer and employee.

Some years ago, an American educator, Professor Dick Schmuck
described schools as formerly 'domestic' organisations which had
now become 'wild' in order to survive in the jungle. For CEOs,
heads and their successors, there will be a more fluid 'jungle' of

employer/employee relationships in which to operate. The occupational and personal competences required will remain the same, however, except that the head is now positioned at the pinnacle of the education career structure where he/she ought to be.

References

Audit Commission (1985) *Good Management in Local Government* Local Government Training Board.

DES (1985) *Better Schools* (Cmnd 9469) HMSO.

DES (1990) *Developing School Management: The Way Forward* School Management Task Force.

DES (1991) *Senior Chief Inspector: Annual Report 1990* London HMSO.

Esp, D. G. (1993) *Competences for School Managers* Kogan Page.

Kirkham, D. in Wilkin, M. (ed.) (1992) *Mentoring in Schools* Kogan Page.

NASSP (1982) *The Effective Principal* National Association of Secondary School Principals.

OFSTED (1993) *The Handbook for the Inspection of Schools* Office for Standards in Education.

Pedlar, M., Boydell, T. and Burgoyne, J. (1989) 'Towards the learning company' in *Management Development and Education* **20** (1).

Training and Development Lead Body (1991) *National Standards for Training and Development Supplement: Standards for Assessment and Development* HMSO.

18 Involving parents in the life of the school

Elsa Davies

One of the nicest things about parental involvement is that it can be such fun. All too often, in concentrating on the more serious aspects of this complex subject, one can forget the warmth of feeling, the confidence of support and the laughter-sharing times which happen when the relationships between people are founded on sufficient trust and respect to become relaxed, understanding and caring. The pleasure and joy in sharing a child's education with parents needs stating, for it is all too easy to become enmeshed in the problems and difficulties which appear to beset the pathway to warm and sincere home school contact.

Having said that, and having acknowledged the complex nature of the subject, it seems both sensible and economical to begin by attempting a definition of terms. This is not easy because parental involvement in school life occurs at every school organisation level and it is subject to widely differing perceptions and interpretations. In this chapter, the term 'parent' is used in the main to refer to the people responsible for a child's welfare, upbringing and education. At times, too, it embraces other members of the family, close family friends, neighbours and members of the community who care about the school. Where the term 'family' is used, children themselves are included, as they are also in the school community which is sometimes referred to as the school family.

In the main, the interpretation of the term 'involvement' follows the standard dictionary definitions based on a significant association with, in this case, an enterprise. In its breadth, it covers practical participation in the school and the classroom during the school day. It also covers the more representative level of participation on home

224

school associations and governing bodies. Both these forms of parental involvement are taken as given, in that they are currently accepted practice in the majority of primary schools. A more personal and idiosyncratic interpretation of involvement allows for the 'significant association' to include less tangible elements of felt support and goodwill to be placed on an equal level of importance as practical participation. In that parents and teachers are involved in a shared responsibility for children's education through schooling, there is assumed in this interpretation, an implied mutual obligation on both parties to work together for the best educational experience for children. It is this 'working together' principle, in its broadest sense, that this chapter on parental involvement addresses.

Perhaps the most pressing argument for headteachers approaching parental involvement in this broader sense is the vital nature of the effect of reciprocal support on children, their parents and their teachers. Parental involvement is so complex, diverse and all-embracing a concept that it pervades the whole ethos of a school. It calls into question the philosophical beliefs underpinning a school's broad aims and, for this reason, deserves the most serious and considered study by headteachers, staff and governors. Alongside these deeper concerns, legislation (such as the *Education [No. 2] Act, 1986* and the *Education Reform Act, 1988*) make it imperative for heads to draw parents more closely into the life of the school. Historically, statements to the effect that schools:

> are more likely to discharge their responsibilities wisely when they ensure that parents and others understand their intentions and the reasons for them (*Curriculum 5–16* DES 1985)

have now been translated into the statutory governors' annual meeting with parents and the National Curriculum profile components. Added to this, there is an intuitive understanding in many teachers that involving parents in school life carries with it many advantages, ranging from the various talents and opportunities parents bring to school life to the important chance it provides for reducing and eliminating areas where children can manipulate conflict between parents and teachers. Other advantages include the opportunity of proceeding more effectively in a child's learning by involving their most natural teachers (parents) and certainly, not the least advantage to a caring professional, is the awareness it raises of not having to undertake the whole weight of responsibility for a child's development when there are others to share it. Finally, there are lessons to be learnt from management research (Peters and Waterman, 1982) which strongly proclaims the importance of an organisation staying close to the client and of listening intently and regularly to them. In order to respond sensitively and to give the best possible service, teachers need to generate a dialogue with families and to listen carefully to them. Teachers also have a responsibility to offer the benefit of their professional expertise as they look together with parents, governors and others for the best way forward for the children in their school.

The essential purpose of good school management is to enable the easier translation of school aims into practice. In relation to parental involvement, this means the creation and maintenance of warm, working and interdependent parent teacher relationships. Therefore, as a framework, the chapter takes broad areas of managerial concern such as communication and decision-making and looks at how they inform and extend the concept of parental involvement and in particular, at how the development of active parental support can help teachers proceed more quickly and lastingly in children's learning.

Communication

One of the major managerial functions of the headteacher's role is the development and maintenance of communications in a school. It forms one third of a manager's executive activity (Mintzberg 1973) and aspects of it pervade almost every area of a manager's work. Interestingly, Mintzberg labels the relevant role category as 'Informational', which serves to emphasise the importance of communications as a means of sharing information. Although the sharing of information may be regarded as an end in itself, it is but the first step in a process which leads towards supportive parental involvement. Through sharing information with school families, a realignment of lay/professional boundaries occurs, which results in an increased commitment of all parties to the primary aim of securing a child's well-being and progress. This common ground is where the mutual respect and trust essential to warm and sincere relationships in a school are nurtured.

Non-verbal communications

Beginning, however, on a contradictory note, there are times when communication is not a matter of sharing factual information in words. Sometimes the items are more tangible. Mentioning a cup of coffee as an important aspect of parental involvement may appear trivial on the surface. Yet, the underlying messages behind the provision of coffee-making facilities for parents at school is very powerful. It is strong and tangible evidence that they are welcomed and it helps people to feel part of the school family. In the same way, similar messages are conveyed by the schools who choose to share space with parents in the form of a parents', family or community room or area. Equally, schools who share their buildings with parents by allowing access to classrooms and corridors are encouraging easement in some parents' intital feelings of apprehension about the school.

Spoken communication

In returning to the theme of sharing information, it is clear from many years of experience that this happens at its most informal and individual level when parents and class teachers meet at each end of the school day. Often such contact is brief and specific but it is a significant and essential feature of parent–teacher communication. It gives both teachers and parents the chance for example, to mention something praiseworthy, to express anxieties and to acknowledge tacitly their mutual support.

Much less satisfying and far less important in relation to encouraging parental involvement are the occasions which arise for formal talking at school functions, education evenings and parent association gatherings. Amongst these events the governors' annual meeting with parents is a significant occasion. At such events there is plenty of opportunity for dissemination of information by professionals but less chance for constructive feedback from families. However, despite their limitations, these events are useful for the other functions they perform in relation to school life (Coulson 1984) and for the starting point in parent contact they provide for some schools.

Equally important, but on a different and rather more individual level, are the opportunities parents have for discussion about their child's development with the head and the teachers. Formal consultations involving individual families and classteachers need still to be a part of our provision as professionals but additionally, there are times when a parent or the head may wish to raise a matter of specific concern, for example, over the provision for a pupil with special educational needs. Access for discussion is important at these times.

It is also useful to offer an invitation for discussion at various times when children have completed particular stages of their learning (Davies 1980a). The National Curriculum designates 7, 11, 14 and 16 years of age as statutory reporting stages but concerned parents and teachers would probably regard this provision as a minimum level of involvement in a child's learning programme. More positively, schools could use the National Curriculum levels of attainment in particular subject areas as bases for offering regular parent/teacher/pupil discussion opportunities.

At these times, the child's school record (which can be initiated in the parents' presence when their child begins school) can enhance discussion with children and parents. Parents appreciate knowing that whenever they need they may have access to any notes which school staff make on their child. There are also times when parents are glad of the chance to add information to this working document. Encouragingly, Macbeth (1984) regards this open access to personal educational data as measure of the degree of success which the parent teacher partnership has achieved.

Written information

Apart from the unofficial 'grapevine', the first contact most families have with schools is their initial visit to enquire about enrolling their child. On this occasion, it can be helpful to give the school's introductory booklet. Such introductory publications not only need to provide enough information for parents to make a considered judgement about their child's early schooling but they should also project the feelings of warmth and purposefulness which characterise a caring, educative community.

The importance of the style, content and presentation of the introductory booklet is also applicable to all forms of written communication with parents, Yet, while clarity of content is highly desirable, it is the welcoming tone and sharing nature of the notes which encourage parental support. Many schools produce regular information circulars which are much appreciated by parents (Davies 1980b). Some newsletters appear two or three times a term and carry information ranging from curricular items and organisational matters to special events and general news. Some also offer opportunities for parents to make contributions to the content as well as summarising meetings where parents have been involved in decision making. A casual and informal style of writing can encourage parents to suggest the inclusion of information items which might be relevant to other families.

It is also worth noting that regular newsletters can be effective in developing the spirit of partnership encouraged through legislation. They can, for example, enable governor concerns to be shared with parents in a natural way which integrates governor activity into the working life of the school.

Even though newsletters serve families in many ways, there is still a need to provide opportunities for parents to make direct contact with other parents as a group. Some schools provide 'family noticeboards' for this purpose and such ideas, along with the brief but friendly notes of home–school associations to families, are initial steps in encouraging parent to parent contact.

However, in order to make progress in this area, some activity by individual parents is to be desired. More advanced stages of parent to parent contact are in evidence when individual or small groups of parents can produce information leaflets or organise educational or social events for children and/or parents. This activity involves parents' communication orally and on paper with each other and is indicative of the extent to which a really trusting bond exists between teachers and parents. Extending opportunities in this particular aspect of communication is one of the future development areas in the progress of parental involvement and an important step towards realising the concept of 'equal partnership' with parents.

Teaching/learning involvement

In recent years, the most significant advances in home–school relationships have centred on maintaining active parental involvement in their child's education once school has begun. The logic behind such moves is the commonsense, economical approach of harnessing the natural talents of the parent-as-teacher in supporting the expertise of the professional teacher. In terms of a child's enhanced progress and motivation for learning the dividends are great and research in the Inner London Education Authority (Griffiths and Hamilton 1984) and Sandwell (Stevens 1984) support personal experience. They are equally noteworthy in relation to the development of purposeful parental involvement through providing parents with a deeper understanding of the joys and the difficulties arising in more formalised teaching. They also serve to emphasise the unity of purpose in the aims of parents and teachers.

Some years ago when the Inner London Education Authority was in existence, the PACT (parents, children and teachers) scheme provided a particularly notable, documented example of continuing parental involvement in a child's learning. In this scheme, children were encouraged to take books home to read with a family member who was then asked to make a brief note of the experience on a progress card. With the addition of the teacher's response, these progress sheets gradually became a form of conversation between parents and teachers which focused specifically on a child's learning. This strategy is still worthwhile and can be adapted to suit the learning programmes of particular schools, for example, where skill mastery is the style of learning, then books accompanied by brief suggestions on specific supportive activities can be made available for parents.

Another method of supporting home learning is for teachers to produce information leaflets on specific educational topics, particularly those concerned with the content, organisation and delivery of the National Curriculum. The possibilities for themes are endless but examples might include leaflets on the contribution of children's play activity to design and technological capability, the value of sand and water play, teaching alphabetical order, activities for developing visual and aural memory and so on. Even further along the path of providing opportunity for the expression of parental desire to help their child's learning is the channelling of a particular and regular professional activity to these ends. In schools where teachers prepare forecasts of work, a brief summary shared with parents can bring rewards, particularly in relation to thematic work. In this way, a child's activities within the family can be complementary to the school based work and parents can also share expertise or knowledge with the class. Brief though such contact must inevitably be, it can give parents an indication of the knowledge and experiences their child may be exposed to as the term proceeds.

In the area of teaching/learning involvement, a considerable onus lies upon the professional to produce tangible output to support active and continuing parental involvement. However, even though the reciprocal input by parents is less visible or concrete, it deserves, nevertheless, to be highly valued. Parental teaching involvement gives impetus and motivation to a child's learning. It also allows teachers time to concentrate on learning areas needing professional expertise. Not least of its advantages is that the dialogue it engenders carries latent messages of trust and understanding between parents and teachers.

Other developments

As technology becomes ever more sophisticated, and the constitution of school groups change, schools will need to consider alternative means of communicating with families. Some schools produce video cassettes to tell parents and prospective parents about their aims and activities. Similarly, audio cassette tapes can substitute in many cases for written information. Such provision can be particularly helpful to handicapped parents. If the cassettes are available in different languages, families from different ethnic groups or from abroad can be made more warmly welcome. On the multicultural theme, where possible, it is both courteous and respectful for the school to try to have all their publications, particularly their news bulletins, translated into the various languages used by parents.

As time proceds, forward-thinking schools will be producing lending libraries of their own computer software packages, specially designed to support their learning programmes. They may also become involved in projecting their school activities through interactive video techniques. In these, and all the aforementioned ways, schools can be engaging in that vital diaglogue with parents which supports a child's learning.

As education business partnerships develop, schools will see ways forward in sharing the teaching/learning elements of their activity with those parents who might find closer involvement difficult. Bulletins outlining new educational developments or school organisation patterns, for example, might be circulated to local companies which employ significant numbers of parents. Similarly, articles in local trade magazines, union bulletins or newspapers can also help share good news about how schools are helping children learn.

Decision-making

Opportunities exist in all aspects of parental involvement for lay professional tensions to emerge, and this is especially so in decision areas which are intimately bound with policy-making. Although teachers have long felt this policy-making function to be a professional preserve, the reality is that schools exist to serve children, and through them, their families and ultimately, society. To achieve the most effective match between parental expectations and professional expertise, teachers need to talk purposefully with parents about ways in which the school can best serve its families. Sometimes the governors' annual meeting is the proper arena for such discussion but, most likely, a slightly less formal setting achieves better results. Whatever the setting, it is important to note that the dialogue can only be sucessful if it is founded on the principle of equality in the home–school partnership. Only then can sincere consultation and genuine involvement over school improvement lead to stronger family commitment to the school in general and more specifically, to the development of the individual pupil.

At present, most schools have two long-established decision making bodies, namely the staff group and the governing body. Schools may also have a relatively newer group in the form of a parents' association which, in relation to the other groups, has the disadvantages of seeking to represent a non-cohesive group of people and of having, for various reasons, a very weak influence base within the structure of school life (Merson and Campbell 1974). In the past, none of these groups fully served the headteacher in discovering the best response the school can make to family needs. Although the new governing bodies could be deemed to provide some answer to this problem, their residual formality and restricted membership constrains their effectiveness in some respects. Consequently, there is still a need for heads and governing bodies to search for innovative ways of discovering and channelling a wealth of talent and goodwill to the betterment of educational practice. An historical example of one creative response was the setting up of school policy advisory body (Davies 1985) which drew all the parties together to look critically and constructively at the school practices and procedures. Discussion areas ranged from the highly practical provision of directional signs in the school building to more complex areas such as transition between schools and supplementary provision in curricular subject areas. The important thing was that, whatever the topic or level of discussion, the school and its families were both the focus and the beneficiaries of the outcome.

Similarly another different but currently valid way of involving parents more fully in school decision-making is to open out areas more closely regarded as professional issues. An example of this kind could be the annual decision necessary on alternative school structure patterns. Parents are often anxious over decisions to undertake such options as 'vertical grouping' of pupils in classes. It can help greatly if they along with the staff, have looked seriously and together for the best option for their school.

Such arrangements not only serve to vitalise parental involvement in school life but they also help to bridge areas between the three distinct decision making bodies previously mentioned. In an ideal world, with everyone working for the best for the child, it would seem sensible for these groups to strengthen and focus their effort through coming together (Davies 1986). Until then, concerned heads and governors will find the ways they can to bring together all who care about the school in the search for continuing school improvement.

Managing conflict

When parents are involved in the various aspects of school life, and in particular, their child's learning, many of the traditional conflict areas disappear. For example, school files on children which once were secret generated far more interest and anxiety in parents than when access to them was available. This was because the teacher trust in according access is matched by parent trust that school documents contained professional statements related to a child's education. In any good working relationship, there are times when differences of opinion may occur. It is then that the role of the headteacher is critical in identifying dysfunctional conflict and channelling all efforts to creative and constructive discussion. If, for example, suggestions offered by parents are unrealistic, impracticable to undertake or at their worst, involve serious compromise of professional knowledge, headteachers and their staffs need to be explicit in defence and justification of recognised principles of educational practice. Likewise, a responsibility rests upon parents to add considered comments to the debate.

In supporting and encouraging both professional and lay contribution to group discussion, the headteacher can lay the foundation for the innovative style of decision reaching which offers the optimum for school improvement. More appropriate for the 'equal partnership' concept is the adoption of a 'worrying at' style of decision making which puts the onus on all parties to contribute. Such a style eschews consensus as it leaves some contributors with little or no commitment to the new proposal. Neither is it based on compromise, with its implication of the outcome being less than the best that can be achieved. When sufficient 'worrying at' the problem to reach an outcome occurs, everyone can take some form of commitment forward into the new scheme, if only that accrued from sharing in the decision making process.

Implementing change

Once decisions involving action have been taken, the work of the headteacher in providing the right sort of organisational environment for these initiatives to flourish is vital. Charged with managing the change process, heads can encourage parents and teachers to be venturesome in making suggestions or trying out new ideas, by arranging flexibility within the school system (Davies 1984). The National Curriculum framework is designed to enable this to happen. Heads can also offer evidence of their trust in parents by delegating authority for undertaking proposed schemes. Such proposals might include the organisation of a group to take responsibility for a school nature area, a 'teach-in' on computer programming, a pre-school family club or a visit to the seaside or the ballet — the list could be endless. If a decision is made to arrange for example, school assemblies involving increased parental and community input, then the head might have to exercise considerable supportive activity with staff and parents as problems are revealed. As well as alerting people to the usual stages of difficulty in the change process, heads are called upon to show tenacity in ensuring the new scheme has a fair chance and fearlessness in deciding to shelve the idea if it proves impractical (Nisbet 1975). Yet, even in these onerous areas, sharing the decision-making responsibility with parents, teachers and governing bodies can alleviate some of the weight of responsibility headteachers often feel (Gray and Coulson 1982). There are times when both groups, either separately or jointly, can be drawn into the necessary formative appraisal which should accompany a new scheme. If, for example, in the early operation of a new style of school assembly, it receives a mixed reception from parents and teachers (despite their initial desire for it), then regular review discussions within the staff group and governing body or policy advisory group can help the headteacher support those people implementing the change.

Conclusion

The benefits of encouraging mutual support between parents and teachers are found at all points within the school system. On an individual pupil level, parental support has its outcome in the extension of natural (and more lasting) learning which enables the professional to proceed more speedily and specifically in a child's learning.

At system level, schools founded on a person centred organisational and educational philosophy, encourage a dialogue with parents which enables them to respond more pertinently and accurately to needs of families. Through sharing information, policy making and even through sharing expertise with parents, such dynamic schools reap the precious reward of active and felt client support and goodwill.

Although this chapter has attempted to look at parental involvement in school life through some areas of managerial concern, it is important to note that effective school management is only valid in terms of the outcomes it achieves. In relation to parental involvement, the outcomes are evident in the friendly, relaxed relationships, founded upon mutual trust, understanding and respect, which enable and support exciting and adventurous happenings in a school. Where such relationships exist, parental involvement is not regarded as a separate aspect of the managerial task: it is, as indeed, it should be, the natural way of life in a caring, educative community.

References

Coulson, A. A. (1984) *The Managerial Behaviour of Primary School Heads*, N.E. Wales Institute of Higher Education.

Davies, E. (1980a) 'Primary school records', in Burgess, T. and Adams, E. (eds) *Outcomes of Education*, Macmillan.

Davies, E. (1980b) 'Primary school self-portraits', in *Where* No. 160, ACE.

Davies, E. (1984) 'The role of the headteacher in the management of change', in Skilbeck, M. (ed.) *Readings in School-Based Curriculum Development*, Harper and Row.

Davies, E. (1985) 'Parental involvement in school policy making', in *Educational Management and Administration* **11**, (2).

Davies, E. (1986) 'The changing role of parents, governors and teachers', in *Educational Management and Administration*, **14**, (2).

DES (1985), *The Curriculum from 5 to 16*, HMSO.

Gray, H. and Coulson, A. A. (1982) 'Teacher education, management and the facilitation of change', in *Educational Change and Development*, **4** (1).

Griffiths, A. and Hamilton, G. (1984) *Parent, Teacher, Child — Working Together in Children's Learning*, Methuen.

Macbeth, A. (1984) *The Child Between — A Report on School–Family Relations in the Countries of the European Community*. Studies Collection, Education Series No. 13 Publ. Office for Official Publications of the European Communities, Luxembourg.

Merson, M. W. and Campbell, R. J. (1974) 'Community education: instruction for inequality', in Golby, M. et al. (eds) *Curriculum Design*, Croom Helm.

Mintzberg, H. (1973) *The Nature of Managerial Work*, Harper and Row.

Nisbet, J. (1975) 'Innovation — bandwagon or hearse?' in Harris, A. et al. (eds) *Curriculum Innovation*, Croom Helm.

Peters, T. J. and Waterman, R. H. (1982) *In Search of Excellence*, Harper and Row.

Stevens, C. (1984) 'All parents as a resource for education', in Harber, C. et al. (eds) *Alternative Educational Futures*, Holt, Rinehart and Winston.

Index